VOICES FR(
THE EXPLOSIUN

The World's Greatest Accidental Explosion
RAF Fauld Underground Bomb Store, 1944

Valerie Hardy

Dedication

This book is dedicated to the memory of the victims and survivors
of the Fauld Explosion.

This 2nd Edition is also in memory of my late husband Colin who suggested the
title and encouraged my resolve to tell the story of a disaster the nation forgot.

Published by Woldscot 2019

2nd Edition
ISBN: 978-1-5272-2969-3

Design: Mark Titterton

Printing: Gomer Press, Llandysul, Ceredigion SA44 4JL

1st Edition 2012 published by Guidelines Books

CONTENTS

PREFACE AND ACKNOWLEDGEMENTS

The Fauld Explosion made history and changed geography.
"The sixth year of war has been noteworthy for by far the biggest explosion to have occurred in these islands."[1]

Whilst staring into the deep, circular crater of Lochnagar near La Boiselle, Albert, France, I made a decision. It was early June 2007 when returning from a family holiday that my husband, a member of the Western Front Association, bribed us with the promise of an excellent dinner and a stay at a fine hotel if he could introduce us to the First World War Somme battlefields. As we stood on the rim of the Lochnagar crater, 'La Grande Mine', site of the largest of the mines which exploded on the opening day of the Somme offensive, he recounted the events of 1 July, 1916. My thoughts however, as I observed our granddaughters walking around the crater, turned to another explosion, another crater, another war, another time, and two other sisters of a similar age two generations earlier.

In 1944 my sister and I had also stared down into a vast and awe-inspiring crater and had known, for the very first time, a highly personal sense of loss. We had gazed down into the depths of a war grave like none other in England. In both circumference and depth it was a significantly larger crater than that of Lochnagar and the surrounding landscape had been totally transformed to the extent that it has been described as resembling a Somme battlefield.

This was the Fauld crater on the Stonepit Hills located near my childhood home of Fauld House Farm in the middle Dove valley in rural East Staffordshire. This crater, estimated at nearly three-quarters of a mile long, half a mile wide and around a hundred feet deep covered an area of twelve acres. Its creation dictated the editing of the Ordnance Survey map. It was the site of the biggest pre-nuclear man-made explosion of the Second World War and the world's largest accidental blast. The Fauld explosion made history and changed geography. The explosion had occurred at eleven minutes past eleven on Monday 27 November, 1944. In Casablanca, fifteen hundred miles away, seismographs variously registered the detonation as being between 4 to 5 and 5 to 7 kilotons. However, this explosion was experienced in an area far removed from the theatres of war and is now largely unknown. Outside of the local area the Fauld crater remains forgotten.

The explosion at Fauld occurred at a time when the Luftwaffe's major bombing raids on Britain's cities had long since ended and been replaced by V1 and V2 attacks. Bomber Command had the Ruhr and Berlin in its sights as prime targets and no-one expected the war to last much longer. Wartime censorship meant that an explosion occurring at what was Britain's major underground ammunition depot was little reported at the time and the findings of the secret military court of inquiry, which had endeavoured to determine the cause or causes of the explosion, were not made public for thirty years. Nearly seventy years later, apart from those who were living close to the scene, most people remain completely unaware of the catastrophe which struck in a rural area of understated beauty in the heart of England; a catastrophe which profoundly affected the people of the village of Hanbury and surrounding farms. It was at Lochnagar that I resolved to fulfil a long-held aspiration

Aerial view of the crater after the explosion
Courtesy of the Imperial War Museum

Aerial View of the crater and the Dove valley
Courtesy of the IWM

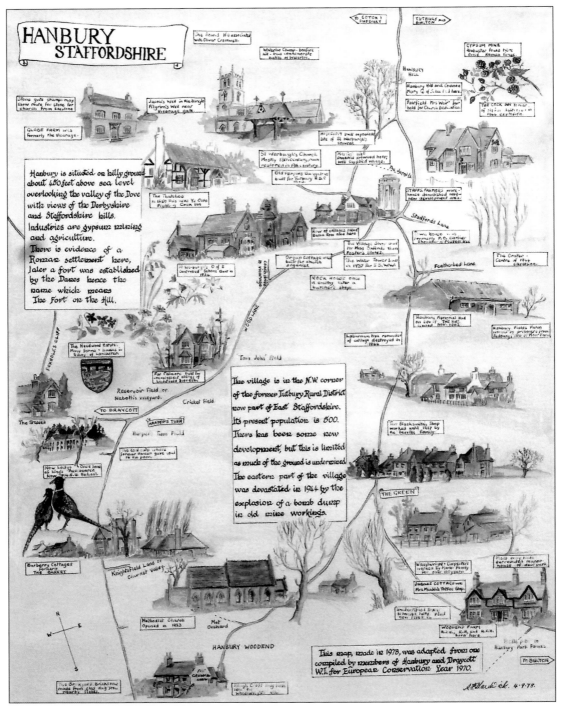

Hand-painted map of Hanbury by Audrey Hardwick, 1970. 'The eastern part of the village was devastated in 1944 by the explosion of a bomb dump in old mine workings.'

Courtesy of Audrey Hardwick

to record the testimonies of those who had experienced Britain's biggest explosion before those memories are lost for ever. Additionally, in ensuring that those voices remain silent no longer, to recapture the impact it made on the close community of the village where I grew up: the village of Hanbury in whose church of St Werburgh I was married and to which I returned for the christening of our daughter Clare.

The terrifying suddenness with which the Second World War came to the village and surrounding farms, on a bright Monday morning in November 1944, changed lives and a landscape for ever. The destruction of our "other Eden", my "demi-paradise" made a powerful impact on my eight-year-old self: I was catapulted into recognition that the war, with which I was growing up, was not simply somewhere "out there" happening to people unknown. It marked the first stage of a loss of innocence. For others, including the child who was my closest friend and who has told me since that she has "blocked out" her memories, the impact was far more traumatic. The Fauld explosion, which had such a profound impact on family, friends and the whole community of Hanbury, appears to have had very little resonance across the nation. However, for many of those who have recalled their personal experiences the memories remain remarkably vivid, and in telling of a disaster the nation forgot a lost world is recaptured.

Voices From The Explosion, focusing on the experiences of the people who were there, pays homage to a particular time and place in wartime Britain. Through their memories it recalls a story with a mystery at its core: a story which remained secret for many years. The testimonies and eye-witness accounts of those who lived through the disaster reveal many stories of heroism as well as tragedy. People's voices reveal the previously untold story in their own words. It is a story seen through different windows of memory, the memories of those who were there.

The true cause of the Fauld explosion will remain a mystery for all time: those who would have been able to confirm the cause were amongst its victims. Although it will never be possible to be definitive regarding the reason, the facts, as far as they can be determined, are known but the testimonies of those most affected are not. People's testimonies of their own experiences are naturally subjective and memories can be fallible but I have endeavoured to cross-reference these wherever possible. *Voices* does not pretend to be an empirical verification of narrative history dealing principally with technical issues and explanations of what occurred. That has been written up by others more qualified than me.[2] However, it is useful for the reader to appreciate the context and framework within which the people's experiences are recorded.

The testimonies include both statements given at the time and those recalled from memory. The people's voices telling the story of their first-hand experiences of Britain's biggest explosion are fivefold. First and foremost they are the spoken recollections of those who experienced the disaster and its consequences. These were garnered by the author in fieldwork undertaken in her former home area between August 2011 and March 2012. Secondly, they are recorded in graphic unpublished eye-witness accounts to which the author has been privileged to be granted access. Thirdly, they include some of the witness statements, made at the Court of Inquiry of December 1944, which were kept secret in the National Archives at Kew until 1974. Fourthly, they are eye-witness accounts quoted in contemporary newspapers. Finally, and of immense value, they are voices from the papers of P.C. Albert Thomas Mackay who worked as the Coroner's officer after the explosion. These include his own recollections and reports together with many witness statements taken down by him at the time. His papers were donated to the Tutbury Museum by his son Donald in 2006 (Ref LH 34).

My research for this book has, in many trips north to the land of my roots, included the delight of renewed contact with many of those who recalled my family and me when we were part of the community of Hanbury up until the late 1950s. Conscious that, in asking people to share their memories, I could be trespassing on sensitive ground where the issues raised caused distress, I was regularly warmed by the welcome I received as one who had also experienced the consequences of the explosion. Particularly moving were the tributes paid by some to my father. I came to feel that the name Hellaby provided a key that opened many doors! Additionally, I have had the delight of meeting others whom I did not know at the time but who have also openly shared their memories with me. I must also acknowledge the friendly welcome and hospitality I always received when, with my head buzzing at the end of a day's fieldwork, I returned to rest at the Shoulder of Mutton at Barton-under-Needwood.

So very many people have generously shared their memories and it is extraordinarily difficult to single out individuals. I do, however, owe most particularly special and warm thanks to my sister, Marjorie Snow (née Hellaby), for the detail, clarity and wealth of her vivid personal recollections. I am also indebted to John Cooper, a former class-mate at Hanbury School, not only for sharing some of his memories but also for allowing access to a wealth of material from his research over many years. Additionally, warm thanks are due to Audrey Hardwick (née Bridges) who, in addition to recalling her own memories and loaning photographs, kindly allowed me access to the unpublished eye-witness record written by her late husband, John Hardwick. Warm thanks are also due to Ida Roberts (née Harrison) both for generously sharing her memories with me and for loaning photographs, and to those many others still living in Hanbury, including Doug Archer, Brian Cooper, Charlie Gibbs, Peter Harrison, Bill Moore, Eileen Pavey (née Bowring), Celia Rutter (née Johnson) and Jim Woolliscroft, who have also shared a wealth of often quite painful memories with me and in a number of instances provided me with photographs. Thanks are also due to my cousin, Rosalie Vicars-Harris (née Jeffery) and Bill Hidderley, for granting me sight of the eye-witness record written by their grandfather, the late William Shelley of Rock House, Hanbury. Very sincere thanks must also go to former Flight Sergeant Neil Robinson and former Leading Aircraftman Ken McCleod, both of whom were stationed at R.A.F. "Maintenance Unit No. 21 Fauld" at the time. Neil Robinson has also kindly sanctioned my use of his own unpublished witness account in addition to recalling his many memories direct and taking me to see the graves of Italian ex-prisoners of war who were victims of the explosion. (I am indebted to Mark Rowe for enabling me to make contact with Neil Robinson.) Ken McCleod, the last person still alive who escaped from the underground bomb store at Fauld, has also, together with his wife Joyce (née Frow) recalled many memories of their experiences in addition to providing me with graphic personal written material and photographs.

I also offer sincere thanks and acknowledgements for the time generously given to me in recalling their own personal experiences and, in many instances, kindly loaning photographs and other material, to many others including Fred Allen, Tom Allen, Hilda Carter (née Watson), Audrey Cooper (née Lindsey), Joe Cooper, Tony Deaville, Dorothy Ede (née Harrison), Hazel Ede (née Worsley), Peter Ede, Joe Foster, Pat Guest (née Major), Henry Hand, George Heathcote, Vivian and David Lowe, Tom Moore, Geoff Marler, Margaret Nicklin (née Cooper), Harry Payne, Ginny Pilkington (née Cowler), Pat Polley (née Foster), Kay Sutton (née Kathleen Hill), Betty Swain (née Lindsey), Margaret Winson (née Bowring), Percy Winson and Jill Woolliscroft. Research has included many days spent at the National Archives at Kew viewing documents, maps and photographs stamped "SECRET" which did not come into the public domain until 1974. Also, many hours have been spent at both the British Newspaper Library at Colindale and the Imperial War Museum. Warm thanks are due to my daughter Clare and family in London for their hospitality whilst I was consulting these archives. Visits to archives in the local area have included searches made at the "Magic Attic" at Swadlincote (Staffordshire Newspapers), the Tutbury Museum (both of which are run by extraordinarily helpful and knowledgeable volunteers) and the Burton-on-Trent branch of Staffordshire County Library. Archivists at the Staffordshire Record Office based at Stafford and Lichfield have also been consulted together with the holders of old air photographs at Bluesky International. I would like to thank staff in all of these archives for providing invaluable guidance in my use of these resources and granting licences for the use of some of the photographic material used in this publication. Additionally, my thanks go to Jolyon Jenkins of BBC Radio 4 for permission to quote from *In Living Memory: Fauld*, a programme produced by him and broadcast on 15 March, 2004, and also to the local radio station in Birmingham, BRMB, for permission to quote from a programme produced by Brian King in 1983. I am indebted to Ida Roberts and Doug Archer for drawing my attention to this broadcast material of 1983 and 2004 and also to Barbara Ashenford for her first-class transcription work. My thanks are also due to author Leah Flemming for permission to quote from her recent novel *The Captain's Daughter*.

Huge and very special thanks are due to Malcolm Lewis, my photographic editor, who has applied his impressive skills to improving many old photographs in addition to annotating air photographs and designing maps and landscape cross-sections.

As with my first book, very special thanks and deep appreciation are due to my husband Colin whose forensic mind, insights, suggestions and objective analysis have proved invaluable in our innumerable discussions at the end of a day's writing. He has given me most tremendous support and encouragement throughout the preparation of this book.

NOTES

1 *Derbyshire Advertiser*, 17 January, 1947 quoting from a Report from H.M. Inspectors of Explosions published as a White Paper 16 January, 1947.

2 (1) N. J. McCamley, *Disasters Underground* (Pen and Sword Military, 2004).

(2) Trevor Jones, "The Great Fauld Explosion", *Staffordshire Studies* Vol. 1, University of Keele, 1988.

(3) John Reed, "21 Maintenance Unit, RAF Fauld, Staffs. November 27, 1944", *After the Battle* Journal No. 18, 1977.

CHAPTER ONE

PRIMROSE TIME

A wonderful sense of freedom in the surrounding fields and woods.
"I can see the cattle on the hillside now."[1]

Fauld House Farm, my home for twenty years, was where I spent my childhood during the Second World War. The farmland worked by my father, Jeff Hellaby, stretched northwards to the River Dove and southwards towards the edge of the Stonepit Hills, Hanbury Hill and Hanbury Common. Upper Castle Hayes Farm, half a mile to the south-south-east, was home to our friends, the Goodwins. Their daughter Marie became my closest childhood friend during the war years and we would spend much of our time, after school and during the holidays, at each other's homes. Upper Castle Hayes Farm on the Stonepit Hills was situated above disused gypsum mines ninety feet underground which from 1938 were used by the Air Ministry as a major munitions store, known locally as the Dump. Active gypsum mining continued in adjacent workings and Peter Ford's and Sons Plaster Works, together with the entrances to their mines, were sited in a narrow wooded valley lying between our two farms.

Life for a child on a farm in the 1940s was in many ways quite privileged and certainly provided a wonderful sense of freedom in the surrounding fields and woods, with walks and rides down to the river or up to the Hanbury fields and beyond. My older sister Marjorie introduced me to the hedgerows where we found the earliest wild violets and also the spectacular bank where the primroses grew in such wild profusion on the lower slopes of the Stonepit Hills below Queen's Purse Wood, the wood which clothed the valley side above Peter Ford's gypsum mines and plaster works. There were other walks on the opposite side of the valley, including one which took us up across the tramway which served the gypsum mines and which crossed our land behind the stable. This walk took us over a low hill and across fields to a fence with a stile where we climbed out of our farmland into Brown's Coppice, which we came to know as the bluebell woods and where, earlier in the spring, the bluebell carpet had been preceded by dainty and wonderfully prolific wood anemones. It was a walk which sometimes included a visit to Mrs Sarah Hill, who lived in one of the Purse Cottages situated between two of the gypsum mine entrances on the edge of Queen's Purse Wood up the narrow valley. Mrs Hill was a dressmaker who, with material purchased with clothing coupons by Mother, made beautiful clothes for my sister and me. She also made clothes for my friend Marie of Upper Castle Hayes Farm. Her youngest daughter Kathleen has recalled that Ford's gypsum mines acted as their air-raid shelters and that the Goodwin family also came down from the farm to shelter in the mines during air raids.

Farmers were required to increase food production during the war and Father acquired his first Fordson tractor, with spiked iron wheels to plough up fields which had previously been used for pasture for dairy cows. However, our shire horses continued to earn their

Geography of the Fauld Area Before the Explosion

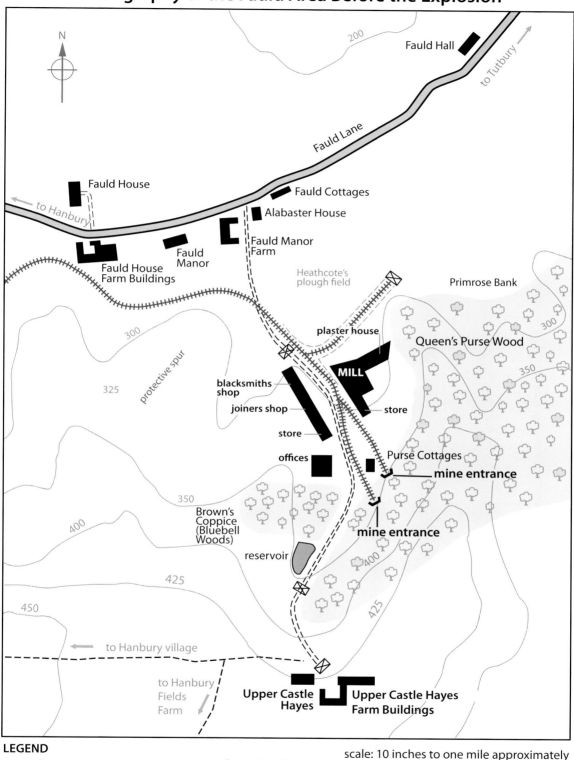

Fauld Hall

to Tutbury

200

Fauld Lane

Fauld House

to Hanbury

Fauld Cottages

Alabaster House

Fauld Manor Farm

Fauld House Farm Buildings

Fauld Manor

Heathcote's plough field

Primrose Bank

300

plaster house

Queen's Purse Wood

300

350

blacksmiths shop

MILL

joiners shop

store

325

protective spur

store

offices

Purse Cottages

mine entrance

350

Brown's Coppice (Bluebell Woods)

mine entrance

400

reservoir

400

425

425

450

to Hanbury village

to Hanbury Fields Farm

Upper Castle Hayes

Upper Castle Hayes Farm Buildings

LEGEND

++++ tramway (single guauge railway)

=== unfenced trackways

--- footpath

⊠ gate

scale: 10 inches to one mile approximately

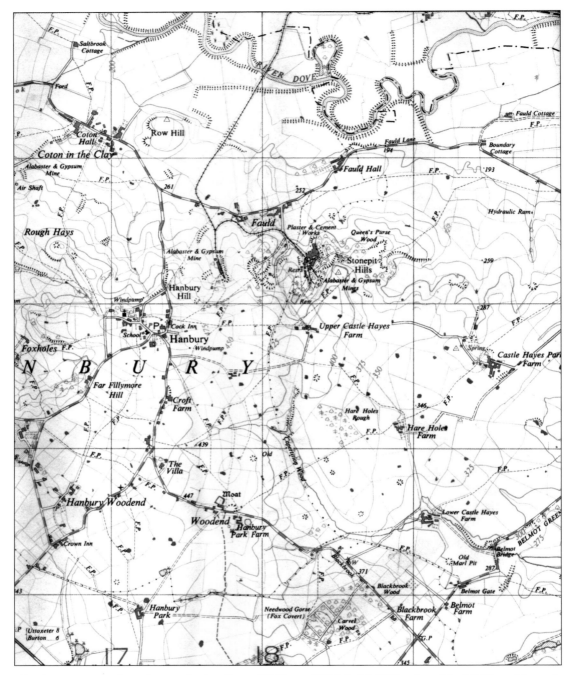

Hanbury area before the explosion from OS Sheet SK12 1:25,000 printed in 1949 and based on six inch map last revised in 1922.

Above: Hellaby sisters Marjorie Snow (right) and Valerie Hardy, 1942

Left: Bernard Harrison at Croft Farm, Hanbury circa 1945
Photo loaned by his daughter, Ida Roberts

Below: Miners with their horses at Fauld blacksmiths circa 1940. Charles Gibbs, who worked down the mine for fifty-nine years, stands on the far right
Photo loaned by his son, Charlie Gibbs

keep on the farm and during the hay harvest we rode on the top of swaying hay-filled wagons pulled by Captain, an enormous grey, or Blossom, a friendly, calm and docile bay: they were my introduction to horses before I learnt to ride my sister's pony, Peggy.

Horses continued to feature significantly for farmers through the 1930s and 40s and there were blacksmiths operating hand-blown furnaces at both Fauld and Hanbury. Horses were also an imperative for the gypsum miners, who used them to haul laden trucks out of the mine before rail lines were installed.

A country childhood was a life lived with animals, and on wet days our Old English sheepdog Nellie was easily encouraged to play in the attics with us. Later, Border Collies, Bob and Meg were the serious working dogs earning their keep on the farm although I always had my own dog as well which needed to kept well away from the sheep at lambing time. Spending time in the fields with Father when he was checking on the sheep I observed his skill when, after a sheep had given birth to a dead lamb, he quickly and carefully removed the skin from the dead lamb and fitted it onto the body of a lamb whose mother had died when giving birth. The motherless lamb was then accepted by the ewe. Sometimes Father brought orphan lambs into the house and revived them with whisky before feeding them from a baby's bottle. The rearing of these "cade" lambs, which became like pets before they had to go to market, was a job I shared with my sister. We became very attached to them and did not seriously discourage them when they tried to follow us to school. Trips to Uttoxeter market regularly involved sharing the back of the car with a bull calf, who always wanted to place a cold wet nose on my knee. Trips to the market at Burton-on-Trent took us along Fauld Lane towards Tutbury where we passed by the securely guarded entrance to the munitions unit of R.A.F. Fauld. On the other side of the road was Boundary House, to which my parents later moved and from where I was married.

The village of Hanbury was a close-knit community where strong links were reinforced through church, chapel, school, the Cock and Crown inns and shared livelihoods in the countryside. My walk to school in the village of Hanbury took me across two of our fields before climbing up the Common to the top of Hanbury Hill. The Common was grazed by sheep and horses belonging to Boko Harrison, who lived in the cottage at the top of Hanbury Hill. He had his sheep branded with a "B" to distinguish them from ours, which had an "H", and sometimes, if he was going to check on his cattle grazing on the primrose bank below Queen's Purse Wood, Marjorie would ride his pony down Hanbury Hill on her way home from school. There were also times when the gypsies with their wonderful old caravans camped at the foot of the Common: they sold hand-made white willow clothes-pegs and told fortunes when they visited Fauld House. My walk to school was initially taken with my sister and the Griffiths children from Coton-in-the-Clay, but when they all went on to secondary school I walked on my own. This was a wonderful opportunity to dawdle, lost in a dream-world, along Martins Lane by the old well where the children used to collect drinking water for the school up until the early 1930s. The lane was a short cut bringing me out near St Werburgh's Church and Hanbury Hall but, with my gas-mask in its tin box bumping painfully on my back, I usually had to run the last few yards to avoid being late.

The two-roomed church school, where Miss Owen and later Miss Fardon was the Head who taught the juniors and Mrs Moseley and later Miss Williams taught the infants,

Hanbury Village
School

*Photo loaned from Rosalie
Vicars-Harris*

Hanbury School Juniors 1945
Back row (left to right): Ken Bowring, Joe Foster, Peter Lindsey, Philip Allen, Roy Marler, Jim Woolliscroft, Fred Lindsey, Tony Deaville, Fred Allen, Bill Moore, Teacher Miss Williams
Middle row (left to right): Les Bowring, George Moore, Bill Hollins, Brian Cooper, Peter Harrison, Ted Moore, Reg. Gibbs, Peter Flint, Ron Harrison
Front row (left to right): Janet Hollins, Beryl Hall, Mavis Winson, Joan Harrison, Brenda Gallagher, Beryl Ede, Margaret Bowring, Rita Shepherd, Pamela Gibbs
Photo provided by Brian Cooper

had around fifty children. It was a welcoming place warmed by large slow-burning pot-bellied iron stoves. Marie, whom I had come to know even before our schooldays, joined her brother Gordon at Hanbury School the term after I had started there. There always seemed to be twice as many boys as girls, as the school photograph of my former class-mates indicates. I remember many of the other children at school. Some of them, the Edes, Hollins and Woolliscrofts, also lived on neighbouring farms and others had fathers who either worked on the land or in the mines and plaster works at Fauld. I recall particularly the Allen brothers; the children with red curly hair of one of the three Bowring families; two Cooper families; the blacksmith's son, Tony Deaville and Peter and Bunty Ede. There was also our friend Pat Foster and her younger brother Joe; Brenda Gallagher; the Gibbs boys and the Harrison twins; Celia Johnson, whom I wished to emulate as the flower monitor; the Lindsey sisters and their younger brother Fred; Roy Marler; the Moore twins and their brothers; Mavis Winson and her siblings and the Woolliscroft boys.

Morning school often included standing in a semi-circle around the stove with Miss Fardon posing quick-fire mental arithmetic and if you got the answer right you moved up a place but if you got it wrong you immediately went down to the end! There also always seemed to be endless sums and "problems" to be tackled directly from the blackboard, which we sat facing in double-bench desks with inkwells. After morning school I went to the Gregsons' farm near the church, where Mrs Gregson had cooked a hot lunch for me. Summer afternoons often included nature-study walks and the collection of wild flowers, which were brought back into school to be sketched with chalks or painted with powder paints; or sometimes Miss Fardon brought in flowers from the vicarage garden for us to paint. Best of all, for a child who always had her nose in a book, were the stories and opportunity for reading at the end of the day where my passion for history was triggered when we were introduced to Captain Marryat's *The Children of the New Forest*. We were always encouraged to bring books home, where they were read in bed by candle light as only half of our rambling farmhouse had electricity.

After school Marie would sometimes walk home with me down Hanbury Common to Fauld House, where we often played in the hay-barn or hay-filled "bings" behind the cowsheds where the swallows and house-martins nested under the eaves of the outer cowshed walls. Or, if the cherries and, later, the plums and first early apples were ripe, we spent time in the orchard and the swing on one of the old apple trees. Alternatively, we regularly took the path behind the Cock Inn across the fields to her home of Upper Castle Hayes. This was an exposed walk across three fields along the open plateau forming the summit of the Stonepit Hills where, looking over the wooded escarpment on our left, the ash and elm and sycamore thinned out to hawthorn and my own home could be spied below. The first part of the path took us along the same route which had been taken earlier in the day by the men from the village who worked at Ford's mines and plaster works.

I would also see many of my school friends and their parents at church, where my father became the vicar's warden in 1945. Some Sundays meant church four times a day, with Children's Church followed by Matins and then afternoon Sunday school and Evensong. Marjorie and I joined the church choir but rarely managed to attend choir practice because of homework. The vicar was the Reverend Crook and Harry Botham, of Hanbury Fields

Fauld House from the Hanbury escarpment
Photo by the author

Hanbury Church Choir 1943
Back row (left to right): Bill Allen, George Rock, Tom Deaville, Bernard Harrison
Second row (left to right): Roy Gregson, Lynn Collier, Lucy Allen, Muriel Collier, Esme Harris, Florrie Rock, Jessie Bowring, Geoff Buckland
Third row (left to right): Vera Harrison, Evelyn Botham, Harry Botham, Rev Crook, Nora Hidderley, Mrs Percy Foster
Front row (left to right): Bill Hidderley, Charlie Gibbs, John Collier, Percy Winson, John Moore, Dennis Bowring

Photo loaned by Bill and Margaret Moore

Farm, was the organist, choir master and vicar's warden until the end of 1944. The verger, George Rock, who worked for Harry Botham, also sang in the choir, as did Bill Allen of Croft Farm, who had a wonderful deep bass voice. Joseph Cooper, who, before he went down the mine, came ploughing and sheep shearing for Father for many years, was a sidesman and the sextant. His son Joe was also in the choir and his youngest son John was a pupil at Hanbury School. Choristers Charlie Gibbs and Dennis Bowring had fathers who worked at *Ford's* gypsum mine and plaster works. (Some of those shown in the photograph of the Hanbury Church Choir feature in the pages which follow.)

By the time my sister had left the village school at Hanbury and started at the High School in Uttoxeter in 1942, the farm at Upper Castle Hayes had become as familiar to me as my own home. During the summer holidays of 1943 and 1944 Marie and I spent most of our time together on one or other of our farms. Those childhood summers, when the war was nothing more than a distant backcloth to our lives, remain extraordinarily vivid: they are memories which take me back to two farms, one in the Dove Valley and one on the Stonepit Hills.

Upper Castle Hayes had, prior to the First World War, been farmed by William Shelley and it was where his daughters were born. His younger daughter Vera married a cousin, Henry Jeffery, and later lived at Aston House, Sudbury. She has left a description of her childhood home in her memoirs: it is a description which rings true to me of what for a few years during the Second World War was my second home.

The farmhouse was moderately sized. We had four bedrooms and a large kitchen and living room and sitting room which was called the "parlour". Also a pantry and large "still" room. The kitchen had an inglenook where the kitchen range was. There was a very large sink in the kitchen and a sort of cellar-like room where smocks were hung and shoes were cleaned. This led out into a vestibule which had a door leading outside and another to a pantry and the still room. Then another door led into a general sort of sitting room or living room which was where my parents spent their evenings because the man who helped on the farm and the maid we had that lived in, used the other kitchen.[2]

Vera also recalled her walk with her sister Nora from Upper Castle Hayes to Hanbury School.

My sister and I went to the village school in Hanbury and when we lived at Castle Hayes we had to walk through five fields, but we didn't mind. When it was very snowy we perhaps didn't go. There was a good path through the fields because the alabaster mines were just below the farmhouse and the men from the village of Hanbury walked to work in the mines. I remember a whistle used to blow at the mines and we used to see how far we could run whilst the whistle was blowing. We quite often met the men coming down to the mines as we were going to school.[3]

The musically talented head teacher at that time, when it was a school for children aged five to fourteen, was Mr Stevens and he, together with his wife who taught the juniors, put on many school productions and trained the successful choir. Vera herself became a teacher at Hanbury School in the late 1920s and early 1930s. Ida Roberts (née Harrison) recalls that Vera Shelley was her teacher and that the school choir competed with other Staffordshire school choirs and regularly won the shield as seen in the photograph. (Some

Hanbury School Choir circa 1936
Back row (left to right): Fred Ede, Frank Cooper, Jeff Foster, Sam Abberley, Reg. Hardwick, Reg. Tipper, Ron Hill, George Ede, Tom Harrison, Tom Deaville, Stephen Carter
Second row (left to right): Audrey Abberley, Rene Needham, Margaret Cooper, Ida Rowe, Celia Stonier, Vera Harrison, Kathleen Hill, Gladys Collington, Doreen Hutchinson, Peggy Owen
Third row (left to right): Barbara Collier, Joan Foster, Lorna Harrison, Mr Stevens, Mrs Stevens, Noreen Bartram, Dorothy Harrison, Alice Harrison
Front row (left to right): Ida Harrison, Doris Archer
Photo loaned by Ida Roberts (née Harrison)

of the children shown in the photograph of the Hanbury School Choir of 1936, Margaret Cooper, Dorothy Harrison, Ida Harrison and Kathleen Hill, recall their memories of the Fauld explosion in the following pages.)

The orchard at Upper Castle Hayes where Marie and I spent many hours playing in her tree-house had been established by William Shelley, as had the garden, with its memorable scent of sweet peas in summer. Marie's parents, Maurice and Mary Goodwin and her Aunt Lizzie, who lived with them, were always very kind to me.

This idyllic childhood was not entirely untouched by the war. Until the end of November 1944, the fact that thousands of tons of bombs were stored beneath the Stonepit Hills made no impact on the innocent lives of the Hellaby children of Fauld House Farm, the Goodwins of Upper Castle Hayes Farm or our school friends in the village of Hanbury. We appeared far removed from the main theatre of war. There were, however, a number of military camps and aerodromes locally and I was aware that air raids were taking place over the Midlands where our relative proximity to the targets of Coventry, Birmingham and Derby did increase our vulnerability. Father became an Air Raid Precaution (ARP)

Warden and no lights indicating the presence of settlements to enemy aircraft could be shown at night. We had shutters for the ground floor rooms but all of the windows on the first and second floors of our large farmhouse had to be specially fitted with blackouts. On some nights, looking out from my parents' bedroom, I saw swooping searchlights from the searchlight station at Draycott-in-the-Clay sweeping the skies for enemy planes. There were other nights when, on waking to the frighteningly eerie wail of the siren warning of an air raid, we retreated rapidly with blankets to the cellar, where only the upper half of the steep flight of steps leading down to the bottom had been properly finished. Some nights, Father carried me on his shoulders and our family of four walked by the light of the stars up Fauld Lane to share Mrs Astle's larger and more comfortable cellar at Fauld Manor. There were a number of allied aircraft crashes in the local area, at Church Broughton in October 1942 and January and February 1943, and also a Wellington bomber crashed at Hoar Cross in December 1943, a Spitfire at Sudbury in January 1944 and a Wellington at Marchington in July 1944.

At Fauld House we had a delightful Italian family, the Gallelis from London's East End, billeted on us. They came to escape the Blitz and the threat of V1 flying bombs; they enjoyed living in the area so much that they settled in the village of Tutbury after the war. At Upper Castle Hayes a sixteen-year-old evacuee from Wallasey, Cheshire lived and worked on the Goodwins' farm. On our farm, the German and Italian prisoners of war who worked for us were very kind to me and one of them made me some wonderful wooden toys.

September 1944 marked changes in our lives when Marie's brother Gordon started at Alleyne's Grammar School in Uttoxeter and I started in the Preparatory Department at the Girls' High School. There were conversations that my mother had with Marie's mother regarding the possibility that maybe Marie would join me at the Prep the following year. However, the end of November 1944 was to mark cataclysmic changes.

On Sunday 26 November, 1944, Father was particularly anxious to finish the milking in time for us all to attend Evensong at Hanbury Church. The Goodwins normally went to chapel and I had accompanied them on occasions when staying with them. However, on this Sunday all of the Goodwin family were going to church and afterwards we would be joining them for supper at Upper Castle Hayes. At church that evening, the vicar, the Rev. Crook, announced that:

Mr Goodwin had offered to advance, free of interest, the balance necessary to provide a new organ, and that after giving a generous donation.[4]

Sunday supper with the Goodwins would be a particular treat for me as I would not have to eat my mother's trifle with its thick whipped cream which was our regular fare on Sunday evenings. It was usually at some time after the vicar had delivered his sermon that, surprisingly as a dairy farmer's daughter and at a time of food rationing, I would start to dread the thought of going home and having to eat cream!

It was quite late in the evening when we finally left Upper Castle Hayes and drove down the steep familiar track, past the reservoir and through Peter Ford's Works. We did not know then that we were leaving for the last time. My sister recalls:

The night before [the Fauld explosion] *after church, we'd all been having supper together with the Goodwins. We often used to go up there for supper and sometimes they came to us. It was quite late when we left, after 10 o'clock. I remember having to get out of the car and shutting all the gates behind us, including the one by the reservoir, because there were young cattle out. I can see the cattle on the hillside now.*[5]

Early the next morning, Marjorie and I were the first to be picked up by the school bus at the end of Fauld House drive. The bus then went up Hanbury Hill where the Hanbury children, including Gordon Goodwin, Dennis Bowring and our friend Pat Foster, were picked up. For Marie and Gordon at Upper Castle Hayes the morning had started even earlier. Ida Roberts (née Harrison), who had left Uttoxeter Girls' High School the previous summer and whose mother worked at the post office, recalls:

Mother was ill and I was delivering the post round Fauld. It was a bright morning and I collected the Fauld post, together with that for Upper Castle Hayes, from the Hanbury Post Office at about seven o'clock and walked down to Fauld. I then walked up to the Goodwins' – they were my last call – and afterwards took the path across the fields back to the village with Marie and Gordon. Gordon needed to be at Hanbury for the school bus to Uttoxeter for about ten past eight, Marie went into Hanbury School and I then had to get back home to get three of my younger brothers and sisters to Hanbury School and three of the older ones onto the school bus to Tutbury.[6]

On that bright and sunny November Monday morning the school day for Gordon and Marie, Marjorie and me started as usual with registration and assembly followed by lessons before morning break from 10.45 to 11.00 a.m. By the end of the day the lives of those children had changed for ever.

At eleven minutes past eleven on 27 November, 1944 I was seated at a table by the window in my form room in the Prep at the High School. I was eight years old and this was my first term. There were around twelve children in the Second Form and we were listening to our teacher, Miss Shevin, when we were all startled by a sudden, inexplicable loud rumbling noise. The table shook under my hands. Was it an earthquake? Or, as had often been predicted by the adults, an attack on one of the nearby aerodromes? After our initial shock and excited questioning, our teacher brought the class to order and we continued with the lesson.

Ida Roberts (née Harrison) 1945
Photo loaned by Ida Roberts

Uttoxeter Girls' High School, 1955
Copyright The Frances Frith Collection

Meanwhile, Marjorie was having a History lesson in the new wing of the main building of the High School. The windows rattled but the imperturbable Miss Thomas continued unruffled with her highly disciplined approach to the teaching of the Tudors to the Upper Fourth.

I am heavily indebted to my sister, who vividly recounted for me her memories of that fateful November day.

Following morning school, some of the girls who lived in Uttoxeter went home and the rest of us went into the old dining room for lunch. A friend who had gone home for lunch came back and told us that "the Dump had gone up". At the start of afternoon school, all of the Upper Fourth [two forms] had to go into the Hall for a harpsichord recital. I remember that the recital was interrupted when a prefect came with a message for me – I was summoned to see the headmistress immediately. Miss Ross told me that Father had rung to tell me that the Dump had gone up and that Mother and he were safe. Father's message was that I was to collect my sister Valerie from the Prep and also Gordon Goodwin from next door (Alleyne's) and that the three of us were to come home early on the next service bus. We were to get off at "Massey's Corner", Sudbury, where we would be picked up and brought home.[7]

Unlike the school bus, the service bus did not go via Fauld. Father had arranged for us to be picked up and brought home by Henry Jeffery, the cousin who farmed at Aston House, Sudbury, near 'Massey's Corner'. This was about five miles from our home.

Marjorie continued:

I remember Miss Ross emphasising very forcefully that "You must not let Gordon Goodwin out of your sight. You must take him home with you."

The three of us left school and caught the service bus but there was no-one waiting to pick us up at 'Massey's Corner'. We started walking and had got as far as the Boar's Head [a pub about half a mile along the road over the River Dove] *when Henry Jeffery picked us up. However, we only got as far as 'Fauld Turns'* [where the road either turns right up Hanbury Hill or continues on to Fauld] *when we were stopped by the police and told that we couldn't go any further. Henry Jeffery stressed that he had children in the car and that he had to get through to Fauld House Farm. When we arrived home the whole length of the drive was full of unknown cars and so we all had to get out by the milk-stand by the entrance to the farmyard. I said to Gordon, "Come with me" but he said, "No, I'm all right now – I'm going home – I can walk from here." He insisted that he was going home and I was becoming quite desperate as he wouldn't listen either to me or to Henry Jeffery. Finally I told you* [i.e. me] *to find Father quickly and you ran up the drive whilst I continued arguing with Gordon. By the time Father had arrived with you at the bottom of the drive, Gordon had already got as far as the gate into the Croft field along Fauld Lane. I remember Father catching up with him and bringing him into the house.*

When we got into the house – Marie was there – our parents had brought her home from school. The police were using the phone, which was the only one left working in the area. There were lots of airmen in the hall near the phone. There were people in the sitting room and the drawing room – there were so many people everywhere – the whole house was buzzing. The windows were all out, chimney pots were down, the roof was pitted, and the cowshed roofs were all pitted.[8]

On my return no longer was Fauld House the safe and comfortable home that had nurtured me. Shattered windows and strewn glass revealed an insecure place in contrast to the one I had left just a few hours earlier. I was greeted by Marie. Innocently, I was delighted to have my best friend staying with me. Only one room in the house, my parents' large bedroom, had glass remaining in the windows. That night, two additional double beds were moved into this room, where all six of us slept fitfully. Before we fell asleep I recall Marie whispering hopefully to me that she thought her parents may have survived because they were due to go the cattle market in Burton market that morning.

It was doubtless painfully clear to both Marie and Gordon that their parents had been lost in this fearful tragedy and it would have been my parents who, I assume, would have had to explain things to them. The story of what had actually happened to their parents was revealed nearly a month later: it was not until shortly before Christmas that year that their remains were found. The Goodwins had been delayed in leaving for the cattle market at Burton-on-Trent that morning as an anticipated delivery of grain was late. Jim Heathcote's young son George, whose father farmed at the nearby Fauld Manor Farm at the time, has reminded me of the story:

The Goodwins had left home for market and had started to drive down the hill but they met the grain lorry coming up. So they went back to the farm and Maurice Goodwin helped to unload the grains. After the grain lorry had left he returned into the house to get changed and then they both left home again to go to Burton market. And the Dump went up – the world came down on them – and the reservoir burst – maybe when they were close to passing it. The grain lorry got away just in time – it had probably got as far as Fauld Cottages, beyond our farm, when the Dump went up.[9]

The Goodwins would have doubtless been concerned to close the two sets of gates behind them both on leaving the farm and Ford's Works yard, to prevent the cattle from straying, just as Marjorie had done the previous evening. This would have delayed them still further when, after the grain lorry had left, they drove down the track from Upper Castle Hayes Farm. They were probably just inside Ford's Works yard when the explosion occurred.

Marjorie continued her recollections:

I went to school next morning. Marie and Gordon stayed at home with you. When I got home all of the Goodwin family – Maurice Goodwin's brothers and sister – were there in the drawing room having tea. The following day I again went to school on my own and the three of you went to Uttoxeter market with our parents. I remember meeting you all after school in Woolworths and noticing that Marie was wearing your clothes.[10]

On the Friday of that week, I returned to school. The timing had obviously been very carefully planned. When I returned home it was to find that Marie and Gordon were no longer with us. I was utterly distraught. My mother did her best to comfort me and explained that the uncle and aunt, with whom they had gone to live at the Hill Farm, Barrow-on-Trent, had a daughter, Doris, the youngest of their family of five, who was just a little bit younger than Marie, and that this cousin would be a good friend to her.

The Fauld explosion, the biggest man-made explosion the world had ever known to date, shattered my "blessed plot" on the border of George Eliot's "Loamshire" and "Stoneyshire" on 27 November, 1944. The blast ripped a huge crater in the landscape and devastated the surrounding countryside. It set off a chain reaction which eventually claimed the lives of seventy people. Shell-shocked survivors witnessed the biggest detonation of conventional explosives in either the First or Second World Wars. On that day, less than a year before the end of the Second World War, almost four thousand tons of bombs tore apart a peaceful landscape: hills, a reservoir, a wooded valley, the Goodwins' farm of Upper Castle Hayes vanished.

NOTES

1 Memories of leaving Upper Castle Hayes Farm on the evening of Sunday 26 November, 1944 as recalled to the author by her sister Marjorie Snow (née Hellaby), 3 August 2011.

2 *Written On My Heart: The Memoirs of Vera Jeffery 1908–2005* (privately published by Rosalie Vicars-Harris and Malcolm Lewis, 2006), p.7 .

3 Ibid., p. 15.

4 *Burton Daily Mail*, 22 December, 1944.

5 Recalled to the author by Marjorie Snow (née Hellaby), 3 August, 2011.

6 Recalled to the author by Ida Roberts (née Harrison), 8 September, 2011.

7 Recalled to the author by Marjorie Snow, 3 August, 2011.

8 Ibid.

9 Recalled to the author by George Heathcote, 19 August, 2011.

10 Recalled by Marjorie Snow, 3 August 2011.

CHAPTER TWO

BENEATH THE PRIMROSE PLACE AND BLUEBELL WOOD

"Most of them had lived in the quiet of an English village all their lives and war had seemed so very far away from them." [1]
"I was in the last war and I've seen some sights but nothing like this. We used to think the 'Jack Johnson' shells were pretty bad but they were like kids' toys compared to this."[2]

In the middle of peaceful farming country in the heart of the English Midlands the small village of Hanbury on the edge of Needwood Forest, land of the Duchy of Lancaster, lies approximately seven miles south-east of Uttoxeter, a comparable distance north-west of Burton-on-Trent and sixteen miles south of Ashbourne. The city of Derby is sixteen miles to the north-west. This hilltop village, with its water tower and ancient church standing out from the surrounding landscape, is superbly located on the highest point of the Stonepit Hills which mark the western end of the Needwood escarpment. The village overlooks the flood plain of the meandering River Dove, the boundary between Staffordshire and Derbyshire, and commands views northwards to the Derbyshire hills of the Peak District and the Weaver hills and moorlands of North Staffordshire. The hamlets of Fauld and Coton-in-the-Clay, within the parish of Hanbury, lie at the foot of the escarpment on a river terrace above the flood plain. Two and a half miles to the east, the continuous edge of the Needwood escarpment is crowned by Tutbury Castle, formerly one of the main seats of the Norman Lord Henry de Ferrers, ancestor of the earls of Derby.

Hanbury is set in a pastoral landscape where farming and gypsum mining have provided the basis of the economy through many generations. Gypsum, which in its massive form is alabaster, has been mined at Fauld since Roman times and the Tutbury seam of gypsum dips southwards beneath the Needwood escarpment. The earliest known use of alabaster in building is revealed in the Norman doorway in the west front of St Mary's Priory Church, Tutbury. The twelfth-century memorial to Sir John de Hanbury in St Werburgh's Church, Hanbury is the oldest alabaster tomb in the county of Staffordshire and maybe in the country. The gypsum mine workings extend in a labyrinth of tunnels under the Stonepit Hills for a number of miles west, south and east of Hanbury and mining at Fauld continues to this day.

In the 1930s and 40s the two main companies who were mining the Fauld gypsum were Staton's and Peter Ford's and Sons. Both companies had established plaster works on the surface using gypsum as their raw material. The Peter Ford's Works were constructed in the lower part of a hidden narrow wooded valley leading off Fauld Lane. Their mine entrances were by way of adits into the Stonepit Hills, where the lower slopes were covered by Queen's Purse Wood above the "primrose bank". At the head of the valley, overlooking the bluebell woods of Brown's Coppice, a thirty-foot-deep reservoir, which covered an area of half an acre, was constructed to service Ford's Works. The wall of the dam, holding back six million gallons of water, was thirty feet high and thirty-five feet thick at its base, tapering to fourteen feet at the top. The roadway through the valley led up to Upper Castle Hayes Farm.

In the years immediately preceding the Second World War the attention of the Air Ministry was drawn to the existence of mine workings at Fauld where the gypsum had been worked out. These disused gypsum mines, ninety feet below the wooded escarpment of the Stonepit Hills, were considered to be well suited to the storage of huge quantities of high-explosive bombs for use by the R.A.F., which, with the prospect of war threatening from the middle of the 1930s, had expanded rapidly.

In 1937, as a precaution against the growing threat of Nazi Germany, the Duchy of Lancaster sold part of one of Peter Ford's gypsum mines to the Air Ministry and arrangements were made initially for the storage of 10,000 tons of bombs, although later that year this

Fauld and Hanbury Location

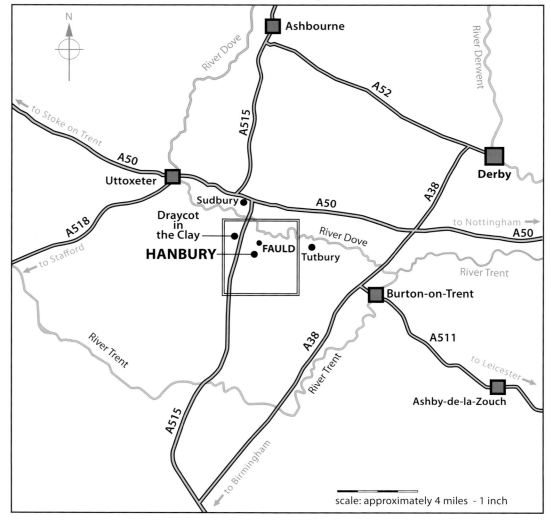

scale: approximately 4 miles - 1 inch

was increased to 24,000 tons. The initial conversion work required for the storage of high-explosive bombs was minimal but later, when the Air Ministry additionally authorised the storage of incendiaries and detonators, further conversion work was required in the mine. This necessitated the construction of a fifty-foot barrier to separate the incendiaries from the high-explosive bombs and a massive one-hundred-and-ten-foot barrier segregated the detonator store. However, whereas in the innermost part of the store where the high-explosive bombs were stored there was an overhead protective cover of ninety feet, the depth of earth cover above the incendiary storage area was only sixty feet and above the detonator storage area, which was the most sensitive of all, the depth was barely forty feet.

The Air Ministry also needed to arrange for vast quantities of bombs to be transported over the river Dove to Scropton, just over a mile to the north, where they could link with the former North Staffordshire Burton to Uttoxeter main railway and eventually to airfields across the country. Peter Ford's and Staton's already transported gypsum, plaster

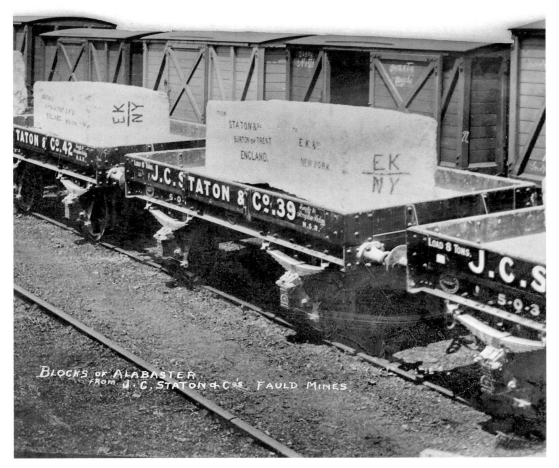

Blocks of alabaster leaving Staton's mine. Fauld alabaster was used in Cornelius Vanderbilt's mansion in Newport, Rhode Island, USA, constructed between 1893 and 1895

Photo courtesy of the Magic Attic Archive

and plasterboard on a narrow-gauge railway to Scropton railway sidings. However, it was essential to construct a new line for the transportation of the bombs linking the underground storage area directly to the railway sidings at Scropton. It also became imperative to purchase land and so extend the facilities at the railway sidings since those used by Peter Ford's and Staton's were totally inadequate for the requirements of the R.A.F. "A light railway was constructed to provide a link with the main line at Scropton and this facility was extended into the underground storage area where it branched into a system of 'roads', 'shunts' and 'loops' which serviced the individual storage locations."[3]

The initial stocking of the old mine with bombs was completed by 1 June, 1938 when Maintenance Unit Number 21 R.A.F. Fauld was scheduled to open as an operations unit. During 1939 the Air Ministry constructed four new entrance tunnels providing access to the high-explosive, incendiary and detonator stores. These entrance tunnels were within the confines of the R.A.F. camp which had been established further along Fauld Lane to the east in the direction of Tutbury and here the dictates of wartime meant that security remained paramount.

Adjacent to the disused mines taken over by the R.A.F. the Company of Messrs Peter Ford's and Sons continued mining the still highly productive seams of gypsum. Their established plaster works on the surface also continued in operation. Ford's mine entrances on the west side clearly needed to be maintained as, in addition to providing access for the miners, they also provided emergency exits and aided ventilation for everyone

Bombs leaving number two entrance of the Fauld mine en route to Scropton Sidings

Photo courtesy of the Imperial War Museum

working underground. Additionally, however, measures designed for security needed to be incorporated at these entrances.

By May 1940, when the remains of the British Expeditionary Force was evacuated from the beaches of Dunkirk, Fauld was storing vast supplies of high explosives, incendiaries, small arms and home defence ammunition of all kinds and it had become "the R.A.F.'s showpiece ammunition store".[4] Even so, by early 1941, additional space was urgently required for the storage of a further ten thousand tons of high-explosive bombs. In June 1941 the Air Ministry purchased an adjacent mine at Fauld from Peter Ford's. Initially, concern had been registered by Ford's directors regarding extension by the R.A.F. into these adjacent disused mine workings. They had pointed out that the roadway to their active gypsum mine workings passed through the new area proposed for further bomb storage and they feared that issues of security would prevent their continuing to mine for gypsum there. In the light of this expressed concern the Air Ministry agreed to construct a blast barrier (which varied between fifteen and fifty feet in thickness),[5] maintaining the bomb store's integrity and also ensuring that Peter Ford's still had use of their roadway in addition to ensuring protection for Ford's miners from the blast of an accidental explosion. This conversion was completed in October 1942 and by this time there had been a relaxation in the regulations regarding safety distances within the mine. Consequently, the combined "old" and "new" mine areas provided sufficient space for the storage of up to 30,000 bombs and explosives and hence Fauld became the largest munitions storage unit in the country.

The "old" and "new" bomb storage areas were separated partly by a hundred-foot-thick pillar of unworked gypsum known as the Castle Hayes Pillar and partly by a hundred-foot-thick artificial barrier constructed by the Air Ministry. It was hoped that if there was an accident in one area the bombs in the other would be protected from the blast. The only access to the "new" area was by two low-roofed tunnels, one of which was constructed through the Castle Hayes Pillar.

It was in the interests of wartime security that the government was concerned to guard the secret of the tiers of bombs stacked in the rocky caverns of the disused mines and officially the existence of the ammunition depot at Fauld was not known to local people. The following description given by a former Royal Engineers officer engaged at R.A.F. Fauld, of what it actually looked like inside the mines where the bombs were stored, was not given until the day after the explosion:

It looked like an Aladdin's cave. You went from one cavern to another by passages ablaze with electric light. In the caverns the lighting had an eerie effect, and in dark corners you could see faintly the enormous tiers of H.E. [high explosive] bombs. In other sections were piles of incendiaries. We often wondered what would happen if an explosion took place in any one cavern. We often had visitors to the place and when they came out they would look pale at the thought of what would happen if an explosion took place.[6]

A former Italian prisoner of war, who later settled in Britain, recalled what it was like working there:

There was a lift shaft which carried the bombs and explosives almost a hundred feet into the former mine and at the bottom of the shaft were long tunnels with storage bays which contained about three thousand tons of explosives, mostly 3,000 lb 'blockbuster bombs'.

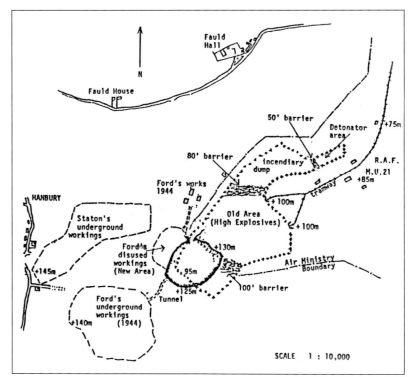

Location of Fauld Workings as compiled from charts submitted to the R.A.F Court of Inquiry in December 1944. The sketch map reveals the "old" area, the "new" area and the outline of the crater formed by the explosion

Courtesy of the National Archives, Kew

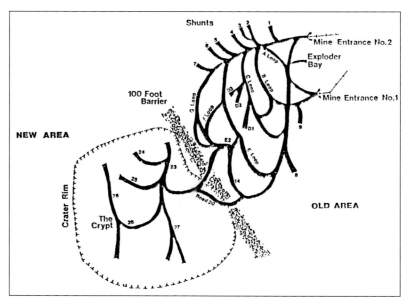

Underground tramways of new and old areas as submitted to Court of Inquiry

Courtesy of TNA

The bombs were hauled from the lifts with chains onto trolleys, then wheeled along the alleyways towards a storage point.[7]

The R.A.F. Maintenance storage unit at Fauld also became the headquarters of the "Master of Provisions Office" of No. 42 Group, with the added responsibility of meeting the demands of all fighter and bomber stations across the country. The significance of this was underlined by visits of senior officers, together with the Duke of Gloucester on 19 February and Sir Archibald Sinclair, the Secretary of State for Air, on 7 August, 1943.

By the spring of 1944, as the relentless demands of Bomber Command intensified in the build-up to the D-Day landings and continuing Allied advance in the months which followed, Maintenance Unit Number 21 R.A.F. Fauld was working at full stretch and handling up to 20,000 tons of bombs per month. The Unit also stored bombs for the United States Army Air Force, most particularly the 4,000 lb "blockbuster" high-explosive bombs, and from early in 1944 a detachment of U.S.A.A.F. personnel was also established there.

However, Fauld was not solely a depot for the storage and issuing of ammunition. It also had a responsibility for the repair of jettisoned bombs. The responsibility for the inspection and repair of all ammunition stocks lay not with the R.A.F. but with a team of civilians employed by the Armaments Inspectorate Department, the A.I.D. The A.I.D. worked as a team of inspectors and viewers responsible for the supervision of the R.A.F. armourers dealing with the hazardous task of dismantling defective bombs. This dismantling could require the removal of the "exploder pocket" containing the composition explosive, a sensitive form of high explosive used in fuses and detonators. It was particularly important

Bombs stored in the old area
Photo courtesy of the IWM

Visit of the Duke of Gloucester to the Fauld Mine, 19 February, 1943
Photo courtesy of the Magic Attic Archive

that the chisel used to chip out the composite explosive from the exploder pocket was made of copper, as other metals would be likely to create a spark which could set off the bombs. The dangerous nature of the job demanded that the damaged bombs should be worked on in an isolated cavern known as the "exploder bay", and it was essential that the correct tools were used in dealing with them.

By May 1944 M.U. No. 21 R.A.F. Fauld was under serious pressure and additional labour was urgently required. The problem was solved by taking on board former Italian prisoners of war, since Italy had now signed an armistice with the Allies. Initially, 46 "co-operators" were brought in from a prisoner of war camp in Hednesford, Staffordshire but in July and September more Italians were employed and many of these were from the P.O.W. camp at nearby Hilton, Derbyshire. By October, 195 Italian ex-prisoners of war (one officer and 194 men) were employed at Fauld. They reinforced the 18 R.A.F. officers, 14 W.A.A.F. officers, 475 other ranks and 445 civilians employed. However, there were very few of the new employees who had more than a basic knowledge of the dangers involved in handling explosives. The rules and regulations controlling the handling of the bombs increased and as the pressures on manpower intensified there was a tendency to a relaxation of standards. "It was difficult enough for experienced men to keep pace with the bewildering succession of technical instructions, but with the influx of new recruits, particularly at viewer level, it was well-nigh impossible. All too often the hard-pressed Chief Examiners found themselves condoning practices that would in times of peace have merited instant dismissal.'[8]

Maintenance Unit No. 21 R.A.F. was known locally as "the Dump". Although most people in the local area were aware that bombs were being stored in the worked-out gypsum mines at Fauld, no-one was in a position to appreciate fully the huge amount of high-explosive bombs and other ammunition stored in the labyrinth of caverns and tunnels beneath the Stonepit Hills. Certainly none of those living locally could imagine what would happen if there was an explosion.

However, an examination of the human geography clearly reveals the extent of the potential dangers. The land of Upper Castle Hayes Farm spread directly over the bomb store and the farmhouse, home to the Goodwins, together with their farm buildings, was supported above the Castle Hayes Pillar. A quarter of a mile to the west, Hanbury Fields Farm, farmed by the Bothams ,was also in a very exposed position. A number of other farms, including Croft Farm, worked by the Allens, Hare Holes, home to the Shelleys, and Fauld House and Fauld Manor Farms, where, respectively, the Hellabys and Heathcotes farmed, were all within a three-quarter-mile radius and potentially vulnerable. The village of Hanbury, with a population of around five hundred, lay half a mile to the west and was most particularly exposed, standing proud at around fifty feet above the general level of the Stonepit Hills escarpment. Additionally, in a valley adjacent to the Dump was Peter Ford's mill-yard, where over eighty men worked in the plaster works and office buildings. Also, Peter Ford's underground workings were only two hundred yards away and the tunnel along which the miners walked to reach the gypsum face took them alongside the reinforced solid rock wall of the "new" area of the bomb store perimeter. Close by the gypsum mine entrances were the Purse Cottages, homes to the Hill and Ford families. Furthermore, the six-million-gallon reservoir, supplying Peter Ford's Works, was perched ominously close to the point where the track led out of the mill-yard and up to Upper Castle Hayes Farm.

Within a mile radius, Lower Castle Hayes Farm, home to the Renshaws, Castle Hayes Park, farmed by the Majors, Fauld Hall, where the Gallimores lived, and Top Farm, Hanbury, worked by the Hardwicks, were also all potentially vulnerable. The R.A.F. administrative buildings, employing up to a thousand military and civilians, and the temporary residential huts, where around five hundred military personnel were resident, lay approximately a mile to the north-east of the Dump. The village of Tutbury lay only two and a half miles to the east and if the whole of the Dump went up then larger towns and cities could suffer widespread devastation.

When, shortly after eleven o'clock on 27 November, 1944 the Dump did go up, not only did it register on seismographs in Casablanca, it was also recorded in Geneva and Rome as an earthquake. A hundred and twenty miles away at Weston-Super-Mare the local people reported an ominous rumble and it was heard in London, Birmingham, Sheffield, Leicester and Northampton and around the Humber estuary. In Coventry glass was shattered. In Daventry people left their homes thinking it was an air raid and many locations across the country noted inexplicable rumbles of sound. It was heard in Lichfield and many buildings in Tutbury were damaged. In Burton-on-Trent the spires of St John's Church, Horninglow and Christ Church in Moor Street were made unsafe and up to a hundred and fifty houses reported damage.

Location of the Village of Hanbury and the Fauld Crater

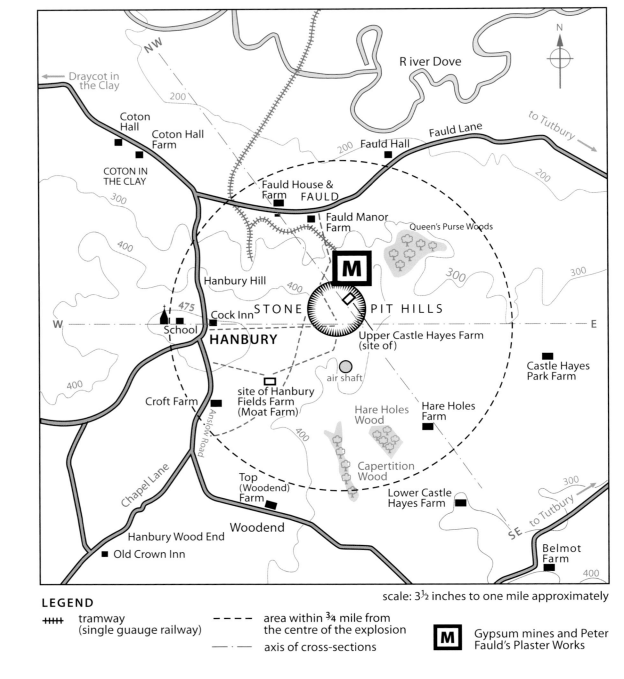

LEGEND

++++ tramway (single guauge railway)

- - - - area within ¾ mile from the centre of the explosion

— · — axis of cross-sections

scale: 3½ inches to one mile approximately

M Gypsum mines and Peter Fauld's Plaster Works

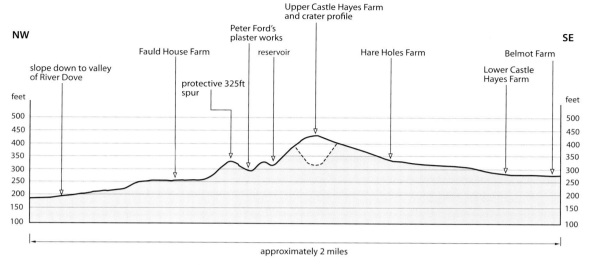

NW

SE

Upper Castle Hayes Farm
and crater profile

Peter Ford's
plaster works

Fauld House Farm

reservoir

Hare Holes Farm

Belmot Farm

slope down to valley
of River Dove

protective 325ft
spur

Lower Castle
Hayes Farm

feet

feet

approximately 2 miles

0.5 inches: 100ft

Section NW - SE through Stonepit Hills

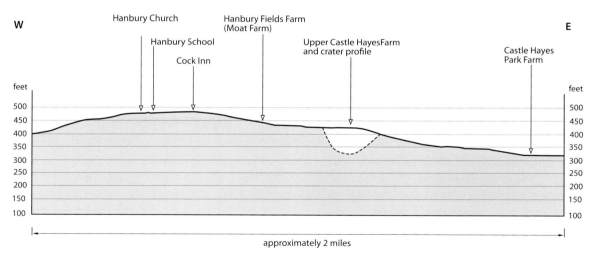

W

E

Hanbury Church

Hanbury Fields Farm
(Moat Farm)

Hanbury School

Upper Castle HayesFarm
and crater profile

Cock Inn

Castle Hayes
Park Farm

feet

feet

approximately 2 miles

0.5 inches: 100ft

Section W - E through Hanbury and the Crater

I lived in Malvern Street, Stapenhill, Burton-on-Trent, approximately ten miles from Fauld and all the houses on one side of the street had a crack in the same position. The older residents told me how they happened – it was when Fauld went up.[9]

The village of Hanbury, together with the wooded valley where Peter Ford's Works had been, presented scenes of appalling devastation. Much of Queen's Purse Wood had been uprooted. The primrose bank, on the lower slopes of the Stonepit Hills below the woods, no longer existed. Fauld House Farm in the Dove valley had been saved by a three-hundred-and-twenty-five-foot intervening protective spur: it was the very same low hill, behind the cow sheds and stable, over which the Hellaby sisters had walked so often to discover the anemones and bluebells in the woods of Brown's Coppice. The Goodwins' farm of Upper Castle Hayes had vanished with a dramatic suddenness into the largest bomb crater in Europe.

Among the material in the National Archives is a report which is simply signed "Test Pilot". It records:

I was sitting in my office attending to the "paper work" of an aeroplane I had just test flown when it happened. There was a sudden distant roar, windows rattled, the metal office doors creaked and shook and a door opened. I ran outside and saw a huge mushroom-like form rising slowly into the air until it had assumed the shape of a giant umbrella. It seemed to remain there for a minute or two before falling steadily and in streaks, back to earth. There were many speculations amongst those of us who saw it, the most popular being that it was a V2 rocket.

About three hours later I had another aeroplane to test, so decided to go and investigate. I judged the explosion to have been about 25 miles distant and did not have much difficulty in finding it as I was guided there by pillars of smoke rising from what might have been a portion of the Siegfried Line after it had been subjected to a 24-hour bombardment by our "heavies" dropping 12,000 pounders, together with an artillery carpet barrage.

On the occasion of this first flight (I have flown over it several times since) I was not aware of what had caused it but that a disaster of appalling magnitude had taken place was obvious. As I flew round at a height of 1,000 ft. the whole thing seemed unreal and reminded me of some fantastic illustration of the Moon or Mars, from one of Jules Verne's books, and indeed, the groups of people I could see working knee-deep in mud might well have been Martians going about their daily tasks in some strange world instead of rescue squads intent on the grim business of searching for the many unfortunate victims of this awful tragedy.[10]

Police Constable Mackay, assistant to the Coroner at the Inquest held in February 1945, recorded:

Most of them had lived in the quiet of an English village all their lives and war had seemed so very far away from them.[11]

However, in November 1944, Bomber Command was still conducting air raids over Europe with bombs supplied from Fauld. There is a certain irony in that it was only six hours earlier, on the morning of 27 November, 1944, that the R.A.F. was bombing Munich when, for the villagers of Hanbury in those same hours before dawn, the war still seemed so very far away.

The *Manchester Guardian's* front-page headline on 28 November, 1944 was:

R.A.F.s Obliteration Bombing

The attack on Munich, carried out by 270 Lancaster Bombers, began at 5 o'clock yesterday morning and was described as a crushing assault.

The *Manchester Guardian* did not report the "R.A.F. Dump Disaster" until 29 November. It was placed on page five.

On 28 November, 1944, the *Derby Evening Telegraph* had front-page headlines of:

BATTLE AT THREE RHINE BRIDGES

and:

VILLAGE AND FARMS ENGULFED

Death Toll still unknown: Civilians in Ruined Area Disappear Without Trace

A Staffordshire village near Burton-on-Trent today lies scorched and in ruins. It is the centre of a district, miles wide, that has been devastated by yesterday's explosion of a bomb and ammunition depot.

The report continued:

I stood on a mass of churned earth which once had been a road and looked on a scene which defied description. I have seen nothing like it on the battlefield. Many of the rescue workers were Servicemen – veterans of several campaigns from Dunkirk and onwards. They had seen towns and countryside torn and blasted by bombs but they too had never seen such destruction at one blow.[12]

The *Uttoxeter Advertiser* reported a veteran of the First World War who, on the morning of 27 November was working at Peter Ford's, saying:

I was in the last war and I've seen some sights but nothing like this. We used to think the "Jack Johnson" shells were pretty bad but they were like kids' toys compared to this.[13]

The *Daily Express* reported:

The woodland valley where the explosion occurred looks today as if it had been scarified by a blast of elemental fire. Around the ridges of the declivity which was once a hill trees stared starkly naked and the desolation below is accentuated by trees pointing their blistered roots skywards like dead giants.[14]

NOTES

1 P.C. Mackay, Report to the Coroner, February, 1945.

2 A witness at Peter Ford's Works (Ernest Smith) reported in the Uttoxeter Advertiser, 6 December, 1944.

3 Reed, After the Battle.

4 McCamley, Disasters Underground.

5 Reed, After the Battle.

6 Evening Standard, 28 November, 1944.

7 Undated newspaper cutting in the Tutbury Museum.

8 Reed, After the Battle.

9 Told to the author by Ginny Pilkington, volunteer at the Magic Attic Archive, Swadlincote, on 2 August, 2011.

10 The National Archives Ref AIR 17/10.

11 P.C. Mackay Report.

12 Derby Evening Telegraph, 28 November, 1944.

13 Ernest Smith, a foreman-loader at Peter Ford's Works, reported in the Uttoxeter Advertiser, 6 December, 1944.

14 Daily Express, 29 November, 1944.

CHAPTER THREE

WITNESSES AND VICTIMS
ON THE SURFACE

"There was a blinding flash and it looked like a great mountain in front of you. The stuff stood up so high – pieces as big as railway engines were going up in the sky – we just stood and watched. It was unbelievable – it looked like it was going over you. There were great lumps of clay. There was stuff landing and making great craters about two hundred yards away. I was holding onto the horse when everything was shaking."[1]

"I shall never forget the sight. I was at the time putting a drain in the field called the Hope when the ground I was standing on shook under my feet and then I heard a great bang and looked across and saw it was like a mountain in the air and then stones and earth fell all about me."[2]

Shortly after eleven o'clock on that cold, bright November morning Jeff Hellaby left the main farm buildings on the opposite side of Fauld Lane and walked up the drive to Fauld House. There was a deafening roar, a huge blast and with dramatic abruptness the sky darkened ominously. He turned to face the thunderous noise. A vast black cloud was spreading outwards and upwards above the Stonepit Hills and across Fauld Lane. It was a terrifying sight.

Jeff Hellaby of Fauld House Farm, 1952

Jeff's immediate concern was for his wife, Ida, in the house. The tremendous blast had shattered all the windows save one and also damaged the roof. However, she had had a remarkable escape from injury. When the blast occurred she was by the cellar door in the passageway between the main and back kitchens and so was safe from the flying glass.

After his initial shock, horrifyingly, he recognised the cause of the blast. The unthinkable had happened: the Dump had gone up. The farm was situated perilously close to the vast arsenal of bombs stored in the disused gypsum mines: it was within 700 yards of what was known as the "incendiary area" close to the mine entrance.[3] However, he knew that there were others in significantly more vulnerable locations: Peter Ford's Plaster Works were only 100 yards from the incendiary area;[4] gypsum mining continued under the Stonepit Hills and the Goodwins at Upper Castle Hayes Farm above the Dump were in a highly perilous position.

Jeff Hellaby's immediate concern, once he was satisfied that his wife was safe, was for the Goodwins. He rapidly returned down the drive to find Dick Utting, who had worked on the farm for many years and lived-in at Fauld House. Dick was turning out the cows after the morning milking as he thought that they would be safer outside and away from the debris falling through the cowshed roof. Stressing the urgency of the situation and telling Dick that *"something terrible has happened at the Goodwins"*,[5] they hastened up Fauld Lane and turned into the narrow valley. Dick was also concerned for the fate of his brother Horace, who was working in the disused gypsum mines where the bombs were stored. However, they only got as far as the wrecked Peter Ford's Plaster Works. It was here, they recognised, that death had struck with terrible effect. The Fauld explosion, the biggest of the Second World War so far, had occurred on a military site but its effects were predominantly the destruction of civilian life and property.

Together with Jim Heathcote, of neighbouring Fauld Manor Farm, Jeff Hellaby and Dick Utting, followed by some American servicemen, were among the first on the scene and helped lead the search for survivors. They faced a scene which almost defied description: above them the Stonepit Hills had seemingly vanished and Peter Ford's Works was almost totally demolished. The scene of utter desolation they witnessed resulted not only from the explosion of nearly four thousand tons of bombs but also the destruction of the dam, releasing six million gallons of water from the reservoir to flood the valley. This huge flood, mixed with fifty thousand tons of blast debris, had destroyed most of Peter Ford's Works and the Purse Cottages, home to the Hills and the Fords. The landscape was totally

Left: Devastation above Peter Ford's mine and Plaster Works

Photo courtesy of the Magic Attic archive

Below: Jim Heathcote with his younger son David, 1952

Photo taken and loaned by his elder son George Heathcote

Above: Jim Heathcote of Fauld Manor Farm, 1952

Photo taken and loaned by his son, George Heathcote

unrecognisable. The farm track up the hill to Upper Castle Hayes Farm, down which Jeff and Ida Hellaby and their daughters had driven the previous evening, had disappeared. The Goodwins' home had gone: it had been blasted out of existence and only a huge crater remained.

Sixteen-year-old Harry Payne was working as a junior in the laboratory at the Nestles factory in Tutbury, two miles away, when he witnessed the explosion. His father, Reg Payne was employed in the ammunition dump at Fauld. Harry, who still lives in Tutbury, has written of his experiences and recalls:

The floor of the laboratory began to heave as I imagine would happen in an earthquake. The windows and glass roof rattled and a few cans of Condensed Milk fell off the storage shelves. Everyone in the laboratory seemed to freeze with a look of bewilderment on their faces, when from one of the laboratory windows which faced over the Dove valley to the hills around Hanbury was seen two long V-shaped columns of smoke. A member of the laboratory staff yelled "My God it's the Dump" and I believe that at the front of everyone's mind was that it had been hit by a V2 rocket.

My immediate concern was for my father Reg Payne who was employed by the Air Ministry as an examiner in the Aeronautical Inspection Department (A.I.D.) and worked along with other team members either in the Fauld mine or adjacent buildings engaged on the quality control and validation of bombs and ammunition before dispatch by rail for wartime purposes. At the time of the explosion I knew that my father would be in the vicinity of the mines in which weapons were stored and without asking for permission, got on my cycle and joined many other factory workers hurrying home.[6]

Harry Payne recalled cycling along Park Lane, Tutbury on his way to the Dump:

At the gate of the bungalow stood Granny and Mother along with my three-year-old sister waiting for news of what had happened. In my haste I remember braking too hard and skidding owing to the icy condition of the road that morning and coming off my bike. I told Mother and Grandma that I would go down to Fauld to see what information I could get, and as I pedalled along Park Lane I vividly remember at almost every gate there were people who had come out of their houses, standing on the pavement looking up and down the road anxious for news.[7]

(Harry Payne recalls, in Chapter Six, what he witnessed when he reached the Dump.)

Police Constable Albert Thomas Mackay (later Sergeant) arrived on the scene in about ten minutes. Little did he realise at that time that he would be searching the site for many months to follow. Farmer's son, John Hardwick, recalled:

The local police were magnificent. Sergeant Mackay walked the devastated area, which was up to a thousand acres in all, every day until the following May.[8]

Police Constable Mackay was cycling through the village of Anslow on his way to the police station at Tutbury when he witnessed the explosion. He was aware of the huge munitions depot at R.A.F. Fauld. He appreciated that, if the arsenal went up, death and destruction would be catastrophic and widespread. The surrounding towns of Burton-on-Trent, Uttoxeter, Derby, Lichfield and neighbouring villages could suffer serious damage. Briefly, he watched the horrifying sight, expecting that the end had come for many thousands of people.

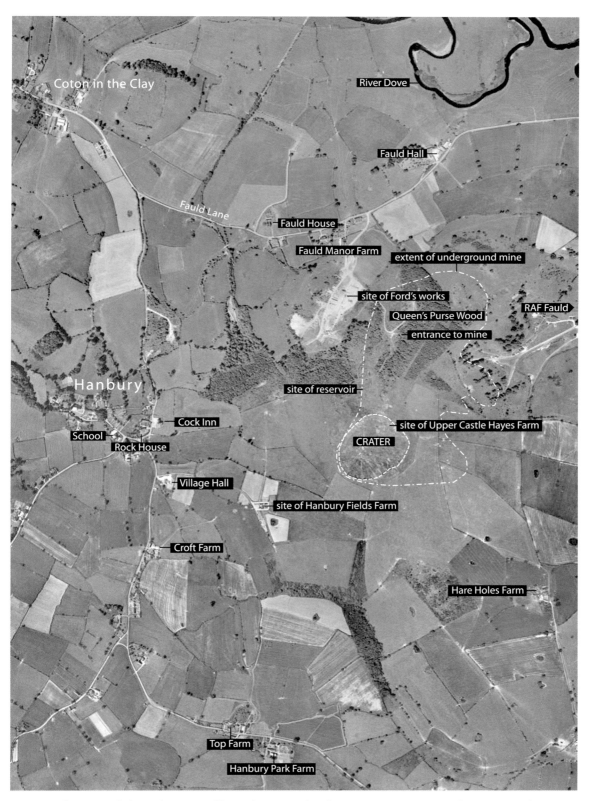

Air Photograph based on Aerofilms photograph taken on 11 June, 1963 from 5,280 feet

Air Photo courtesy of Bluesky International Limited and annotated by Malcolm Lewis

Time seemed to stand still for the next few seconds and then quiet reigned again. By a miracle, death and destruction had passed thousands by. By what a narrow margin was never known or even suspected by these people and only now can this closely guarded secret kept by the few who knew, be disclosed.[9]

In his report to the Chief Constable of Staffordshire P.C. Mackay wrote:

On the morning of Monday, 27th of November, 1944, I was on cycle and passing through Anslow village on my way to Tutbury Station, when, at 11.09 a.m., I heard and felt a violent explosion followed by five lesser ones. Simultaneously, I saw thick volumes of what I thought to be black smoke billowing up into the sky for thousands of feet, from the direction of the R.A.F. station at Fauld, about two miles away. A white cloud spread slowly over a large area near ground level and the "black smoke" was shot with many colours.

I knew something serious had happened and I cycled to the main entrance of the R.A.F. station – arriving there about 11.20 a.m. Flames were visible in two places among the hills of the station and I could hear the "pop", "pop" of incendiaries going off.[10]

When P.C. Mackay arrived at R.A.F. Fauld it was to witness thirty-foot flames from the burning incendiary store near the mine entrance and the workers, military and civilian, walking down the roadways for roll call. All telephones at the R.A.F. station were out of order. However, Police Sergeant Kelly of Tutbury, also realising what had happened, had telephoned his headquarters and calls had gone out from there to the local Report Centre and the Fire Station. Recognising the urgency of the situation Air Raid Precaution vehicles, fire engines and servicemen from a nearby American Camp descended on the R.A.F. station at Fauld.

P.C. Mackay continued his report to the Chief Constable:

Full realisation of the extent of the disaster was not known until about 12.30 p.m. when Sergeant Kelly reported that he had been informed by Charles Gallimore, a farmer, of Fauld Hall, that the Works of Messrs P. Ford and Sons Ltd, had been destroyed. These Works were situated about three quarters of a mile beyond the R.A.F. station, towards Uttoxeter, and lay in a small valley half a mile off the Fauld Lane up a dirt track. A.R.P. services and U.S.A vehicles had passed this track but none had observed the condition at Ford's Works owing to this isolation and the survivors had had no means of communication except by word of mouth.

Superintendent Vodrey, Sergeant Chamberlain and Sergeant Massey of Uttoxeter had also arrived and I immediately went with them and Inspector Webb to the Works, which were totally destroyed.

A large reservoir had existed above the Works and supplied water for all necessary purposes. The explosions had hurled thousands of tons of soil onto the Works site and the water from the destroyed reservoir had poured down into it turning it into a valley of sticky mud. Two cottages [the Purse Cottages] had been built in one corner of the Works yard but these had gone. When I arrived, an American officer with other ranks was carrying Mrs Nellie Ford (an occupant of one of these cottages) out of the mud on a stretcher. I helped them get her away to hospital and then joined in the general search. Shortly afterwards the body of George Lawrence Cockaine (50) of 11, Church Street, Tutbury was found and I loaded him into a C.D. ambulance.

I climbed through the wood and emerged into the fields forming part of Moat Farm,

Hanbury and found the whole area to be a scene of utter devastation, Moat Farm was shattered by the blast. [Moat Farm was also known as Hanbury Fields Farm and farmed by Harry Botham.] *Large and small craters existed everywhere with dead cattle dotted about but all were badly injured and required to be destroyed. I also observed that a gigantic crater now existed on land formerly part of Castle Hayes Farm and that the whole of the farmhouse and buildings had completely vanished. It was evident that the main explosion had occurred here and that a vast amount of High Explosives had exploded in one of the underground workings and that the "black smoke" that I had observed was in fact millions of tons of soil.*[11]

P. C. Mackay recorded that he had known the Goodwin family and Miss Elizabeth Smith at Upper Castle Hayes and had visited the farmhouse many times, including a week's wartime harvesting holiday spent there.

A confidential report by the Ministry of Home Security into the Fauld explosion dated December 1944 but not released until 1974 stated:

Considerable damage by blast and debris was caused in the immediate vicinity above ground, whilst extensive damage by debris and earth shock was caused to property within a radius of approximately a quarter of a mile from the point of explosion. Maximum debris damage extended to a radius of approximately 1420 yards [over three-quarters of a mile] *from the seat of the explosion, Hanbury village being particularly affected. Messrs Peter Ford's Lime and Gypsum Works to the North of the incident was practically demolished together with Purse Cottages immediately adjacent. Upper Castle Hayes Farm, which was on a pillar of unworked ground to the North of the section of workings affected, completely disappeared into the huge crater made by the explosion. Apparently, the top of the pillar mentioned sheared off and fell together with the whole of the Farm.*

The main crater was surveyed by the R.A.F. Works Service by means of two theodolites and has been accurately plotted on 25-inch map tracings. The crater is some 900 feet [over half a mile] *in length by 700 feet wide with a depth of approximately 80 feet.*[12]

At other times the depth of the crater has been variously estimated at anything between 100 and 400 feet. It was known that there had been 90 feet of earth cover above where the high-explosive bombs were stored in the mine and later figures have estimated the depth as probably at least 100 feet. The sign outside the Cock Inn in Hanbury describes the crater as 400 feet deep. Varying dimensions of the length and breadth have also been quoted, including an estimated length of three-quarters of a mile and a width of nearly half a mile. It is generally accepted that it covers an area of approximately twelve acres.

Jeff Hellaby knew that his friends the Goodwins had intended to go to the cattle market in Burton that morning. If all had gone to plan they should have left before the explosion occurred. He hoped and prayed that they had got away in time. The same would not be the case for the men working on the farm or, indeed, for Mary Goodwin's sister, Marie's Aunt Lizzie (Elizabeth Smith).

The four men working at Upper Castle Hayes that morning were: Stephen West, originally from Mill Farm, Cubley, Derbyshire who lived-in with the Goodwins; his younger and recently married brother, John, who lived in Hanbury; sixteen-year-old evacuee Russell Miles from Wallasey, Cheshire, who also lived-in at the farm; and sixty-eight-year-old

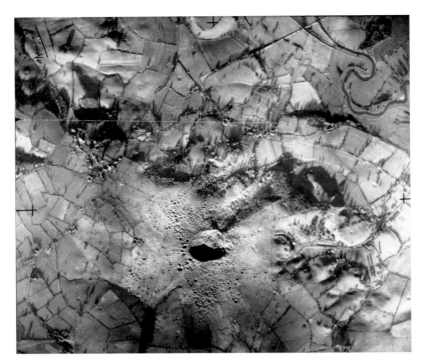

Fauld crater and surrounding area from the air on 2 December, 1944

Photo courtesy of the National Archives

Fauld area from the air on 2 December, 1944

Photo courtesy of TNA

Robert Wagstaffe, thatcher and hedge-cutter, who lived at Draycott-in-the-Clay and did casual work for many farmers in the area. Bob Wagstaffe had arranged to do some work for Maurice Goodwin that morning and the last sighting of him had been by young George Ede, who worked with his father at Coton Hall Farm and who, twenty minutes before, had seen him striding across the fields to Upper Castle Hayes. All four were victims of the explosion: the bodies of Robert Wagstaffe and Russell Miles were never found. That of John West was found on the following Friday and that of his brother Stephen nearly three years later in August 1947.

In addition to Jeff Hellaby at Fauld House and his neighbour Jim Heathcote at Fauld Manor Farm, the families who lived in the Fauld Cottages along Fauld Lane were also witnesses to the explosion. Two of them were Tom and Dorothy Harrison. Dorothy, who subsequently married a younger brother of George Ede, who had seen thatcher Bob Wagstaffe taking his last walk across the fields to Upper Castle Hayes, recalls her memories of the morning when the Dump went up.

Dorothy Ede now lives near Ashbourne. At the time she was twenty years old and a volunteer in the Women's Land Army. Both she and her brother Tom were working at neighbouring Fauld Manor Farm on the morning of 27 November. She recalls her experiences of that fateful day:

By rights I shouldn't be here today if I'd done what Mr Heathcote told me to do that morning. I'd already got the horse to the stable from Shady Common Field. He then told me to go and move the sheep and cows up into another field. [This field was much closer to the centre of the explosion.] *I didn't do that, which was a good thing, because all of those sheep and cows were killed. Instead, I went back home to get some cream for the developing sty on my eye. I took George Heathcote* [Jim Heathcote's four-year-old son] *with me. When the Dump went up I lay on top of George because I thought the house was going to go on top of him. Both my parents were home when I got there with George. The front door of the house had blasted out in my dad's face. He went off walking and we didn't see him again until I got home that night.*

Dorothy Ede (née Harrison) when she joined the Land Army in 1942 aged seventeen

Photo loaned by Dorothy Ede

Quickly I went back to the farm and there met Dr Carera's wife. Dr Carera was in the Air Force at the time. She'd parked in the hay-barn and was on her way up [to Ford's Mines and Plaster Works] *to see what she could do to help. The hay-barn hadn't gone but part of the roof of the house and buildings had gone and doors had been blown off. And then, the Americans came up. I thought I'd never seen so many Yanks in my life. Mr Heathcote guided them up to where it had all gone up. There were lots of people came up the lane. The Yanks were first and then the A.R.P. Big boulders and trucks were coming down. My brother Tom and I went up before Mr Heathcote – up the lane. My brother picked up half a body. He shouted to me not to look and I'm glad I didn't. There were people and traffic going up and down the lane for weeks afterwards. There were the diggers – trying to get the bodies out – they used to wake me up at night.*

Together with Tom and Mr Heathcote we all tried to walk up to Peter Ford's. We couldn't get across Shady Common Field from where I'd collected the horse earlier that morning and all of the sheep had gone. We never found any sheep. We went across the fields to Hanbury – my brother Tom, Jim Heathcote and me. We couldn't find out where all the fields had gone – all the boundaries had gone. We walked through all this devastation. All the sheep had gone and nearly all the cattle – there were only about four cows left and we tried to bring them back down to the farm.[13]

In December 1944 the Ministry of Home Security recorded that approximately two hundred cattle were killed or injured by the explosion. Those in the vicinity were killed by blast and debris with their lungs completely collapsed, and heavy bruising was observed on the carcasses. Those immediately over the centre of the explosion were blown to pieces and their body parts were found in fields adjacent to the main crater. Several cows which found their way back to the various farms were found to be suffering from shock and damage from flying stones. In some cases debris was embedded in their hides and they had very severe bruising as though they had been hit by large boulders.

Five cows which were taken in off the fields of Fauld Manor Farm on the night following the incident were found to be in a dazed state and the following morning they were found to be dead.[14]

Dorothy Ede continued her recollections:

We went on through the devastated area up to Hanbury and saw all the horrors of the Cock Inn and the blown-up Hut [the Village Hall was always known as the Hut]. *We saw that the Harrisons' house* [home to Ida Roberts (née Harrison), who had walked to Hanbury from Upper Castle Hayes with Gordon and Marie Goodwin earlier that morning] *was almost completely destroyed – it was nearly opposite the Hut.*

We came back to the farm [Fauld Manor Farm] *and we all sat down. Then Fred* [Ede] *came up. I was engaged to him. People* [in the area] *had told him that it was rumoured that all of the people at Heathcote's farm had been killed.*[15]

Fred Ede, from nearby Coton Hall Farm, had been working on his father's land in a field at the foot of Hanbury Hill at the time. Dorothy told of Fred's experiences and these were confirmed by his younger brother Peter, who described the huge boulders of alabaster which landed in the field where his brother was working when the horses, Charlie and Nigger, bolted back home to Coton Hall Farm.

Fred had been muck-carting in their field at the bottom of Hanbury Hill. Everything went dark and there was this horrendous noise. And the horses took off with the muck-cart right across that field – straight back to the farm. His brothers, George and Jim, were also on the farm and Peter was at school at Hanbury.[16]

Dorothy's experiences were separately confirmed by Jim Heathcote's son George. Although only four years old at the time, he has a recollection of that Monday and also recalls what his father told him of what happened.

I was playing in the ash ruck [cold ashes cleared from the open fire which heated the cottage] *visiting my Auntie Dot – this was Dorothy Harrison of Fauld Cottages. She was a land girl who worked for my Dad. She'd taken me to her home to get some cream for her eye. We'd been up to Shady Common, the land which joined your Dad's, when we heard this great boom.*

I remember they used my Dad's garage to put the bodies in for people to identify them and there was a caravan serving tea in the farmyard. There was also this great block of alabaster which had been blown out. It was in front of the house for years. [The Heathcotes lived in Alabaster House whilst farming the land of neighbouring Fauld Manor. Alabaster House was established as an incident base.]

My Dad lost seventeen cows. There were ten dead in the field and seven died from shock and their injuries in the sheds the next morning. They couldn't get them down through our fields. They took the road up to Peter Ford's. My Dad took the Americans up the road to Peter Ford's. He was the first on the scene and he met up with your Dad and Dick Utting. When my Dad took me up to Hanbury I remember seeing the bed hanging out of the Cock Inn.[17]

The following day, the *Daily Telegraph* reported:

At one farm I spoke to the farmer's wife [Mrs Heathcote of Fauld Manor Farm] *who said "it was terrible. I thought our last hour had come. The explosion killed nine or ten of our cows and the whole flock of our fifty sheep. The farm is ruined and there is no doubt that we shall have to leave."*[18]

This was George Heathcote's mother, who didn't tell of the additional cows which had died. The Heathcotes did not in fact leave their farm.

George continued his story:

My Dad had a terrier dog and the dog found some bodies. I also remember Jack Gorton – he came out of the mine alive and swore he'd never go down the pit again.[19]

After the explosion Jack Gorton came to work for Jeff Hellaby at Fauld House Farm. His story is told in the following chapter.

A graphic eye-witness account is also given by Doug Archer, who has spent his life in farming and who still lives in Hanbury. As a boy he had attended school at Church Broughton with Steve West, who lost his life at Upper Castle Hayes. He was sixteen years old when he witnessed the explosion when working on Grange Farm about a mile to the south-east of the Dump. He recalls:

I was working at Grange Farm beyond Belmot Green [on the road towards Tutbury]. *We were about to move into Hare Holes Farm* [half a mile south-east of Upper Castle Hayes Farm]. *When it happened we were muck-carting – we spread it by hand in those days – we had a horse and cart. It was a lovely morning. It was Jack Tunnicliffe's farm. He was raking the muck piles and we were on the third row. I was holding the horse when everything started shaking – the chains on the cart and the harness were all rattling. I said "Eh up sir, the Dump's going up!" We looked across the fields towards the Dump – there was a blinding flash and it looked like a great mountain in front of you. The stuff stood up so high – pieces as big as railway engines were going up in the air – we just stood and watched. It was unbelievable – it looked like it was going over you. There were great lumps of clay. There was stuff landing and making great craters about two hundred yards away. I was holding onto the horse when everything was shaking. We took the horse back to the farm and found Mrs Tunnicliffe and her young son John under the stairs – they thought it was the German bombs.*

We walked over the fields up to Hare Holes Farm – there were holes everywhere. There

Doug Archer, 1949

Photo loaned by Doug Archer

were holes in the roof of the house. The cowshed roofs and buildings were wrecked. Jack Shelley and his daughter Annie were there at the time. There was a V-shaped piece knocked out of the roof of the house. All of the fields had craters in them. We were due to move in the following March. At Hare Holes old Jack Shelley came from behind some buildings. His first words were – "Ain't they made a bloody mess!" He thought it was the Germans. From Hare Holes we [Doug Archer and Jack Tunnicliffe] continued walking right up to the crater where Upper Castle Hayes Farm had been. The territory was all mangled. We saw a body in a crashed tree. In the crater you could see the remains of the actual concrete blocks from Peter Ford's Plaster Pits. The entrance to Peter Ford's pit [mine] was just below the crater and the bottom end of Peter Ford's was at the bottom end of the crater.

My Dad, Donald Archer, had a lucky escape that morning. He worked for Renshaws at Lower Castle Hayes Farm but, because it was such a lovely morning, they were all down in the fields near the Anslow Road at Blackbrook [Hanbury] spreading lime on the fields there. If they had been up at Hare Holes Wood they would have been killed.

Twelve months afterwards, the worst part of it was you had to be careful where you jumped – we used to go shooting over there – foxes and rabbits – you were likely to jump on a rotting cow.[20]

The official report on the damage to Hare Holes Farm stated:

Chimney stacks cracked and pots dislodged. Ceilings damaged. Roofs holed by debris. Farm buildings damaged by debris. Holes in corrugated iron sheeting to Dutch barn.[21]

Former Flight Sergeant Neil Robinson, who now lives in Stapenhill, Burton-on-Trent, was stationed at R.A.F. Fauld from March 1943 to January 1945. Twenty-one years old, he was about five hundred yards from the mine entrance to the ammunition dump when the explosion occurred. After helping the fire-fighting parties at the mine entrance he joined one of the stretcher parties and went up to the crater and later came across the Shelleys at Hare Holes Farm. He recalls:

We were told to go with one of the stretcher parties up over the top to the crater taking two sten guns and two rifles to slaughter the sheep that were in trouble. Later we came across Hare Holes Farm and discovered the Shelleys in a state of shock. They had the remains of a meal on the table and there was a gaping hole in the roof through which you could see the sky.[22]

Flight Sergeant Neil Robinson, 1945

Photo loaned by Neil Robinson

Neil Robinson has written of his experiences in a short, graphic unpublished memoir.

Flight Sergeant Bill Allen and I were to arm ourselves with sten guns and rifles and take three or four airmen with us to carry the ammunition. Our job was to cover the outer area of the mine, search for any animals that were injured and to put them out of their misery by shooting them. Our small party set out and started to climb the black rubble that had once been the side of a hill. When we reached the top we saw the crater for the first time. Near the edge of the crater we found several sheep, some dead and others badly mutilated.

It was apparent from our position that the entire mine had not been destroyed completely by the blast, the hills housing the mine had disappeared leaving an uneven surface in all directions with the crater in the centre. We could not see the base of the crater due to the grey smoke still hanging about.

One of the worst sights we came across was a horse impaled upon some iron railings.

It had obviously been lifted up by the force of the blast and dropped onto the railings. Bill made doubly sure that it was dead by emptying the contents of his sten gun into the horse's head.[23]

It was later in the day when they came across Hare Holes Farm where:

The roof beams were still intact but there were gaping holes in the roof. When we entered the room, we found to our utter amazement a couple sitting at the table and staring into space. The debris from the roof was piled high on the table which contained the remains of a meal. Although they were uninjured they were in a state of shock.[24]

There was no warning of the colossal forces unleashed by the explosion which lashed the hilltop village of Hanbury and nearby farms. Hanbury Fields Farm lay half a mile to the east of the village and its land adjoined that of Upper Castle Hayes. Frequently known as Moat Farm, it felt the full force of the blast. At ten o'clock on the morning of the explosion, Mr and Mrs Harry Botham had left for Lichfield market with their young daughter Lucy. However, Mr Harry Botham's mother did not go with them as, being a Monday, Mrs Mary Cooper from the village was due to come to the farm to do the weekly washing. Working on the farm that morning were Sydney Chawner, who worked full time for Mr Botham, and George Rock, who did three days a week. Mrs Mary Cooper recounted her experiences to P.C. Mackay, who recorded it in a police statement.

About ten fifty a.m. on Monday, the twenty-seventh of November, 1944, I arrived at Moat Farm, Hanbury. I found that Mr and Mrs Botham had gone to Lichfield Market, leaving "Granny" Botham alone in the farmhouse.

At eleven a.m., I went across the yard to get a bucket of slack for the copper fire. I saw the farm labourer, Sydney Chawner, standing by the chop house [where root crops are prepared for fodder], *the door of which was open. Chawner had a pitch fork in his hand and he was smoking a pipe. I spoke to him about the weather – it was a very nice day – and George Rock (whom I know very well) shouted from out of the chop house, "Hello Mrs Cooper, how are you?" I said, "All right, George, going to be busy like you." I did not see him at all, but I knew his voice well and he knew me. I heard him say to Chawner, "Is that all, Syd?" and Chawner said, "Yes, let's go."*

I went back in the house and went on with my work there. About eleven ten a.m., I was in the wash-house when I heard what I thought was the chimney pot falling down the roof. Then I heard an awful roar and saw dirt and stones going past the window. Granny was with me and we stood together with my arm around her. I heard more awful noises and then saw the legs of a bed and other bedroom furniture show through the floor above and I put Granny under the table and got under myself.

Left: Mary Cooper with her youngest children John (left), Joe and Joyce

Photo loaned by Margaret Nicklin

Right: George Rock in the Hanbury Church Choir, 1943

Taken from photo loaned by Bill Moore

Everything went dark for several minutes and I thought we were buried alive. Gradually light came back and I crawled out from under the table and looked out across the yard and saw everything in sight was in ruins with debris everywhere. I got Granny out into the yard and then Mr Hunt [a neighbouring Hanbury farmer] came.

I shouted for Chawner and Rock and went to the chop house for them but saw neither of them. It was then that I looked across the fields towards Goodwins and saw the farm had gone and all the fields torn up in all shapes.

I met Mrs Cox and together we got Granny away to a friend's house, then I came home. Later I heard my husband, Joseph, had died in Peter Ford's mine, where he worked as a loco driver.

The farm was burning when Mr Hunt came – I don't know what started the fire and as all the water supply had gone it could not be put out.[25]

Mary Cooper's eldest daughter, Margaret Nicklin, who witnessed the signing of her mother's statement to P.C. Mackay, recalls:

My mother and Granny Botham were very lucky. They hid under the table. My mother said to Granny Botham – "I think there's a plane coming over." I helped my mother afterwards with the bodies and the coffins.[26]

For three months afterwards, Mrs Mary Cooper exhibited truly remarkable inner strength and great courage.

From that day on until the end, Mrs Cooper gave an exhibition of moral courage greater than any heroic deed. She attended daily at the mortuary, lighting the boiler fire and keeping the mortuary scrupulously clean, notwithstanding the presence of bodies of other victims which must have reminded her vividly and frequently of her own loss.[27]

Mary Cooper's son Joe also recalls:

I don't know how my mother and old Mrs Botham – she was in her eighties – survived. They got under the table. They never found George Rock. My mother thought he'd been in the barn beforehand getting hay down. They didn't find a trace of poor old George. They found Sydney Chawner. Mr and Mrs Botham and Lucy – she would be about three or four – had gone to Lichfield market.[28]

Neighbouring Hanbury farmer John Hunt, who lived at what used to be known as

Ebernezer House which was beyond Croft Farm on Anslow Road before the junction with Chapel Lane (see map of the location of the village of Hanbury and the Fauld crater in Chapter Two), also witnessed the explosion and stated:

At eleven ten a.m. on Monday the twenty-seventh of November, 1944 I was at home when I saw a huge column of something black shoot up into the air in the direction of the dump. Then I heard a loud explosion.

I guessed what had happened and I thought Botham's farm would be affected so I ran there to see if they were safe. I found the farm in ruins but saw "Granny" Botham and Mrs Cooper by the side of the wash-house door. I was told that Mr and Mrs Botham had gone to Lichfield market. I asked Mrs Cooper where the men were and she said she didn't know.

I saw smoke coming from the hay-barn so I went there and made a thorough search all around and on top of the hay-barn, but neither labourer, Chawner or Rock were there. I can swear to that.

I knew the work these men did and guessed they would be cabbage cutting and carting so I went towards the cabbage field. It was now a field of holes and hills. I saw Mr Botham's horse lying dead and the remains of the cart yards away. I knew then there was no hope for anyone who had been in that field, so I came back to the farm then.[29]

Left: Devastation at Hanbury Fields Farm. Farmhouse bottom right
Photo courtesy of TNA

Right: Harry Botham of Hanbury Fields Farm
Photo:- Hanbury Church Choir 1943

Above: Hanbury Fields Farm buildings Photo courtesy of TNA
Below: Hanbury Fields Farm panorama Photo courtesy of TNA

Sydney Chawner and George Rock had left the chop house and taken the horse and cart to work in the cabbage field which adjoined the land of Upper Castle Hayes Farm.

On the Bothams' return from Lichfield market at around three-thirty that afternoon, they found their home in ruins. Sydney Chawner's body was found but that of George Rock was never found. Harry Botham reported to P.C. Mackay:

I learned then that Chawner had been found dead but that Rock was missing. I looked in the chop house and saw that the knife always used by him was missing but that the gorse-hook always used by Chawner was still there. From this I concluded that Rock had gone cabbage cutting with Chawner acting as carter.[30]

P.C. Mackay reported:

At one fifty p.m. I saw the half buried and mutilated body of a farm labourer, Sydney Chawner, on land forming part of Moat Farm. I also saw a dead horse about thirty yards away with fragments of a cart about another thirty yards away in a different direction, but saw no signs of the missing man, Frederick George Rock.[31]

The Vicar of Hanbury, the Rev. Crook, had been one of the earliest on the scene from the village of Hanbury searching for the men working on Botham's farm. P.C. Mackay told how, with the assistance of one of the Italian ex-prisoners of war, he had dug Sydney Chawner out of his half buried position before the vicar organised diggers to free him and arranged for his body to be taken to the school, which had now become a mortuary. The Vicar's story was reported:

I continued my search and found the body of Mr Chawner, who was buried head first in the ground with a dead horse and cows lying around him. He lay between the ruins of Mr Goodwin's farm and Mr Botham's farm. I then went in search of my own man, George Rock, [verger at the church] *who was working with Mr Chawner but could not find him. I organised digging parties and got Mr Chawner out. He was dead. There was no sign of Rock. The body of Chawner was taken to the Mission Room* [Parish Room next to the school].[32]

Before the official inquest, which took place in early February 1945, P.C. Mackay, the Coroner's assistant, reported:

On many dates since the twenty-seventh of November, 1944, I have made search for Frederick George Rock, in all directions from Moat farmhouse, but without trace of him. On the thirteenth of January, 1945, with three other police officers and thirty Civil Defence personnel, I again made a foot by foot search of a hundred yards flagged square around the area in which his colleague, Sydney Chawner was found, but there was no trace of the missing man.[33]

Hanbury Fields farmhouse and buildings were 650 yards (less than half a mile) to the south-west of where Upper Castle Hayes house and buildings had been. Sited at the same altitude as the neighbouring Goodwins farm, they experienced the full force of the blast and were completely beyond repair. They were subsequently demolished and later the Bothams moved to farm near Belper in Derbyshire.

The house and farm buildings of Castle Hayes Park lie 1,450 yards (over three-quarters of a mile) to the east-south-east of where Upper Castle Hayes had been. They were sited a hundred feet lower down the escarpment and were less exposed than the neighbouring Hare Holes Farm, which was at a slightly higher altitude and within only half a mile south-east of where Upper Castle Hayes had been (see map of location of the village of Hanbury and the Fauld crater in Chapter Two). These slight differences in altitude, distance and degree of exposure proved critical. Castle Hayes Park was farmed by the Majors. Their three-year-old daughter Pat (now Pat Guest and living in Tutbury) recalls what she was told of what had happened.

There were some sheds down and the chimney pots were down. We had to evacuate the house for three days. There were all these animals that had gone – they needed to be destroyed. There was a great boulder which landed in the cart where the men were working in a field of root crops. They lay down in the rows of roots and the boulder crashed through the cart and the horse bolted. It was fortunate that the boulder didn't land on them – they could have been killed.[34]

Farmer's son Roy Gregson of Church Farm, Hanbury was seventeen and had recalled:

Yes, I remember the sound. It was an enormous HOOOOOOMP and up she went . . . and up . . . and up. The sky went black as the soil went up and I could see boulders rolling about above me – boulders in the sky. A piece of alabaster weighing twenty tons came down three-quarters of a mile away.[35]

Roy Gregson also told how:

I was working on my father's farm with a horse and cart carting cabbages for the cattle – and there was this almighty shake and then this explosion and everything rolled up like a volcano erupting. My horse ran away – me after it – I didn't know what had happened.[36]

Roy Gregson and Tom Allen at Church Farm, Hanbury circa 1945
Photo from Percy Winson

The late John Hardwicke has left an unpublished handwritten record of what he witnessed on the surface. His parents farmed at Top Farm (also known as Woodend Farm) at the top of Blackbrook Hill in Hanbury. John was twenty-one at the time:

I can only tell my story – give my eye-witness account. On that particular Monday morning I was working on my parents' 100-acre farm. Our farm was to the south of the ammunition dump and we farmed about 500 feet above sea level on the hills over the alabaster working. Access to the dump and to the mine still being worked was by drift from land lower down and near to the river [the River Dove].

Because our neighbour [William Woolliscroft of Hanbury Park Farm] *was ill, and he still had a root crop not yet harvested, we* [John and Fred Ford, who lived in a cottage close to Top Farm and worked for John's father Bert Hardwick] *were sent to help and by 11 o'clock were in the fields cutting and lifting turnips and mangolds.*

Shortly after 11.00 a.m. on this bright, sunny, frosty morning there was an explosion quickly followed by a second and we knew that the Dump had gone up. First of all we ran for cover. All we could do was get down into a ditch. We saw the edge of Hare Holes Wood – some two acres of trees – being blown into the air and out of sight. The bright morning was gone and in a matter of minutes all the virgin soil which had been blown into the air now started to come down like a dust storm. Our distance from the source of the explosion would be about a mile and eventually we were walking through about two inches of soil.[37]

In 1989, sharing his recollections with Byron Rogers of *The Guardian*, John Hardwick

[Handwritten witness account in left panel]

Above: John Hardwick and his parents at Top Farm, Hanbury circa 1944
Photo loaned by Audrey Hardwick

Left: From John Hardwick's witness account *Loaned by Audrey Hardwick*

pointed out that had he been working on his father's land, which was much closer to the crater, he could well have been one of the victims instead of just being an eye-witness.

Our land went two thirds of the way down to the crater and the only reason why I'm still around to tell you this story is that I was on the land of a neighbour who was ill. I was cutting a field of roots for him.[38]

The home of the Harrison family was quite close to the Village Hall and Featherbed Lane which led to Hanbury Fields Farm. Mrs Clara Harrison was alone at home at the time. She was recovering from an extended stay in hospital. The two eldest of her ten children were away from home, sixteen-year-old Ida was in Uttoxeter, her youngest, three year-old Colin, was with a neighbour and the rest were at school. She recalled:

I was sitting by the fire and my hearth rug just went backwards and forwards and then my fender went across the room. And I went through the door and I thought it was an aeroplane bursting in the sky. It was a terrible noise and I walked down to a gate and the gate came after me. I made haste and stood in the cowshed – in the corner of the cowshed.[39]

In the critical seconds following the explosion Clara Harrison's instinctive reaction to run from the house, where a massive boulder and debris had crashed through the roof, had probably saved her life. Her home was rendered uninhabitable. When she became aware that the noise and the vibration had stopped, she continued:

I'd thought well, perhaps everything's over and I'll go and see. I got to the cowshed door and the earth was coming down and it was as black as night. You couldn't see anything only dust and dirt – and all that coming down. It was all jet black as though it was night time. In fact I couldn't open that door. I had to stand and all the dust and dirt was coming down on you.[40]

William Shelley was another Hanbury resident who witnessed the explosion. He had formerly farmed at Upper Castle Hayes and his elder brother Jack was still farming at Hare Holes. In 1958 he completed writing his life story and included in his account a vivid description of the explosion. The original handwritten unpublished document is held by his grandson Bill Hidderley and his granddaughter Rosalie Vicars-Harris also has a copy.[41]

Until 1916, William had lived and farmed at Upper Castle Hayes Farm and also managed the greater part of the land of Hare Holes Farm. His wife Sarah (née Foster) was from Hanbury Fields Farm. He bought land and property in Hanbury and in 1944 was living at Rock House, Hanbury, which suffered extensive damage as a result of the explosion. He lost animals and buildings and much of his land was seriously damaged. On the morning of 27 November he was working on land which was within three-quarters of a mile of the explosion. He was in the "Hope" field at the top of Hanbury Hill and across the road from the Cock Inn (see aerial photograph of Hanbury in this chapter). He also had a barn and cowshed known as the Stalford Buildings on his Hanbury land which were totally wrecked. He had been in these buildings minutes before the explosion. He described his experiences:

I shall never forget the sight. I was at the time putting a drain in, down in the field called the Hope, when the ground I was standing on shook under my feet. I then heard a great bang and looked across and saw it was like a mountain in the air, and then stones and earth fell all about me. I was about three-quarters of a mile away from the explosion. After a few minutes I opened my eyes and never saw such a transformation. The field was all covered with burned soil, several inches deep. So I started for home. When I got to the top of the field I saw there was a sheep lying on its side. It had been hit by a stone or earth and as I went up the village towards home

William Shelley's witness account
Courtesy of Bill Hidderley

the damage was awful to see. All the roofs were damaged. Part of the Cock Inn was knocked down, and part of our kitchen was knocked in and the roof of our house was down in the living room. Some fields which I owned between Hanbury and Castle Hayes had holes in them all over nearly the size of a room, and all my buildings in that land were all to pieces. I had one ram killed. A cow we kept for milk for the house was in the fields at the time and had escaped without hurt. Our house was unsafe, we stayed there for the first night but our people came over the next day and would persuade us to leave as there was a cottage at liberty which had recently been completed for the Chapel House Farm in Tutbury.[42]

Left: William Shelley's devastated Stalford Buildings behind the Cock Inn
Photo courtesy of Magic Attic archive

Above: Bill Hidderley from Hanbury Church Choir photograph

Left (left to right): William Shelley, Sarah Shelley, Maud Foster, Joseph Foster (brother of Sarah Shelley) outside Hanbury Church
Photo loaned by Bill Hidderley

Chapel House Farm was the home of William's elder daughter and son-in-law – Nora and Ted Hidderley. William's wife Sarah had run out of Rock House when she heard the explosion, but when she saw the debris flying she ran back into the house to hide under the table just before the roof collapsed. The bedroom floor fell in but the carpet held the bulk of the rubble suspended above the table.[43]

William Shelley's grandson, Bill Hidderley, has filled in some details of his grandfather's story.

Grandfather was in the Hope Field at the top of Hanbury Hill. It was close to the Cock Inn. There was a tree there at an angle – we used to play there as children – and Grandfather sheltered there when the Dump went up. He'd taken some tools from the Stalford Buildings. There was one cow in those buildings – she'd walked out unhurt. He'd taken his tools and then decided to walk down to The Hope to clean the spring out. It was a damn good thing he did. [His Stalford farm buildings were completely wrecked.]

Granny was standing in the scullery at Rock House when it happened. She ran out into the yard and then ran back again and hid under the dining room table. Then the bedroom floor above collapsed but the rubble was held up by the carpet. My grandparents moved into an empty cottage close by Chapel House where my parents farmed.[44]

Joyce McCleod, who at the time was Joyce Frow and living in Tutbury, was working in Burton-on-Trent in a factory making parts for fighter planes when, from the factory fire escape, she witnessed the explosion. Lewis Frow, her fifteen-year-old brother, had just left school and was working at the Dump as a trainee electrician. Joyce, who now lives in Burton, has written the following account and recalls:

Aerial view of Hanbury Village 4 December, 1944

Photo courtesy of TNA and annotated by Malcolm Lewis

On Monday, 27 November, 1944 I remember it was a lovely sunny day. At about 11.10 a.m. I felt the building shake and the machines were shaking. We all thought it was bombs being dropped somewhere. We went outside onto the fire escape. You could still feel a tremor and then we saw a dark cloud a long way off. After a while we were told that it would be safe to go back to work. Later news got about that the Dump had blown up. The Dump was 21 MU R.A.F. Fauld where bombs were stored during the war.

Knowing my brother worked there and would be in the mine I spoke to the foreman and asked if I could go home. I was given permission to go. I had a long walk to get a bus and when I got home my mother said "What are you doing here?" She had felt the ground shaking but had not heard the noise because she was deaf. She told me to get on my bike and go there. When I got to the Fauld Ministry of Defence I was told that my brother was all right and would be home at the usual time. When he did not come home we knew it was serious, we had seen emergency services going there.

By now it was a dark, miserable night. We sat up all night – going out each time we heard a noise. We could not find out much about what was happening; during the war things were kept secret, very few people had telephones. After a few days we received a telegram to say my brother was missing, presumed killed. My mother screamed and said "I do not believe it" and threw it in the fire.[45]

Fifteen-year-old Lewis Frow was the youngest of the eighteen victims whose bodies were never found and for whom the Fauld crater is their grave.

The morning of Monday 27 November, 1944 was cold and bright. The local weather was reported as a westerly wind of three miles per hour, shade temperature of thirty degrees Fahrenheit, visibility of 1500 yards and generally fine without cloud.[46] Overnight the weather changed and rain fell heavily. It turned the hundreds of acres of devastation into horrendous bog reminiscent of the battlefields of the Somme and Passchendaele.

NOTES

1 As told to the author by Doug Archer, Hanbury on 11 September, 2011.

2 Handwritten account by William Shelley, 1958 formerly of Rock House, Hanbury.

3 The National Archives: from a report on a visit to the Air Ministry Site at Fauld on 31 July, 1945. Appendix C: 'It will be seen that the outskirts of HANBURY (The Cock Inn) are 975 yards from the nearest edge of the High Explosives area and 1100 yards from the the of the Incendiary area. The TUTBURY road is 550 yards from the Incendiary area, and the fairly substantial buildings of FAULD HOUSE, FAULD HOUSE FARM, MANOR FARM AND FAULD HALL are all within 700 yards.

4 Ibid.

5 As recalled by Marjorie (née Hellaby) Snow to the author on 3 August, 2011.

6 Memories of Harry Payne lodged in the Tutbury Museum. Whilst researching this book the author spoke with Harry Payne on 19 August, 2011.

7 Memories of Harry Payne as recorded on 13 May, 1999 and lodged with John Cooper.

8 From the unpublished record of John Hardwick who farmed in Hanbury. This handwritten record was kindly loaned to the author by his widow, Audrey Hardwick.

9 From the report written by P.C. Albert Thomas Mackay, who was the Coroner's Officer working for J.L. Auden, Coroner at the Fauld Explosion Inquest of February 1945. The Mackay Papers were donated to the Tutbury Museum by his son Donald in 2006.

10 P.C. Mackay's report to the Chief Constable of Staffordshire, 7 December, 1944.

11 Ibid.

12 The National Archives Ref AIR 17/10.

13 Recollections of Dorothy Ede (née Harrison) as recalled to the author on 19 August, 2011.

14 The National Archives Ref AIR 17/10.

15 Recollections of Dorothy Ede.

16 Ibid.

17 Recollections of George Heathcote as told to the author on 19 August, 2011.

18 *Daily Telegraph*, 28 November, 1944.

19 George Heathcote to the author on 19 August, 2011.

20 Recollections of Doug Archer as told to the author on 11 September, 2011.

21 National Archives Ref AIR 17/10.

22 As recalled by Neil Robinson to the author on 20 March 2012.

23 Record of Neil Robinson.

24 Ibid.

25 Mary Cooper's statement to P.C. Mackay on 23 January, 1945.

26 Recollections of Margaret Nicklin (née Cooper) as told to the author on 31 August, 2011.

27 P.C. Mackay's Report to the Coroner, February 1945.

28 Recollections of Joe Cooper as told to the author on 10 November, 2011.

29 John Hunt's statement to P.C. Mackay on 30 January, 1945.

30 Harry Botham's statement to P.C. Mackay on 30 January, 1945.

31 P.C. Mackay's Report.

32 Reverend Crook as reported in the *Burton Daily Mail*, 28 November, 1944 and *Daily Telegraph*, 29 November, 1944.

33 P.C. Mackay's Report.

34 Pat Guest as recalled to the author on 16 August, 2011.

35 *Sunday Telegraph Review*, 27 November, 1994.

36 BRMB radio recording from Birmingham, programme produced by Brian King, 1983.

37 Unpublished record of John Hardwick.

38 *Weekend Guardian*, 11–12 March, 1989.

39 BRMB radio, Birmingham, 1983.

40 Ibid.

41 From a handwritten autobiography of William Shelley. His grandson, Bill Hidderley, kindly allowed the author sight of this document and his granddaughter Rosalie Vicars-Harris kindly loaned a copy.

42 From unpublished life story of William Shelley.

43 *Written on my Heart: Memoirs of Vera Jeffery* by Rosalie Vicars-Harris and Malcolm Lewis.

44 Recollections of Bill Hidderley as recalled to the author on 21 January, 2012.

45 From Joyce McCleod (née Frow) when visiting her on 18 August, 2011.

46 The National Archives Ref AIR 17/10.

CHAPTER FOUR

WITNESSES AND VICTIMS AT FORD'S MINE AND PLASTER WORKS

"Conditions are like Passchendaele. The men are buried under ten feet of mud. We cannot hope to reach them."[1]
"So terrible was the scene of desolation all around him where huge craters overlapped one another as far as one could see and all the familiar landmarks had disappeared that he did not know his way home."[2]

Shortly after eight o'clock on Monday 27 November, 1944, sixty-four-year-old Joseph Foster left his Hanbury home to walk to Peter Ford's and Sons mines and plaster works at Fauld, where he was the Works Manager.[3] It was a walk across a familiar landscape, taking him along footpaths crossing Botham's and Goodwin's farmland, continuing on down the track from Upper Castle Hayes Farm, passing the reservoir on his left-hand side and the Purse Cottages on his right. He also passed the main mine entrance on the right, which was at the top of Ford's yard. It was the same walk which a number of other Hanbury men who worked in the mine and plaster works had taken even earlier in the day. All of them had passed by an air shaft from the mine nearly a hundred feet below, little realising the significance it would play in the lives of some of them later that day. At about the same time as Joseph Foster had left home, his granddaughter Pat was about to join Jeff Hellaby's two daughters on the school bus to Uttoxeter. A little later his grandson Joe would be walking to Hanbury School.

Joseph Foster
Photo loaned by his grandson Joe Foster

Later that morning Joseph Foster had a remarkable escape.

At about 11.00 a.m. I was helping the joiner, Harry Wetherill, to put up plaster boards when Frank Cartwright, a clerk, came to me and said I was wanted in the office. I went to the office and then hurried back to Wetherill in the mess room behind the mill. I did not see Cartwright again after he gave me the message. I had only been back in the mess room about two minutes when, at ten minutes past eleven I heard a sound which I thought was a large number of planes "dive-bombing" the works followed by what I thought were explosions.

Everything went quite dark for three or four minutes, then it gradually began to get light again. Wetherill and I went to the door and I saw water rushing all around the mess room and there was

59

about two feet of debris over everything near me. The mill was badly damaged with trees and other stuff piled up against it. The mill had kept all this heavy debris off the mess room so saving Wetherill and me. I saw a workman named Hurstfield lying on the tramway trapped by timber and with the assistance of another workman, James Ratcliffe, I got him out. Water kept coming down and it was knee-deep by the time we got him free. Some parts of the [work] shops were totally destroyed and also the offices. Water hid most of the yard and it was dangerous to attempt any search in the mess. I listened but heard no sound from any trapped person.[4]

Frank Cartwright, who was from Uttoxeter, returned to the office after giving Joseph Foster the message that he was wanted on the telephone. He was the transport manager at Peter Ford's and had worked in the office since leaving school. His body was never found. He was forty-one years old and left a widow. His forty-six-year-old elder brother Reginald was the head clerk in Peter Ford's office and was also from Uttoxeter. He also lost his life and left a widow and three daughters. He had spent twenty-six years in the offices at Peter Ford's.

The story of Joseph Foster's remarkable escape was reported the following day:

It is difficult to realise that anyone could have emerged from that holocaust unscathed. Mr Foster had one finger trapped and may lose a nail – that is all!

A man of over seventy and a youth of seventeen escaped without a scratch but a man two yards from Mr Foster escaped uninjured and others were killed.

"I didn't feel anything really", said Mr Foster. "One second everything was normal and the next everything was coming to pieces. We went to the help of the injured, and it was the fact that we were giving them what attention we could that kept our thoughts off ourselves.[5]

Peter Ford's mill-yard was only a hundred yards from the centre of the explosion. The surface workers had little warning of the disaster to come. As thousands of tons of bombs exploded the shock waves broke the bank of the reservoir supplying the works and the water plunged through Queen's Purse Wood and Brown's Coppice gathering trees, boulders and earth as it formed a twenty-foot wall of mud. It careered right through the plaster works, burying the workers and destroying the buildings.

The explosion of the Workings apparently had the effect of bursting a Reservoir situated above Peter Ford's Lime and Gypsum Works, the blast travelling down an outside access tunnel on the West of the R.A.F. Workings, the contents of the Reservoir flowing into the valley of the Works and taking with it considerable quantities of earth and trees, thus causing an avalanche effect. This, together with the blast and debris from the main crater, practically destroyed the Works and the adjacent Purse Cottages.[6]

Shandy Harrison was working at the far end of the yard:

We were just shoving a crate of plasterboard into the drier at the time and we felt the earth shake. Nobody talked to one another. All that we did was run outside and there was all this stuff up in the air. There was water coming into the place before we got outside and all this stuff was coming down. It seemed to be hours before it finished but it wasn't many seconds but it seemed to be that long and dark. It went very dark with all this stuff coming down. And then afterwards, when it was all over, we could see a couple of blokes floating down in slurry and all that.[7]

Devastation above Peter Ford's mine and plaster works
Photo courtesy of the Imperial War Museum (IWM)

Joseph Foster told of how he found men in the plasterboard room and then went along the side of Queen's Purse Woods to search for survivors. He was looking particularly for the Purse Cottages which belonged to the Company. The cottages had totally disappeared but, hearing shouts for help:

I saw Mrs Ford sitting astride a heap of earth about twenty yards in front of her cottage site and ten yards from the other side of the yard. It was quite impossible to reach her; I tried to go to her but was waist deep in mud in about two yards. American soldiers with an officer came along this other side and I shouted to them and the officer immediately went through the mud with another soldier and rescued her.[8]

Jeff Hellaby and Dick Utting had also reached this point in their search for survivors. Jeff's elder daughter Marjorie recounts her father's experiences as he and Jim Heathcote led the search parties of American service men:

Father and Dick and Jim Heathcote were prodding in the mud leading the way. They found Mrs Ford from Purse Cottages. She was still alive in the sludge opposite to where the reservoir used to be. She'd been held up by the remains of the wall which had been there on the left where you went up to Goodwins.[9]

Mrs Ford was seriously injured and taken to hospital, where initially she appeared to make a remarkable recovery. It was many months later when she eventually died. Her death was attributed to the shock of her traumatic experience. Her name appears on the memorials to the victims of the explosion. The local press reported that:

Mrs Ford was blown through the air a distance of about a hundred yards. She was found lying unconscious with her clothes ripped off. She is detained in the Derbyshire Royal Infirmary suffering from broken ribs, a broken arm and lacerations to the scalp.[10]

Mrs Nellie Ford's husband William, who was at work at Peter Ford's, lost his life. Mr Harry Hill in the offices was also a victim of the disaster. His wife, Mrs Sarah Hill, was at home at the time. Both she and her neighbour were anticipating a visit from the insurance agent, Mr Frederick William Harrison. Mr Harrison had worked for the Prudential Assurance Company in Burton-on-Trent for thirty-two years and on that Monday morning had arranged to visit clients in the Fauld area. At eleven o'clock he had visited Mrs Pegg, who lived at the Fauld Cottages on Fauld Lane, and then proceeded up the track to Peter Ford's to see Mrs Hill and Mrs Ford at the Purse Cottages. For fifty-eight-year-old Frederick Harrison it was to be a doomed visit. He and Mrs Hill, like Mrs Ford, were blasted out of the cottages but they did not escape alive. It was a month later before either of their bodies was found.

Police Constable Mackay recorded:

Immediately prior to the explosion Mr Frederick Harrison, an insurance agent, made his very first visit after his promotion, to the cottages. He called upon the occupant of the first cottage, Mrs Sarah Hill, and hearing him, Mrs Ford entered her front room to get her own insurance card and money for Mr Harrison. Without any warning the walls of this room fell outwards, and Mrs Ford was sucked out and upwards. She descended upon top of a huge piece of soft slag, twenty yards from her cottage, which, together with its neighbouring one had completely disappeared, as had the nearby reservoir, the water from which was swirling around her. Why she was not buried by the descending debris is beyond understanding.[11]

One of the two Purse Cottages had been home to the Hill family for eleven years prior to the explosion. At the time their two elder sons, Bill and Jim, were in the armed forces, their eldest daughter was married and their youngest children, twins Kathleen and Ronald, were doing their National Service away from home. Their younger daughter Kathleen recalls:

I was at Coventry at the time, doing my National Service working for the Hospital Co-operation. We heard this terrific noise and dashed outside. Subsequently we were told that it was an explosion near Burton-on-Trent. I immediately knew what it was. I tried to telephone my parents but it was midnight before I could get through when I was told that both my parents were "missing".

Prior to the explosion I'd had a dream – it was that my father had been out on his motorcycle and he'd had a horrendous accident. I remember phoning him and saying – "Don't go out on your motorcycle." The hall porter of the place where I was living also told me that he'd had a dream that something terrible was going to happen to me. It's quite amazing that I should have had that dream about my father and that the porter should have had that one about me.

My brother Bill was in the R.A.F. in the Middle East at the time and he came home on compassionate leave. My brother Jim was in the Navy – on submarines and up in Northumberland at the time. My brothers had to cope with the estate. My sister Eileen was married with three young children and living near Abbot's Bromley. She never really recovered from losing our parents. I went to stay with her for a couple of days and then I stayed with the Edes at Coton Hall Farm. I stayed with them at the time of the funerals.[12]

Left: Kay Sutton (née Kathleen Hill) (left) in front of Fauld Manor circa 1940 *Photo loaned by Kay Sutton*
Middle: Bill Hill (left) with brother Jim in Purse Cottage garden circa 1940 *Photo loaned by Kay Sutton*
Right: Sarah Hill in September 1944 *Photo loaned by Kay Sutton*

Kay Sutton (née Kathleen Hill) told how two months before the explosion her mother, Sarah Hill, had had her photograph taken and had given a copy to all of her children. It is the only picture of their mother the children ever had. The only one of their father is on a group of the workers at Peter Ford's dated 1937 (see end of chapter). Strangely, Kathleen also said that:

My mother, when a girl, went to book a ticket for the Titanic *but she couldn't get one and so she booked on the* Lusitania *instead. She went on to Canada and on her arrival there was a tornado and her parents sent her a cheque for a hundred pounds because they were so worried about her. She first met my father in Canada, he was working on the Canadian Pacific Railway, and their first three children were born there. Ron and I were born in Draycott-in-the-Clay. I think there was something very brave and courageous about living in the Purse Cottages – we went there when I was about eleven. My grandfather worked at Ford's and was involved in a terrible accident there.*[13]

Harry Hill circa 1937

Photo from group picture of Ford's workforce loaned by John Cooper

It was not until shortly before Christmas that it became possible for rescue workers to burrow down through the mud to locate the shattered remains of the Purse Cottages. The work had to be performed by hand and the great slabs of earth thrown clear. The body of Mrs Sarah Hill was recovered on Boxing Day and that of the insurance agent, Mr Harrison, the following day. The body of Mrs Hill's husband Harry was not recovered until 3 January, 1945.

Joseph Foster's statement for P.C. Mackay continued:

I saw our mine entrance and reservoir had disappeared and that there was a huge gap where the reservoir had been. I went on towards Upper Castle Hayes Farm and saw a huge crater where the farm had been and the countryside for a mile around was torn up into unrecognisable shapes. It was then apparent that the explosion had taken place at the R.A.F. Station.[14]

Marjorie Snow (née Hellaby) continued her recollections of her father's experiences in searching for survivors and victims:

The first one they found was the blacksmith – Cockaigne – Father said he had the anvil in his back. In Peter Ford's yard, the first building you came to was the blacksmith's shop, then the joiners and then the offices – they were all on the right-hand side as you went through. On the left was the Mill with the Plaster-House, sheds and store. At the end were the Purse Cottages – where the Fords and the Hills lived. The Cottages and the Mill were flattened and all was devastated on the left-hand side as they went up. At the end there had been the open-fronted tin sheds where the plaster was crushed and rolled into powder and put into barrels at the far end of the Mill. Dennis Bowring's father, Tony Bowring, ran up the slag heaps and down the other side and there was another man also – they were all right. They jumped into the powder barrels – they pulled the lids over themselves. Others working in the powder house included Norman Worthington; it was his first job and he was only seventeen. He was the youngest working there. He, with others, got inside some of the big plaster barrels and suffocated. The Worthingtons are still farming at Coton.[15]

Damage at Ford's Plaster Works

Photo courtesy of Magic Attic archive

Although there were very few survivors from the flattened Ford's Mill, there were some lucky escapes from other of the Ford's Works buildings. Betty Swain (née Lindsey), who lived in Hanbury and was at Tutbury School at the time, recounts the experiences of her father, Fred Lindsey, who had worked down the mine before transferring to an above-ground job in the plasterboard room:

He worked in the plasterboard room. It wasn't a very sound structure but none were killed in there. The bicycle shed where he left his bike was not touched.[16]

Betty Swain's sister Audrey Cooper, who was also at Tutbury School at the time, confirms what she remembers of her father's experiences. Their Uncle Arthur, Fred Lindsey's brother, also had a lucky escape from the plaster works. At the time he was spreading plasterboard at a large table in an adjacent building.

Fred Lindsey

Photo loaned by his daughter Betty and taken from the group photo of workers involved in reclamation in the mine after the explosion

"What a team you've got", he cracked to a mate of his at the top of a high loft. "I'll come down and see you in a minute", came the retort. He never did.

The earth shook and everything went up. The walls caved in, the roof buckled and then a reservoir started to flood into them. Arthur's mate was killed on the spot.[17]

Ernest Smith from Uttoxeter was a foreman loader at the works and the *Uttoxeter Advertiser* reported his story:

I was helping Frank Woolley, of Church Broughton, to load a lorry with plaster boards when there were two terrific explosions. Woolley said "What's that? Let's run round here." We made a dive for the board department and got among rolls of paper. The ground was quaking and then the roof fell in all around us. Two other chaps were in the building – Cyril Leedham from Hanbury, the foreman of the board department, and another I can't remember. It was pitch dark and Cyril said, "Quick, get through here." I think we dived through a small window but I shall never know. It all happened in seconds and when your life is at stake you don't stop to think or take notice. If we had not been quick we should have been trapped.

We floundered about 1,000 yards through the slurry up to our knees and eventually got out in the lane leading up to the works. All the time there were rumblings underground and debris was falling all around.

I was in the last war and I've seen some sights but nothing like this. We used to think the "Jack Johnson" shells were pretty bad, but they were like kids' toys compared to this. By Jove I'm lucky to be alive. No-one who has not been to the scene can have the slightest idea of the havoc. A huge boiler full of oil was flung 50 or 60 yards, as if it was a cork. Rumbling explosions were going on underground all day and white smoke was coming up from the ground behind where the hill once stood. It was the water from the reservoir which made things worse: it poured into our place, and that and the gas did our chaps in.

The Americans were wonderful: nothing stopped them. A lot of our chaps were marooned on the far side of the lake of slurry, which was ten feet deep in places, but with the help of the Americans we laid a track of planks, trees and other debris and got them to safety. It was a terrible experience – one I shall never forget. How my mates and I escaped I don't know.[18]

For thirty-six-year-old Ernest Bennet it was his first day at the plaster works. Arriving at Fauld at eight o'clock he started immediately on his job of making plaster boards. At ten past eleven half the workroom blew up and many of his colleagues were buried. He stayed all night helping with the rescue work.[19]

Brothers Tom and Fred Bowring were from Hanbury. Fred worked down the mine and lost his life. His brother Tom worked above ground making plaster and cement. He stated:

I started work on Monday, the twenty-seventh of November, 1944, at eight-thirty a.m. I saw William Gent about an hour later in the cement place in the Mill. About eleven a.m. Percy Cooper of Hanbury came to me and we talked about various matters for several minutes, then we parted. He went up the Mill and I went outside. [Ten minutes later both William Gent and Percy Cooper would be dead.]

I saw little bits of something falling on the ground all around me and I looked up to see what was happening. I saw that the sky was full of huge lumps of dirt and debris of all kinds and it seemed right over the Works. It looked a tremendous height up in the air. I dashed across the yard to the bag room where there were some corrugated tins reared up and I got under them just as the stuff came down and knocked these tins down onto me. Everything went very dark and I heard terrific noises.

It seemed a long time to me before the light came back and I crawled out from under the tins. I then heard the noise of water rushing down the yard and I ran to the top of the tip [the slag heap of gypsum rubble and waste] *and down it and into the field at the bottom* [Heathcote's plough field – see map of Geography of the Fauld area before the explosion in Chapter One] *where I went waist deep into mud and had to turn back up the tip and I then saw the Works were destroyed and most of it had disappeared under thousands of tons of soil and rock. Millions of gallons of water was flooding the site and I guessed our reservoir had been broken.*

I went back to the bag room which was still standing and met Mr Foster and I went with him to the [Plaster] *Board Room where I saw several more workmen. The Board Room was badly damaged but we went through it and onto the hillside where I could see that most of the buildings had gone, also the two cottages where Mr and Mrs Hill and Mr and Mrs Ford had lived, also our reservoir. There was a huge gap at the top of the Works yard and our mine entrance was not visible.*

I felt ill then and after walking round to Gallimore's Farm [Fauld Hall] *and onto the road, I then went home and later heard my brother, Fred, had died in the mine, and that all that had happened had been the result of an explosion at the R.A.F. station at Fauld.*[20]

Plaster works devastation showing shattered remains of the Mill
Photo courtesy of the Magic Attic archive

Nearly eighteen years later, Tom Bowring recalled:

A plane had been buzzing about a few minutes before and we thought it had dropped a bomb. I ran outside and threw myself down, and at the same moment the whole hill seemed to explode. I saw a huge ball of flame going end over end into the sky and then bricks, earth and stones came crashing down half burying me. [21]

Had Tom Bowring returned to the Mill where he had started work that morning, instead of going outside, he too would have lost his life. There were very few survivors from that part of the Works. Another worker, Jack Key, should also have been there on the fateful morning. However, Jack, who was always known as "Doddy", had not turned up for work. He rarely did so on Monday mornings as it was his normal practice to drink rather too much at the Crown Inn at Hanbury over the weekend. All who remember him in Hanbury tell the story of how Doddy Key claimed that "he owed his life to Marston's Ales".

Joe Cooper, one of the sons of Mary Cooper who was at the Bothams' farm at the time and who lost his father, Joseph Cooper senior, in the mine recalls:

Tom Bowring got out alive. He was working outside and every stitch of clothing was torn off him. Your Dad [Jeff Hellaby] provided him with clothes. He found him an army greatcoat. [22]

Tom Bowring escaped with a bad case of shock. There were others who suffered even more traumatic experiences and had miraculous escapes from death. William Phillips was the electrician at Peter Ford's:

He had just left his office when the explosion hurled him a hundred yards away and buried him in the thick mud. Unknown to him, one hand remained above the mud and this hand was seen by a survivor who rushed to it and pulled Mr Phillips out seconds before water covered the spot. Mr Phillips suffered serious injuries but finally recovered. [23]

William Phillips, who was living at Marchington at the time when he worked at Peter Ford's, recalled his experiences eighteen years later:

I was standing about two hundred and fifty yards from the mine entrance talking to a friend when I heard a muffled crump. I looked up and in that split second saw the whole hill burst open. I saw a whole tree, roots intact, flying through the air. There were stones and bits of fence and machinery, all jumbled up together. Then the blast reached me and, though I tried to grab a telephone pole, I was torn off and flung ninety yards into a ploughed field. [24]

This was the same ploughed field, farmed by Jim Heathcote, where Tom Bowring had found himself. However, William Phillips lay there unconscious. He had been swamped by the rapidly engulfing flood wave from the burst reservoir, which was now mixed with over fifty thousand tons of debris and which had already destroyed much of Peter Ford's plaster factory and their working mine entrance. He was, as P.C. Mackay reported, eventually saved because a rescuer saw his raised hand above the mud and slime and pulled him out.

Of all the buildings at the Ford's works, it was the Mill which suffered worst and it was the area from which very few escaped with their lives. One of the lucky ones was thirty-seven-year-old William Lovatt of Uttoxeter, who reported that:

I was at work on Monday, the twenty-seventh of November, 1944, when I saw John Redfern at work on the bank at about twenty minutes to nine in the morning. I did not speak to him. At about eleven a.m. I spoke to William Gent in the Mill. I was still in the Mill at eleven ten a.m. when the explosion occurred but know very little about it as I was trapped by a beam across one foot. I was released later and got away safely. I only know that the Mill started to shake and then parts fell in, then the lights failed and all was pitch dark. I have not seen either Redfern or Gent since.[25]

Both William Gent of Tutbury and John Redfern of Marchington Woodlands were victims of the explosion which totally wrecked the Mill. John Redfern was a skilled craftsman. He worked as a stone-dresser preparing alabaster for a range of ornamental purposes. Evidence of his presence in the works yard prior to the explosion was provided by his colleague William Lovatt. His body was never found: he is recorded, on the memorial erected by the side of the crater, as one of eighteen whose bodies were never recovered.

There is, however, an intriguing postscript regarding the "missing" John Redfern. The Coroner's assistant, P.C. Mackay, recorded him on a "supplementary list of persons whose deaths can be presumed to have occurred at 11.10 a.m. 27.11.44" and added: *"With reference to the above missing man attention is drawn to the body of 'unknown' man recovered from the above works yard on 2nd January, 1945."*

Over a month had elapsed before the body of this "unknown" man was recovered. The Works Manager, Joseph Foster, who knew his staff well, failed in this one instance to identify the body. John Redfern's workmates, William Mosely of Tutbury, Jack ("Doddy") Key of Hanbury and Ernest Gibbs of Draycott also failed to identify him: all attempts at identification proved futile. However, although the physical description of the body is limited, the description of the clothing worn by the "unknown" man is more revealing in terms of suggesting the type of work he may have been engaged in. He was wearing "a brown serge jacket, grey pin-striped worsted waistcoat, white shirt with thin black stripe, grey socks, size eight studded black boots with iron tips at soles and heels. He was also wearing a portion of sacking taken from a cement bag and tied to his person as an apron." (The description is taken from P.C. Mackay's records.) The nature of the clothing worn might well suggest a skilled man who prepares alabaster for ornamental purposes. However, even his sister, Daisy Kirk from Draycott-in-the-Clay, was convinced that it was not the body of her brother John Redfern.[26] The "unknown Man" was laid to rest in Hanbury churchyard on 5 January, 1945.

Mr G. J. Walker of Hanbury was also one of the workers at Peter Ford's who escaped unscathed from the works. He ascribed his safety to the fact that he was working against a machine that was embedded in concrete and which therefore gave him some protection.

It was the water from the reservoir that was the worst. When the reservoir was blown up, the water came down just like a sea. It came up to my knees and we could not get out from water and wreckage. But after we had struggled for about ten minutes, some Americans came up and yanked us out.[27]

Twenty-six of the surface workers at Peter Ford's lost their lives that day: they were either trapped in the twisted wreckage of the buildings in which they were working or buried under thousands of tons of sludge. Mrs Sarah Hill and insurance agent Frederick Harrison at the Purse Cottages also died and Mrs Nellie Ford, who was seriously injured, died eighteen months later. Works Manager Joseph Foster had spent the whole of his working life there and knew all his workers well. He had had a miraculous escape from death. His only injury of a torn fingernail was doubtless sustained in helping to liberate a trapped workman from being drowned by the water from the burst reservoir. In addition to those from Hanbury and neighbouring villages there were many from Tutbury. Nine of the victims working in Ford's plaster works and mine were from Tutbury. In addition, there were seven Tutbury men who lost their lives in the R.A.F. ammunition dump.

It was shortly after two o'clock, a delay of nearly three hours, when the Civil Defence Mutual Assistance Control received the following message:

Explosion at Burton on Trent – brunt of explosion borne by Peter Ford and Sons Plaster Pits. Please send Heavy Rescue Parties at once as men are trapped. Parties will be met at Kingsley, Rolleston Road, Burton on Trent.[28]

The *Burton Daily Mail* reported later in the day that the number of casualties was feared to be high and although the total number was not yet determined they surmised that Peter Ford's Plaster and Cement Works had suffered the most casualties:

The worst part of the damage seems to have occurred at cement works where practically every building was either completely demolished or too badly damaged to be repaired. It is understood that here casualties were very heavy but the actual number has not yet been ascertained. A roll call is being taken.[29]

A reporter from the *Daily Telegraph* recorded what a rescue worker had said to him:

Conditions are like Passchendaele. The men are buried under about ten feet of mud. We cannot hope to reach them.[30]

In addition to the destruction which affected the surface workers, those working underground were also affected. The working mine lay further underground beyond the disused mine now used by the Air Ministry as part of the ammunition dump. However, the working gypsum mine shared a ventilation system with one of the disused mines now used for bomb storage (it was the part of the Dump known as the "new" area). When the explosion occurred in the "new" area the enemy for Ford's miners was poisonous gas. To access the working mine, Peter Ford's miners used an underground road which ran parallel to the worked-out abandoned mine now used for ammunition storage. The barrier between the roadway used by Ford's miners and the mine used by the Air Ministry had been reinforced to ensure it was blast proof. It certainly proved its value in that none of the miners were killed as a result of blast from the explosion.

At the secret Military Court of Inquiry of December 1944, the resident engineer of the Air Ministry Works department, Eric Bryant, was asked:

Approximately where were Ford's working underground in relation to the High Explosive area?

In reply he stated:

To the best of my knowledge and belief they were working approximately half a mile to the south-east with a portion of solid ground between.[31]

Twenty-one of Peter Ford's workers had entered the long tunnel leading to the working mine that morning. The tunnel took them alongside the reinforced wall before branching off towards the gypsum workings. Their route took them by a ventilation shaft which could also act as an emergency exit if necessary. When they reached the gypsum-face, one hundred and forty feet below Hanbury Fields farmland, the miners split up into groups. Jack Gorton was a leader of one of the groups and George Shepherd and Charlie Gibbs were working with him. Charlie Gibbs told how:

It was just one big vibration which just lifted us off the ground a bit. The foreman [Arthur Harris] *came up and said "What was that?" I said "I think the Dump's gone up." I said "go up the air shaft" and he did but came back saying "there's nothing in the air shaft – just a barrowful or two of soil" and then he said "perhaps a V bomber* [Hitler's assault with the pilotless V bombs had commenced just a few months previously] *has been over and dropped a bomb near." I said I thought it was nothing of the sort and we carried on working until gone 12 o'clock.*[32]

This was the air shaft which the miners had passed on their way to the gypsum-face earlier. The miners had come to the conclusion that the vibration had probably been the result of blasting in some remote part of the workings. If they had left the mine immediately by the ventilation shaft they would all have been saved. Their decision to continue working would prove a fatal mistake. Unknown to them the carbon monoxide gas resulting from the explosion was creeping insidiously towards the miners via the access tunnel along which they had walked earlier.

Shortly after 12 o'clock a small group of miners decided to leave the mine to try and discover what had caused the vibration nearly three-quarters of an hour earlier. Making their way along the tunnel they passed under the air shaft and walked on towards the deadly gas. Jack Gorton and Charlie Gibbs were among those who stayed behind but after a while, when none of the group who had gone to investigate had returned, Charlie Gibbs decided to investigate for himself. When he discovered the gas on the roadway he returned and informed the rest of the group, suggesting they go and try to help rescue the other miners.

On the surface, Peter Ford's Works Manager, Joseph Foster, reported to P.C. Mackay:

We have an air shaft on Moat Farm [Hanbury Fields Farm] *and as this was still visible I went there to try and contact the miners working below but I got no response to my calls. I sent a man for ropes and lamps so that we could go down and I came back to the works yard so that we could do this. While doing this, two of the miners, Alfred Page and Fred Lowe, succeeded in climbing the shaft and came towards Fauld.*[33]

When the explosion occurred Ford's miners were three-quarters of a mile from the mine entrance and one hundred and forty feet below Hanbury Fields Farm. They had already excavated four tons of gypsum and this was loaded onto narrow-gauge trucks ready to be hauled by locos back to the surface. Their electric light failed. Jack Gorton from Tutbury was one of the miners who escaped with his life, but not before he had helped many of his workmates to escape from the poisonous gasses emanating from the exploded bomb store.

Jack Gorton was a witness at the Military Court of Inquiry which was held *in camera* in early December. He was the only one of Peter Ford's employees who was a witness at the Inquiry, although it was not until thirty years later that the witness statements became public. However, his story was reported in the *Daily Herald* of 30 November, 1944 under a heading of:

I got out alive after the dump blew up

We work my pals and me separated by a solid door of cement seven feet deep from those thousands of tons of stored bombs.

On Monday morning, me and my mate George Shepherd walked into the galleries. A hole in the hillside is our way in. We go with wicker food baskets flung over our shoulders with pieces of string and it's a walk of five and twenty minutes to our job 160 feet down. There are miles of galleries like an underground maze.

George and I got on the job. We talked about the weekend football results and joked a bit.

We heard a thump, a terrible thump. It sent me flying into the rock face. I got up and said to my mate – "What the hell is this?" But we were still alive. We could slap our thighs and feel that our bones were still unbroken.

We decided to go into the main roadway to see if we could get to the boys – there were twenty-one of them – to see if we could get out into the daylight and fresh air.

Charlie Gibbs, a loader, took a light in his hand and walked off. Soon he came back and said: "Boys, there's gas in the main roadway." Charlie Gibbs faced us squarely and asked for volunteers to go into the main roadway to see if we could find our friends. We heard Charlie saying: "We must have some more help."

Charles Gibbs's son, also known as Charlie, recalls that his father escaped from the mine via the air shaft. Additionally, although still suffering from the effects of gas, he returned on the days following in order to guide rescue workers searching for survivors. His too was a story of heroism.

Jack Gorton's story continued:

We walked on and found Willy Watson, a loco driver, lying in the main roadway. He was unconscious. They took him back. I walked on another two hundred yards and smelt gas, like sniffing burnt sugar.

We took Willy Watson through a relief door, because we knew that on the other side of it there was fresh air and laid him down. We twisted his ears and worked his left arm around like a pump. We saw his eyes flicker and then we knew that Willy was still alive.

We went for two other men who were on the same roadway, through two pockets of gas before we got to them. I saw George Smith crouch down, unconscious. And this is where I started to go under. A piece of rock fell on one of my hands. I suddenly realised that that piece of rock had never caused me any pain. Then I went under.

I don't remember anything more but I know that my mates dragged me back to safety.

Up on the surface, a farmer who is a Civil Defence worker had refused to leave the mouth of the tunnel because he thought that some of us might get a message up to him. Somebody did shout. It is ninety feet down there but the farmer heard the cry.

They got a rope lowered down and the boys tied it round me and I was hauled up – my wicker food basket with me. There it was, perched on my chest on the stretcher when I came round.

I must be the luckiest man alive. I've heard people say that before but now I know. I managed to get out of an explosion that churned up our bit of countryside into a mud heap. Five of my mates are down there dead.[34]

The farmer who was a Civil Defence worker may well have been Bert Hardwick of Top Farm, Hanbury.

Jack Gorton's statement to the Court of Inquiry gave full details as follows:

On the morning of Monday 27th November 1944 I was working in Ford's mine when, just after 11 o'clock I heard an explosion. This explosion was not sufficient to stop us

Bert Hardwick,
Royal Observer
Corps 1942

Photo loaned by Audrey Hardwick

working but a second explosion occurred just a few seconds after the first which was very much greater and even lifted up a wagon containing about four tons of gypsum. During the second explosion the electric light went out and we were left to use tallow candles which were normally carried as emergency lighting. The point where I and my party were working was about three-quarters of a mile south, south-east of the fan opening which exists between Ford's main line and the new area of the H.E. [High Explosive] mine.

I first sent one of my men forward towards the entrance to find out what was happening, but he did not come back, so I went forward myself. After passing the suction shaft, which lies about a quarter of a mile south, south-east of the fan, I came across gas and one unconscious man [William Watson]. I brought him back to safety which means to the south-east of the suction shaft. I presumed that the gas would be coming through the fan opening and it did not seem to be coming further south-east than the suction shaft, as it was being dragged up to the outside area through this shaft. At this time I was carrying a lighted tallow candle; this did not go out when I entered the gas area. The gas tasted like burnt sugar.

I made a further trip forward to find out what was happening. I came across two dead men [George Smith and Harry Shepherd] and then had to return as I was becoming overcome by fumes. We then decided to send two men up the suction shaft for help. They did not return and after about half an hour had elapsed two Air Force men came down the shaft and managed to rescue me, by which time I had almost lost consciousness.[35]

William Watson was the last one to be rescued via the air shaft. He lived at Hanbury Woodend and was the father of three children. On 21 December he told his story to P.C. Mackay, who incorporated it in full within his report to the Coroner:

I have been employed as a loco driver, for Messrs Peter Ford and Sons, Ltd, Fauld, in their gypsum mine for many years. About eleven ten a.m. on Monday, 27th November, 1944 I was with my loco in the mine and about a mile from the main entrance with other miners, when I felt the loco sort of waver about and the lights went out. My loco engine was running and I didn't hear any noise.

I drove my loco and wagons towards the next man to collect their stone. The men were Fred Bowring and Percy Priestley. They were upset and said they had been thrown about the hole by something. We talked about it and decided to go out towards the entrance and find out what it was.

Fred Bowring, Harris and Percy Priestley went on, then Priestley came back and said the gobs [sic] had been blown by the air shaft and the loco would not be able to get by. This was about eleven twenty-five a.m. He also said Bowring and Harris had gone on towards the main entrance on foot.

We passed the air shaft by about two hundred and fifty yards, and then saw Fred Bowring lying by the side of the track. I turned him over and undid his shirt but he died while I was doing this. I could see a light from a lamp just around a bend a little further on and I said, "There's someone else not gone very far."

Joe Cooper and Jack Wright went on to see who it was but before they got to him they shouted back, "It's Massey – meaning Harris – and he's dead." Wright said to Cooper, "It's gas, come on Joe let's get out" and he came staggering back. As he passed me he said, "It's got me." Cooper did not come back.

I said to Harry Shepherd and George Smith, who stood by me, "Come on let's get out or it will have us." Morris had gone back to help Jack Wright along.

We set off to go back, with Shepherd and Smith behind me. I had only gone about forty yards when both legs suddenly went funny and I fell down but started to crawl along but I lost consciousness. When I came round, at one twenty p.m., I was about seventy yards past the air shaft towards the end of the mine. George Smith, Harry Shepherd and Fred Bowring lay dead by me. Other miners were with me and a few minutes later a rescue party of Air Force and Firemen came along and took me out of the mine on a stretcher by way of the air shaft.[36]

In recording William Watson's rescue from the mine, P.C. Mackay stated:

So terrible was the scene of desolation all around him where huge craters overlapped one another as far as one could see and all the familiar landmarks had disappeared that he did not know his way home.[37]

When the gas reached the main gypsum mine all the miners were suffering and many were too weak to climb unaided up the iron ladders which led to safety over eighty feet up the air shaft. By the time that two R.A.F. corporals, who had set out across country in search of survivors, descended the air shaft the gas had claimed the lives of five of the miners. The airmen, together with firemen and local people, worked as the gas fumes grew thicker to bring dazed miners to safety.

In his eye-witness account, John Hardwick recorded:

We got to the air shaft just as Mr Watson, a miner, was emerging. He would be about forty then [actually 46] and had lived in Hanbury all his working life. The shaft was in fields which he walked every day on his way to work. He came out of the shaft and had no idea where he was. It was not surprising. He came out to a sort of moonscape. Land contours had changed. Familiar trees had gone. Nearby should have been a 300-acre farm, home of those two schoolchildren [Gordon and Marie Goodwin]. House, cowsheds, barns, implement sheds – all had gone. In place of a farm was a great crater shaped like an ice-

cream cornet. In the bottom were twisted railway tracks used for internal transport. It is said that 93,000,000 tons of soil had been ejected from it. Some half a mile from the crater were pieces of alabaster each weighing up to 15 tons.

Mr Watson was the last man to come out of the air shaft. He told of the bodies below and of gas which would prevent any chance of reaching them. No-one was alive down there.[38]

Fifty years later John Hardwick was interviewed by the *Sunday Telegraph*:

See that air shaft? A chap called Bill Watson was last up from that mine and when he got out he looked around him and didn't know where he was. It wasn't shock, it was the landscape he walked through every morning was so changed he didn't recognise anything.[39]

Hanbury farmer Leslie Shotton of Knightsfield Farm, who was the Chairman of the Parish Council, was also involved in the rescue of miners via the air shaft on Hanbury Fields farmland. They were all suffering, to a greater or lesser degree, from the effects of gas. The rescuers erected a system of pulleys to haul up the survivors.

We stayed down for a twenty-minute period [because of the gas]. *I was tying ropes round men, who were brought there by their uninjured colleagues, to be hauled to safety.*[40]

The *Daily Sketch* reported:

All the villagers are talking of a man who rescued seven men. He is the 52-year-old Chairman of the Parish Council. Returning from Burton at the time of the explosion, he threw ropes, ladders and other rescue gear into his car and made for the area where he knew men were engaged.[41]

Airmen from the Dump also repeatedly went down the iron ladder in the mine shaft into the gas-filled chamber to rescue the miners, and Corporals S.B. Rock and J.S. Peters were awarded M.B.E.s. Flight Lieutenant J.P. Lewin aided in the rescue operation of miners via the air shaft after he had carried out prolonged searches at the Dump under extremely hazardous conditions and his award of the George Medal was well merited.

Site of air shaft on former
Hanbury Fields farmland *Photo by the author*

Jack Gorton, George Shepherd, Fred Rowe, Alf Page, Jim Treadwell, Percy Priestley, Charles Gibbs and William Watson were among those rescued via the air shaft (see map of location of the village of Hanbury and the Fauld crater in Chapter Two). Charles Gibbs's son, Charlie, who still lives in Hanbury, finds it distressing recalling the circumstances of the rescue and the following days:

And then a policeman had my dad in his arms – it was terrible – he never spoke. He'd come up the shaft with George Shepherd and Bill Watson. The doctor said we must give him plenty to drink and let him rest. They closed the road off – there were the Mines Rescue, the Voluntary Services, the Police, the Fire Service – I can see it all now. My

Dad settled down. The following morning the Mines Rescue came and said – "Could we have a word with him? Could he come with us to guide us back in the mine?" I went with him to the gate. They had these four cages of canaries. They came back with dead canaries – all dead. They came back again the next day to ask him again to act as a guide in the mine and the police carried me, protesting, back into the house. My father went down again with them – this was the Wednesday and they got two more bodies out. On the Thursday, they got quite a lot out – the gas had gone. He never spoke about it. They got them all out including one they couldn't recognise. My father wouldn't go to any of the funerals and wouldn't go to the services in the Church. Poor old Dad. He started to recover from his gassing. He'd lost all his mates.[42]

It was reported on Wednesday, 29 November:

One of the survivors of the plaster pits [gypsum mine] is Charles Gibbs, of Woodend, Hanbury, whose father, Charles Gibbs senior was foreman at the pit up to seven years ago.

Charles Gibbs junior was slightly gassed but managed to make his way out of the pit, when he had to receive attention, but immediately volunteered to go back to try to help his workmates. He knew that Cooper, Harris and others were still there but he was sent home. Today, however, he was allowed to join a gang. His father said that his son felt the force of the first explosion and decided to make his way towards the shaft, as did the other men, except one or two who kept working for half a minute or so. Then, came the second explosion and the fumes. Cooper and Harris appeared to have got some distance towards safety, but were overcome before they could cover the last few yards, so no-one could help them.[43]

Charles Gibbs
Photo loaned by his son, Charlie Gibbs

The National Press also reported that thirty-nine-year-old Charles Gibbs had continued working for half an hour with a party of men after the explosion had rocked the workings.

No alarm had been given and so we thought that everything was alright. We did not know that the offices and all the other buildings had been wiped out and flooded. I carried one man out [to the air shaft] and then went back to look for more. I found two men dead and others unconscious. We carried several out but then the fumes were getting hold of me. I went back to try to find my pal, Fred Bowring, but could not. He was found dead today [Tuesday 28 November] and leaves seven young children, the youngest only a few months old. With me were James Treadwell and Percy Priestley. Our heads were buzzing with the fumes and we had to crawl part of the way dragging the unconscious men with us.

Then we heard the rescue squads and they lowered ropes so that we could clamber up and raise the unconscious men.[44]

Mr Charles Gibbs was one of those unhurt. Man after man he carried to safety on his back and he gave in only when he collapsed through being gassed; he was himself carried home by R.A.F. men.[45]

Following the explosion, Charles Gibbs returned to work in the mine. His son Charlie recalls:

My father was a blaster at the pits. He used to give a blast at around five o'clock as a signal to my mother that he was about to leave work and would soon be home.[46]

There were five miners who died from carbon monoxide poisoning in Ford's gypsum mine that day. Harry Shepherd and George Smith had cycled from Tutbury earlier that morning and Fred Bowring, Joseph Cooper and Arthur Harris had walked across the fields from Hanbury. Arthur Harris was the mine foreman and his daughter Esme, who sang in the Church Choir (see photograph in Chapter One), lost her father that day. Harry Shepherd was the oldest, a veteran miner still working at seventy-three who had lived in the district all his life. He left two daughters. His son William also lost his life that day but on the surface. Sixty-one-year-old George Smith had three sons serving overseas and two married daughters. Joseph Cooper left a widow and eight children. Fred Bowring left a widow and seven young children. Their eldest daughter, Eileen, was eleven years old.

Fred Bowring

Photo loaned by his eldest daughter Eileen Pavey

Eileen Pavey nee Bowring circa 1946

Photo loaned by Eileen Pavey

Still living in Hanbury, Eileen Pavey (née Bowring) recalls her vivid memories:

I'd had peritonitis in the August holiday after leaving Hanbury School. I should have started at Tutbury School in the September but I didn't go to school all that Autumn Term. I was at home with my mother. We were just bringing the baby – seven-and-a-half-months-old Linda – downstairs. Mother was at the top of the stairs and the great noise of the explosion shocked her so much that the baby was thrown out of her arms and I caught her [baby Linda] *halfway down the stairs. The washing was already on the line and it was covered in brown soil which was everywhere. Jean and Margaret and Kenneth were at school at the time.* [As well as the baby Linda, Eileen's younger sisters, Phyllis and Doreen, were also at home.]

I remember Mr Hardwick and his son John coming up the road and we asked them what had happened. We said we didn't know and they said they were going across the field to find out. John's Mother and Dad were very good to us.

On the morning of the explosion, Mr Woolliscroft had wanted my Dad not to go to work in the mine but to stay and help him with the milking. [The Bowring home was located between the Hardwick's at Top Farm and the Woolliscroft's at Hanbury Park Farm.] *But Dad went to work – to the mine. My Dad was a man of fifteen stone. He was gassed down the mine. It would have been difficult getting him out from the mine shaft on a stretcher.*

My mother and Gran went up to the school after the explosion and I had to look after the children – the baby Linda and Doreen and Phyllis. My brother Ken remembers running out into the playground with the slates falling off the school roof.

Childhood for eleven-year-old Eileen terminated with dramatic abruptness that Monday morning.

I looked after the children night and day. Mother went to pieces and Grandma was no better – she was in an awful state as well – she was even worse than my mother. [This was Eileen's paternal grandmother.] *The worst thing about it was afterwards and how we had to manage. Mother was allowed a pound a week for each child and to get the extra money we used to have to go to Court. People were very good to us – the Hardwicks, the Mycocks, and even old Mrs Bullock. The neighbours were all very good.*

Wilfred and Lesley Bowring were my cousins – they lived at the Brickyard Cottages at Hanbury Woodend. Thomas was their father – he was my father's brother. He got out alive [from the plaster works].

I did go back to school after Christmas but left when I was fifteen. I went to work at the Mycocks [farmers at Barton-under-Needwood].

A couple of years afterwards Mother was ill – she had thyroid problems and spent six weeks in hospital. We didn't know where the next penny was coming from. The family were all split up. Margaret and Jean went to the Hardwicks; Phyllis and Ken to Mr and Mrs Ford and I went with Doreen and Linda to live with my aunt – Mrs Tom Bowring – Dad's brother.[47]

Bowring children: (back row left to right) Jean, Margaret, Eileen; (front row left to right) Ken, Linda, Phyllis, Doreen

Photo loaned by Eileen Pavey

Writing fifty years on John Hardwick recorded:

Ordinary people rose to the demands. We were our own social services. I say to people that if this had happened in peacetime, we should have been overrun with social workers, expert counsellors and especially the media. As it was we took care of ourselves. A relief fund was set up to meet the needs of bereaved families while there were dependants.[48]

Joseph Cooper left a widow and eight children, four of whom were still at school. His youngest son, nine-year-old John, was at school at Hanbury and his son Joe and daughters Sibyl and Joyce were at school in Tutbury. His eldest son, Frank, was in the Royal Army Service Corps and his three elder daughters, Margaret, Pat and Vivian, had started work.

Joseph Cooper had worked as a loco driver in the gypsum mine for only three years. Before that he had spent his life in farming, firstly on his own and then doing agricultural contract work for William Shelley of Rock House, Hanbury and also ploughing and sheep-shearing for Jeff Hellaby of Fauld House Farm. He was well known for his skill as a sheep-shearer and also for his ploughing both by horse and tractor. His son Joe recalls his father coming down to Fauld House at sheep-shearing time and also the ploughing he did with Jeff Hellaby's first Fordson tractor. William Shelley's grandson Bill Hidderley also recalled:

Joe Cooper worked for Grandfather and Father. He was a wonderful ploughman.[49]

Joseph Cooper had volunteered during the First World War and served in India with the North Staffordshire Regiment. Twenty-six years later he lost his life in the gypsum mine due to gas. His body, together with that of Arthur Harris, was not recovered for four days. His widow Mary, who had helped save the life of Granny Botham of Hanbury Fields Farm, received the bodies, including that of her husband, into the temporary mortuary of Hanbury School. His youngest son John, who became the mining engineer at the Fauld gypsum mines, still finds it distressing to speak of the disaster which took his father's life and turned his mother into an unsung heroine.

Joseph Cooper senior circa 1941

Photo loaned by his eldest daughter Margaret Nicklin

The Coroner told of how Mrs Mary Cooper:

. . . cleansed and scrubbed a very gruesome temporary mortuary every day for 72 days. The work has been indescribable. She helped with the undressing and also the washing of the clothing removed from the bodies. One of the first victims that she had to deal with was her own husband. She survived the wrecking of a farm at which she was looking after an old lady, and it is probably due to her cool action that the old lady's life was saved.[50]

The Coroner recommended that she be considered for an award in consideration of her heroism. The Under Secretary of State for Air wrote commending her outstanding service and also made a financial award.

All of the miners who escaped did so via the air shaft on Hanbury Fields farmland. About half an hour after the explosion some of the miners had decided to walk back towards the entrance knowing that, en route, about half a mile from the entrance, they would pass an air shaft. This shaft provided an escape from the mine by a series of ladders which they could have climbed. However, the miners observed that the door to the air shaft was damaged and consequently passed on towards the mine entrance. There was a terrible irony in ignoring this means of escape by passing on beyond the damaged door as, unknown to them, the shaft remained intact. Had they examined it more closely, five lives would have been saved and the rest of the miners would have been spared a terrifying experience.

It was the shared ventilation system between the Air Ministry Mine and Ford's working gypsum mine which had allowed the seepage of the poisonous gases to which many of the miners succumbed. After the explosion, Jack Gorton vowed he would never return to the mine. He did work for a number of farmers, including William Shelley of Hanbury and his son-in-law and grandson Ted and Bill Hidderley of Tutbury. William Shelley's grandson Bill recalls:

Jack Gorton worked for me. He was very brave in rescuing people. He kept going back down to rescue people by the air shaft on Botham's farm.[51]

Finally he came to work for Jeff Hellaby at Fauld House Farm, where he was highly regarded by all the family and all who knew and worked with him. Known as "Big Jack", he was a gentle giant and, according to George Heathcote, now of Hartington Hall Farm, who also remembers him from his time at Fauld, he:

. . . was the "bodyguard" for Tutbury Hawthorns football team when they first started.[52]

One of the loco drivers who had a remarkably lucky escape was Mr Beck of Tutbury who, for thirty-eight years, drove a locomotive that carried gypsum from the mine to Scropton railway sidings. On 27 November, 1944 he missed death by ten minutes through delay at Scropton.

I used to drive the loco from Scropton, first to Staton's mine. Ford's was ten minutes beyond. Because of the delay we were at Staton's when the explosion nearly rocked the engine off the line. Rocks like wheelbarrows were flying about and it went dark with dust and smoke.[53]

The walk to work, which Joseph Foster and many others had taken earlier that day, by footpaths crossing the familiar fields of Hanbury Fields and Upper Castle Hayes land and on down into the wooded valley to Peter Ford's, would never be repeated. In the weeks and months which followed, Joseph Foster spent his days both in advising the Staffordshire County Surveyor, Robert S. Murt, O.B.E. (who had taken on the task of managing the recovery of victims) and also in the agonising task of identifying the bodies of those with whom he had spent all of his working life. Bulldozers, mechanical diggers of every type (many loaned by the Americans) and dumpers appeared in the works yard of what had been Peter Ford's and Sons and many of the survivors of Ford's men helped in the heart-breaking task of recovering the bodies of their former work mates. The work proceeded in what was often bitter weather in the following months. It was a colossal task as around ten thousand tons of debris had to be removed in order to recover the bodies. Twenty-six

Ford's Workers
Photograph probably taken circa 1937 as Charlie Gibbs' grandfather is still working there
Front row seated on the ground (left to right): 5th Charles Gibbs senior, 10th Harry Hill, 11th Douglas Foster (with spaniel) **Second row** seated (left to right): 6th Harry Wetherill
Third row standing (far left): Ford brothers, 4th 'Doddy' Key *Photo loaned by John Cooper*

bodies were recovered from the works yard of Peter Ford's and Sons and five from Ford's gypsum mine, which together comprised over forty per cent of the total loss of life. The last recovery from the works yard was made on 5 February, 1945, which was just one day before the Coroner, Major L.D. Auden, officiated at the Inquest into the cause of death of the victims of the explosion. Both Joseph Foster and Peter Ford took to driving to the devastated works each morning with a dark suit in the back of their cars in order to attend the many funerals which took place in the months which followed. Maud Foster, Joseph Foster's wife, spent time helping Mrs Mary Cooper in the mortuary at Hanbury School.

NOTES

1 *Daily Telegraph*, 29 November 1944.

2 P.C. Mackay's report to the Coroner for the Inquest of February 1945.

3 Joseph Foster was the Great Uncle of Bill Hidderley. "Uncle Joe used to walk down to Peter Ford's over Goodwin's land": quoted to the author on 21 January, 2012.

4 Report signed by Joseph Foster and taken down by the Coroner's assistant, P.C. Mackay at Fauld on 22 January, 1945.

5 *Burton Daily Mail*, 28 November, 1944.

6 National Archives Ref AIR 17/10.

7 BRMB radio documentary broadcast from Birmingham produced by Brian King, 28 November, 1983.

8 Report by Joseph Foster to P.C. Mackay.

9 As recalled by my sister Marjorie Snow (née Hellaby) on 3 August 2011.

10 *Burton Mail*, 29 November, 1944.

11 From report of Coroner's assistant, P.C. Mackay.

12 As recalled by Kay Sutton (née Kathleen Hill) on 1 September, 2011.

13 Ibid.

14 Joseph Foster's report as taken down by P.C. Mackay.

15 As recalled by Marjorie Snow (née Hellaby) on 3 August 2011.

16 As recalled to the author by Betty Swain (née Lindsey) on 24 October, 2011.

17 Article by John Turner in *Staffordshire Weekend*, 23–29 January 1963.

18 *Uttoxeter Advertiser*, 6 December, 1944.

19 Reported in the *Daily Express*, 29 November, 1944.

20 Report signed by T. W. Bowring and taken down by P.C. Mackay on 22 January, 1945.

21 *Sunday Mercury*, 3 June, 1962.

22 As recalled to the author by Joe Cooper on 10 December, 2011.

23 Report of Coroner's assistant, P.C. Mackay, February 1945.

24 *Sunday Mercury*, 3 June, 1962.

25 Signed statement reported by William Lovatt to P.C. Mackay on 31 January, 1945.

26 As told to the author by John Cooper on 20 March, 2012.

27 *Burton Daily Mail*, 29 November, 1944.

28 Staffordshire Record Office F4/1C/G.

29 *Burton Daily Mail*, 27 November, 1944.

30 *Daily Telegraph*, 29 November, 1944.

31 National Archives Ref AIR 17/8.

32 BRMB radio documentary broadcast from Birmingham 28 November, 1983.

33 Signed report of Joseph Foster taken down by P.C. Mackay on 22 January, 1945.

34 Jack Gorton's story as reported in the *Daily Herald*, 30 November, 1944.

35 National Archives ref AIR 17/8.

36 Signed account of William Watson as reported to P.C. Mackay on 21 December, 1944.

37 P.C. Mackay's Report.

38 Unpublished record of John Hardwick.

39 *Sunday Telegraph*, 27 November 1994.

40 Reported in the *Daily Express*, 29 November, 1944.

41 *Daily Sketch*, 29 November, 1944.

42 As related to the author by Charlie Gibbs on 25 October, 2011.

43 *Burton Daily Mail*, 29 November, 1944.

44 *London Daily Mail*, 29 November, 1944.

45 *News Chronicle*, 29 November, 1944.

46 Charlie Gibbs as told to the author on 25 October, 2011.

47 As related to the author by Eileen Pavey (née Bowring) on 8 September, 2011.

48 Handwritten record of John Hardwick.

49 Bill Hidderley recalled to the author 21 January, 2012.

50 Copy letter (in John Cooper's papers loaned to the author) from the Coroner, Major J. L. Auden, to the Hon J. F. Gretton M.P., 7 February, 1945.

51 Bill Hidderley recalled to the author 21 January, 2012.

52 George Heathcote recalled to the author 19 August, 2011.

53 *Sunday Mercury*, 24 July, 1960.

CHAPTER FIVE

CHILDREN AND THE VILLAGE

"The battlefields of France and Germany are reproduced in this corner of England where a little village was partially wrecked by the force of the explosion."[1]
"We shot out of the school, flung a porch door open and were looking towards the explosion site. We shut the door and ran out the other side. I distinctly remember that I fell over as tiles clattered all around us. But none of us got hit. We shinned over a six-foot fence and ran for just a few yards. In less than 20 or 30 seconds, everything that was big that was going to come down was down. The village was devastated. About an hour and a half later, the dust from the explosion blotted out the sky, which went a sort of brown and settled a quarter of an inch thick all over the village."[2]

For the village children at Hanbury School the bright sunny morning of 27 November, 1944 started like any normal Monday morning. However, it would be the last day of school at Hanbury until spring 1945 and for many of the children it would be the most traumatic day of their lives.

The stark record from the head teacher, Miss Fardon, in the Hanbury School Log Book states:

27/11/44 – About 11.15 this morning a violent earth tremor was felt followed by a loud explosion. I got the children under the desks as stones etc. came through the school roof. About 4 mins. later a storm of dust, stones etc. came from the sky. The Vicar came to school immediately but no child was hurt. Later the children were sent home. The school was then prepared for a mortuary.[3]

The large iron pot-bellied stoves which heated the school had been lit by the caretaker, Mrs Mary Cooper, before she left to walk to Hanbury Fields (Moat) Farm to do the weekly washing for the Botham family. Mrs Cooper's youngest son, John, would be attending school as usual that morning. Her husband Joseph had left for work at the gypsum mine earlier. After registration and the issuing of National Savings stamps, lessons began for the juniors with Miss Fardon in the "big room" and, through the sliding doors, the infants with Miss Williams in the smaller room.

Painting of Hanbury School by Vera Jeffery (née Shelley)

Photo of painting loaned by her elder daughter Rosalie Vicars-Harris

After morning break, lessons again proceeded as usual from 11 o'clock. Ten minutes later they were terminated dramatically. Tony Deaville, the blacksmith's son, was seven years old and recalls that he was sitting next to Marie Goodwin when:

The school started shaking and the blackboard came crashing down. It went dark and we heard this great explosion. I and one or two others jumped up and ran into the cloakroom with the teacher shouting after us to come back. We came back into the classroom and stayed there until my Dad came up to school. He ran back to the Bothams' and stayed with Grandma Botham until the emergency services arrived. I then walked home with the Moore twins George and Ted together with their brother Bill. We walked past the Harrisons' house and saw the destruction and also the great boulder of alabaster which had landed in a field where, we later learnt, Bill Allen of Croft Farm had had a lucky escape as it had gone right in front of his horse and cart. The horse had shied. The alabaster boulder remained in the fields for many years. Behind where we lived it was Bert Hardwick's land and we saw this tree – the branches were in the ground and the roots were in the air. There were dead sheep and cattle everywhere.[4]

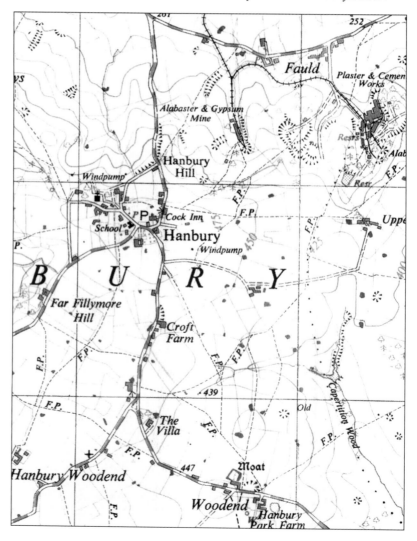

Enlarged portion of OS Sheet SK12 last updated from six-inch map in 1922

John Cooper circa 1943
Photo loaned by Margaret Nicklin (née Cooper)

John Cooper was nine years old and recalls that he and a number of other boys, including Peter Flint, Peter Harrison and Philip Allen, ran out of school:

We were starting an English lesson when it happened and there was this tremendous bang – you can't really say anything else but it was just a colossal bang. All through the war we had been trained to dive under the desks but that didn't happen in this case for about five or six of us. We just took to our heels and dashed out of the school through what we used to call the boys' porch and we opened the door on the east side which was on the side facing the explosion. If you stood in this doorway you looked over a big old oak tree by the side of Rock House [home to the Shelleys, which received a great boulder through the roof and where the kitchen, which was built onto the side of the house, was totally wrecked] *and we saw this great cloud of black smoke and debris being thrown into the air against what had been a beautiful blue sky. For some reason, you know, kid's logic, we slammed the door on that side and went out the other side. It didn't make any difference but we ran out of the other side of the porch and as we ran some of the debris had started landing and there were tiles crashing round those of us running through the school yard.*[5]

Remarkably, none of the boys who ran out of school was seriously injured despite the fact that several heavy coping stones on the steep gables of the school roof slid off after the explosion. John Cooper also recalls that the falling debris had driven through the roof of the school, shattering one corner of the teacher's solid oak desk. It was the desk on which the teacher would regularly sit to tell a story. One of the boys who did receive a slight injury from a tile flying from the roof was Bill Woolliscroft. His younger brother Jim, now farming at Knightsfield Farm, Hanbury was in the infants at the time and remembers:

Above: Damage to the Shelleys' home, Rock House
Photo courtesy of the Magic Attic archive

Right: Damage to Rock House extension
Photo courtesy of the Magic Attic archive

We dived under the desks. We ran home to Hanbury Park Farm. My Dad was coming back from Burton market with a horse and cart – he'd been fetching grain or something. When we went home the road was terrible – the Harrisons' house had gone. My brother Bill had been cut on the head by a tile from the school roof.[6]

Two of the boys who ran out of school with John Cooper were seven-year-olds Bill Moore and Brian Cooper. Bill was the sixth of seven boys and the family lived further down the road from Croft Farm opposite the former Ebernezer Farm. Minutes before Bill went home with his twin brothers George and Ted, together with Tony Deaville, his eldest brother John had had a remarkable escape: he had been in the cart with farmer Bill Allen of Croft Farm, when, seconds before the explosion, the horse had refused to move. Brian Cooper's father Percy worked at Peter Ford's Plaster Works and, like John Cooper's father Joseph, had left for work earlier that morning.

Bill Moore and Brian Cooper recall:

We ran out of the back door through the cloakrooms. There were tiles flying everywhere. It's amazing how they never hit us. The teacher was Miss Fardon and the blackboard fell over. She told us to get under the desks but we didn't.[7]

Brian Cooper remembers:

I ran to Mrs Buckley's – the house near the church. She was standing in the doorway and all her washing was covered in soil. I remember the soil coming down. I can't remember going home but I know my mother came to collect me. We were living at the time close to the old Crown Inn. My father worked in the cracking sheds at the plaster works – they cracked the gypsum for plaster making. He was killed but they didn't find his body immediately. I was seven at the time. We didn't go to school again until March.[8]

Bill Moore recalls:

My Dad was in the R.A.F. He was on leave at the time. I can recall him saying that there were lads who'd been fighting all over the world but they'd never seen anything like that [the devastation after the explosion]. When we got home – to the council houses beyond Croft Farm – we'd seen on the way the big hole in the roof of the house where the two Miss Harrisons lived – they were sisters and they lived next door to Celia Johnson's cottage "Sunny Breeze". A great rock of alabaster had gone through the roof and through the bed and there was a great hole in the ground.[9]

Bill Moore taken from photo of Hanbury School Juniors 1945 *Taken from a photo loaned by Bill Moore*

Fred Allen, who was eight years old at the time, also recalls:

I ran out of school with John Cooper and Bill Moore. The teacher told us to get under the desks but I ran out. There was this great rumble and bits coming through the roof. I've never run so fast in all my life. We went round to the Cock Inn – it was wrecked. We didn't know whether it was Germans or not. I ran to Mrs Bowen's because I knew my mother was doing the washing there. It's the cottage near the church – the washing was hanging out and it was all covered in dirt.[10]

Ten-year-old Celia Rutter (née Johnson) lived at Sunny Breeze, a pretty cottage just beyond Croft Farm, and she tells:

I remember Miss Fardon told us to get under the desks. She barred the door because some people panicked. I don't remember the noise. It's the dark I remember most. It was black – you couldn't see. There were holes in the roof and the dust was coming down. After we got out from under the desks Miss Fardon gathered us round the stove and got us singing – we sang "There'll always be an England". She was trying to comfort us I suppose. We just thought it was a bomb – one of those V2s. I remember the vicar came quite soon afterwards. I can't actually remember getting home. I do remember all the sludge on the road. The Moores' boys, who lived near me, and Peter Harrison and Fred Allen – they all ran out. They saw the trees upside down and they went to see the crater soon afterwards. My mother wouldn't let me go. My mother was working at a munitions factory in Burton – someone told her that she'd better get home because the Dump had gone up. She was told that the children at school were all right. My Auntie Lucy [Lucy Allen at Croft Farm] was doing the washing. Her young son Bill, my cousin, was at Mrs Rock's, who lived close by – she was "baby-sitting" him.[11]

Mrs Rock's husband, George, had gone to work at Botham's farm that morning but was never seen again.

Eight-year-old Peter Harrison, a younger brother of sixteen-year-old Ida who had walked with the Goodwin children from Upper Castle Hayes to the village earlier, also remembers the blackboard crashing down in the schoolroom, dust coming down, diving under the desks, singing round the stove and the vicar coming. He recalls running home:

The water pipes had burst in the road and there was sludge everywhere. I ran down home and the pigs were out. I got them in. I saw all the devastation of our own home – it was totally wrecked and subsequently it was demolished. Mother was ill and only recently out of hospital. I waited for my Dad to come home. He came home about half an hour after it happened. He was down the mine – Staton's not Peter Ford's. [Unlike Ford's mine there was no damage to Staton's mine.] We moved into the Roebuck Inn – my Auntie Annie kept the Roebuck at Draycott. Ida went to the vicarage where our sister Gladys was working. Our sister Vera was away from home in the A.T.S.[12]

Above: Peter Harrison

Photo from Hanbury School Juniors 1945

Right: Damage to the Harrisons' home

Photo courtesy of the Magic Attic archive

Peter Harrison's sister, Ida Roberts, recalls that after delivering the post around Fauld that morning, walking back to Hanbury with the Goodwin children and getting her younger siblings off to school at Hanbury and Tutbury, she had gone into Uttoxeter.

There were ten of us in the family and I was number three. Because my mother was ill I had to leave the High School at Uttoxeter early. It was my seventeenth birthday the day after the explosion. It should have been wash day. There was going to be a social in the Village Hall that I was going to that evening. I'd gone to fetch my dress from Uttoxeter – it was being altered. I didn't know anything about the explosion until I got to Draycott on my way back from Uttoxeter. I was picking up my bike from Draycott. I biked as far as "Harpur's Corner" – where New Lodge and the private school Howett House used to be – and I couldn't cycle any further. There was so much sludge on the road – the water pipes had burst. Mother was at home on her own – I discovered that she'd run into the cowshed. When I got home – I saw the roof had gone – our home was destroyed. Our home was about two hundred yards past the Village Hall and that was completely flattened. My youngest brother, three-year-old Colin was with the Archers. Father was down the mine – Staton's gypsum mine.[13]

Remains of the Village Hall
Photo courtesy of the Magic Attic archive

Peter Ede, nine years old at the time, recalls:

We heard this great noise and it went pitch black – blacker than black. Miss Fardon told us to get under the desks. We were told that a German bomber had gone over. And then we were sent home. The Hut [Village Hall] was flat; the Cock was very badly damaged. I went home to Coton [Coton Hall Farm] down Hanbury Hill. My brother Fred had been working in the field at the bottom of Hanbury Hill – there were huge boulders in that field. The horses he was working with both bolted. I was one of the first who went up to see the crater.[14]

Later in the day, John Cooper's eldest sister, twenty-one-year-old Margaret (now Margaret Nicklin) also remembers going down Hanbury Hill to Coton. Their eldest brother, Frank, was in the Army and he was stationed at Birmingham, from where he used to transport tanks to Leeds. Their mother was anxious to contact her eldest son and Margaret recalls:

I was working in a shop at Horninglow, Burton, when it happened. Getting home was terrible – there was so much sludge everywhere. My sister Pat was working for Miss Brace at Coton Hall and I walked down to Coton to see if she could contact Frank. Miss Brace ordered a taxi to pick up Frank from Burton station at midnight and she lent me her bike so that I could get home.[15]

Joe Foster, grandson of Peter Ford's Works Manager, Joseph Foster, was also in school at Hanbury. He was still in the infants:

Grandfather was the mine manager. Douglas, my father, was the assistant manager, but was on war service in Kenya. He came home to help with the rescue work. I was at Hanbury School in the village. A loud bang was heard and Miss Williams ordered us under our desks as "the Germans were bombing". This was quickly done as we had had a practice several times. A second noise, more of a rumble, was heard and the roof of the school was holed and debris was falling in, after which it went quiet and the teacher sent us into the cloakroom which had a lower roof and was intact. We thought this was fun as we had no idea what "war" really was. Eventually some of us were allowed home if we lived more distant from the bomb dump. I had to take home a cousin called Marion [known as Marie] *as the teachers expected her family had been killed as their farm was above the mine workings although this was not yet confirmed. She was later picked up by another member of her family and it was confirmed that her parents had not been found.* [It was Jeff and Ida Hellaby who collected Marie Goodwin from the Fosters.] *The walk of half a mile was difficult as the whole area was covered in mud several inches deep. I also remember that my other grandfather's family farmed over the mine also.* [This was Joe's grandfather, William Shelley's elder brother Jack, who farmed at Hare Holes Farm, which was badly damaged. His grandfather William Shelley's home of Rock House was also badly damaged in Hanbury village.] *Our house was only slightly damaged when the tall chimney fell down over the lawn and garden.*[16]

Joe Foster's elder sister Pat was at school in Uttoxeter. Not quite eleven years old, Pat (now Pat Polley) was in her first term at the High School.

Being November, it was dark when I got home. Our home had not suffered any serious damage and the village shop which Auntie Dolly kept had only a few tiles off, but other properties had more damage. The rescue of the many who had died continued for a long time and Granny Foster (Maud) was in the Parish Room laying out the bodies as they were brought up from the mine and the buildings. Dad and Uncle Joe were both in the Army doing National Service in the Medical Corps and Dad was sent home to help in the identification of those who had died as he and Granddad knew all the people who worked there [at Peter Ford's]. *Dad took me to Botham's Farm, behind the Village Hall which suffered great damage, to search for someone missing. I think it was Jim Ford, the verger.* [I suspect she meant George Rock. Jim Ford became the verger after George Rock.] *I had to wait outside the sheds while he went in, but we didn't find anyone. The area around was completely changed – mud and mess – and where Goodwin's farm was, was this enormous crater, so deep you could see the railway lines at the bottom of the mine.*[17]

The Vicar of Hanbury, the Reverend Crook, has left a graphic story:

I was just leaving the vicarage garden at about 11.15 a.m. when a terrific pressure of air struck me. The earth began to shake, bricks fell all around me and a pinnacle fell off the church. There was a violent explosion like an earthquake. A huge cloud of dirt and smoke shot into the sky to a terrific height. I made my way to the school nearby to see about the children. It took me about four minutes to get from the vicarage which is nearby.

During that time there was a terrible upheaval of the ground and what appeared to be shells, stone and rock were falling in all directions. Then there was a falling of fine earth which covered me from head to foot. The whole place was shrouded in dirt and before one could think about it holes appeared in house roofs and the recreation room [Village Hall] vanished. At one moment it was there and the next it was not. Chimneys began to fall, telephone and electricity wires went and the whole landscape was changed in fifty seconds. Where there had been trees and grass there was nothing but bare earth and craters.

I went into the school and found the children wondering what had happened. The schoolmistress, Miss Fardon, had got the children under their desks. Their song was "There'll always be an England". As soon as the danger seemed to be over I had them all sent home.

Then I went in search of casualties. I found the roads blocked, water mains burst and I came across a number of parents looking for their children. I was able to reassure them.

Left: Reverend James Crook 1943 *Taken from a photo loaned by Bill Moore*
Right: Damage to St Werburgh's Church and Mrs Bowen's cottage opposite
Photo courtesy of the Magic Attic archive

The Vicar's search for casualties took him to Hanbury Fields Farm and he then arranged for the School and the Parish Room to be used as a mortuary.

By this time the rescue parties and fire parties arrived from all over and I went back to the school to clear it ready for the reception of casualties.

The police were wonderful and so were the R.A.F. personnel and the Americans. One cannot speak too highly of them. The women of the village also gave us wonderful help.[18]

The Vicar worked unstintingly during the hours and days and weeks that followed. He personally visited all of the bereaved. John Cooper recalls that it was about eleven o'clock that night that the vicar knocked on the door and said:

"I'm afraid Joe won't be coming home tonight."

Shortly after the explosion, twenty-one-year-old John Hardwick and his father of Top Farm, Hanbury walked up to the village to see what assistance they could render. He has written:

On our way we passed cottages where there were widows who as yet did not realise it. Their husbands were at work in the alabaster mine adjacent to the dump and many of them had been killed in the workings.

Then I began to walk up the village and met one lady leaning over her gate. I could see from her face that she suspected the worst, for her husband was in the mine. He was dead and they had seven children under twelve. She [Rose Bowring, see Chapter Four] *still lives in the village.*

The road to the village was strewn with debris. What few telephone lines we had in those days were down. Structural damage towards the village was greater and one cottage was damaged beyond repair. [This was the Harrisons' home.] *It was eventually taken down and for thirty years its only memorial was a laburnum tree which survived in what had once been the garden.*

Our concern was for the men in the mine and we made our way down Featherbed Lane towards an air shaft for the mine which should have provided an escape route for the gypsum miners.

At the end of Featherbed Lane, the "Hut", our village hall, which was in a 1914–18 war creosoted long shed with slow combustion stoves, was just a pile of timbers. In it we had had all of our village functions. We had celebrated the Coronation [of George VI]. *Now it was gone – piano keys littered the path and a pot-cupboard had been blown yards away, but the pots survived.*

As we went towards the air shaft we passed what had been a 60 acre farm [Hanbury Fields, also known as Moat Farm], *this was now in ruins. A three-bay Dutch barn, full of valuable winter fodder (wartime) was on fire and it didn't seem to matter. At that point I clearly remember about us winning the war – and it didn't seem to matter.*[19]

In walking from their home of Top Farm into the village of Hanbury, past Croft Farm, the Harrisons' house, the Stalford Buildings (cow sheds and Dutch barn belonging to William Shelley of Rock House) the Village Hall and Hanbury Fields Farm, John and his father Bert Hardwick had been climbing very gradually uphill. Further on from the junction with Featherbed Lane, Rock House and the Cock Inn were also at a slightly higher level. It was this slightly elevated position, coupled with the fact that all of these buildings were on the eastern side of the village, which made them particularly vulnerable to the blast and the debris from the explosion. This more exposed part of the village suffered the most severe devastation and the fields between Hanbury and the crater were pitted with many smaller craters. The confidential report by the Ministry of Home Security, December 1944 stated that:

Hanbury Fields Farm was very extensively damaged by debris and blast whilst Hare Holes Farm and Croft Farm and the cottage adjacent [the Harrisons' cottage] *were extensively damaged. Property in Hanbury Village which was extensively damaged by debris included the Cock Inn, Rock House,* the *Village Hall* and *Stalford Buildings (Cow Sheds and Dutch Barn).*[20]

Bill Allen's eye-witness account is recorded in a contemporary report from the Directorate of Aeronautical Inspection Services:

An eye witness account given by William Allen of Croft Farm, Hanbury, who was in the road near building No. 34 [the Harrisons' cottage] *describes having seen blue flashes and smoke rising in the vicinity of these craters.*[21]

At the time of the explosion, Bill Allen was driving his horse and cart between Croft Farm and William Shelley's warehouses, which later became the "Staffordshire Farmers" building, located opposite the Cock Inn. He was accompanied by the oldest of the Moore boys, John, who had recently started working on the farm. Two of John Moore's brothers, Bill (at school in Hanbury) and Tom (at school in Tutbury), confirm the remarkable story of their eldest brother's experience. In the words of Tom Moore:

Bill Allen of Croft Farm in the Church Choir
Taken from a photo loaned by Bill Moore

My brother John, who was fourteen and had left school, was working for Bill Allen at Croft Farm. They were on their way to William Shelley's warehouses in the horse and cart and were just beyond the Harrisons' when the horse backed and wouldn't go any further. Everything went black. They got under the cart. A great boulder dropped across the road in front of them. Had the horse continued they would all have been under the boulder.[22]

Bill Allen's niece, Celia Rutter who, as Celia Johnson, was at Hanbury School at the time, also tells of her uncle's extraordinary experience.

Uncle Bill was in his horse and cart. He had young John Moore with him. They were just beyond the Harrisons' when the horse refused to go. Then there was this explosion and a great boulder dropped down in front of them. They would have been in its path if the horse had gone on. Uncle Bill's hand was cut by flying shrapnel. He had to go to the American Hospital [at Sudbury].[23]

The late Mildred Buckley was close to the Village Hall and had observed Bill Allen and his horse and cart. She related later:

I was just about to start my washing in the shed adjoining the Village Hall that morning. Thank goodness I hadn't started. I was at my daughter-in-law's when the whole house shook. I grabbed her baby and we both ran under the stairs for safety. I thought it was a doodlebug at first [a name commonly used to describe the V1 pilotless flying bombs]. *When I emerged the soil shower had started. Outside in the road a farmer and his horse and cart stood between two craters. He was covered in black dust. There wasn't a chimney left standing anywhere and dust was coming down so heavily that I was covered.*[24]

The Cock Inn and buildings close by suffered serious damage. The late Mrs Ena Wetherill, who lived in a cottage almost opposite the inn, had recalled that she and her baby son John had had a miraculous escape when debris weighing several hundredweight crashed through the roof of her home. She had just put her baby out in his pram and managed to snatch him to safety only seconds before the pram was crushed by boulders.

When I first heard the explosion I ran to see if my three-month-old baby was all right. As I left the room the debris fell through the ceiling. I picked up the baby and as I did so the bottom fell out of the pram.[25]

At exactly the same time, baby John Wetherill's grandfather, joiner Harry Wetherill, had also had a lucky escape when he was with Joseph Foster putting up plaster boards at Ford's works.

At the Cock Inn two wings were completely destroyed by falling debris and the roof ripped off those parts remaining standing. Mr and Mrs Melvin Zucca had only taken over the pub the previous June. Mrs Zucca and her two young children had a remarkable escape. She had recalled how she had just brought in the washing and made a cup of coffee when she felt a terrific vibration. She tried to get into the cellar but before she could do so there was another shock and she dived under the table with the children. Mrs Zucca escaped with a cut hand and the terrified children escaped unhurt.[26]

Left: Damage to the Cock Inn
Photo courtesy of the Magic Attic archive

Below: Rescue of rocking horse from the Cock Inn
Photo courtesy of the Magic Attic archive

Only two of the rooms remained undamaged but that evening the pub opened for business as usual and with the help of neighbours and additional borrowed glasses customers were served by candlelight.

The Blitzed Inn Carries On!

The old Cock Inn was practically demolished but the tap room remained intact, and the landlady began serving with the remaining supplies and glasses as soon as possible.

Above, a bed protruded crazily from the wall of a shattered bedroom.[27]

It was also reported that in the unharmed tap room:

There still hangs a darts board from which the darts hung by the last customer still protrude.[28]

The *Gazette* reported that cycling by the Cock Inn:

An airman [L.A.C. J. Gair] who was blown off his bicycle, seeing flames in the bar rushed to the rescue with two other men and between them they extinguished the fire.[29]

Margaret Nicklin (née Cooper) recalls:

Margaret Nicklin nee Cooper
Photo loaned by Margaret Nicklin

There was only one room which could be used in the pub. I arranged to stay with Mrs Zucca when Mr Zucca had to go down to Wales to take their two young children to their other grandparents. Mrs Zucca and I slept under a tarpaulin. I helped her in the pub when it opened and after it closed. I went to work from there – to Fauld. I stopped at home for a bit so that I could help my mother at the school where all the bodies were taken.[30]

Above: Sign outside the re-built Cock Inn
Photo by Lindsey Porter

Right: Mural of local area at the Cock Inn
Photo by Lindsey Porter by kind permission of the landlord

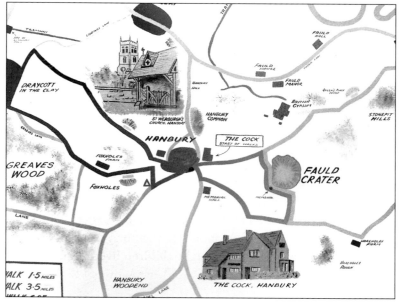

At the village school at nearby Sudbury, nine-year-old Betty Fradley (née Astle) recalls the experiences of her brother Arthur when he visited Hanbury later that afternoon and remembers:

I was a little girl at Sudbury School. In those days they brought in the milk from a local farm for the children. I remember the milk being brought in and poured into beakers which were on this big table with a shiny top. There was this big rumble and the table rocked up and down – the milk in the beakers swashed around. We all wanted to rush outside but the teacher told us to get under the desks. We went outside afterwards and saw these great clouds over Hanbury. When I got home to the farm I found that a door had been blown off and windows smashed. My parents were concerned for our relatives, the Gregsons, who farmed in Hanbury – it was the farm opposite the church. When my older brother Arthur came home from school [Alleyne's in Uttoxeter] he cycled over to Hanbury. The road into the village was blocked off but they let him through. He found that the Gregsons' cattle had their backs covered in soil. He was told that it was twenty minutes before the soil stopped coming down. My cousin Roy Gregson went down to help in the rescue from the mine shaft.[31]

Betty Fradley recalls that over twenty years later, when she worked as a warden at Field Study Centres in Derbyshire, she used to take children down into the crater to study the natural history and it was not until sometime in the 1970s that permission was withdrawn. She also recalls that her Uncle Len Gregson was filling in small craters on his land right up to the 1980s.

The explosion was also heard and witnessed at the primary school at Hatton, next to Tutbury on the Derbyshire side of the River Dove. Audrey Hardwick (née Bridges) was nineteen years old and teaching a group of twenty junior school children. She recalls:

My group of middle junior level children included several London evacuees. John Tillman was late coming back from break – he said: "Miss, I can see trees going up in the air." I didn't know what was happening. I remember my Head coming in – Mr Peters – he said: "Don't let (certain) children go home because it's the Dump that's gone up and some of their fathers work there." Their fathers were okay. It was felt rather than heard. The children were quite calm – there was plaster coming off the ceiling – some of the children were continuing to come in with their bottles of milk from break. My father worked at Tutbury Station. He came up to see if the Hardwicks were all right. There was not a lot of damage to the buildings but the land was damaged [Top Farm, Hanbury]. I first saw all the devastation of Hanbury on the following Sunday – there was an open air service by the wreck of the village hall. On the day that it happened, everyone had the fear that more bombs would go up.[32]

Margaret Winson (née Bowring) was a child at Hatton School and recalls:

I was walking across the playground to wash the beakers that we'd had for milk. All I remember was that it went dark and everything shook and there was a noise. When I came home at lunch-time nobody knew what had happened.[33]

Many of the children at Hanbury School had older siblings at the secondary school in Tutbury. The Winson family of eight children lived near the Coopers in Hanbury and the eldest son Percy was at Tutbury School at the time. He recalls:

We'd just come in from break. There was this big rumble – we thought it was an earthquake. We'd always had a drill for going into the Anderson shelters and as soon as there was this

Left: Nineteen-year-old Audrey Hardwick (née Bridges) when a teacher at Hatton School
Photo loaned by Audrey Hardwick **Middle:** Percy Winson, chorister, 1943 *Taken from a photo loaned by Bill Moore*
Right: Joe Cooper circa 1943 *Photo loaned by Margaret Nicklin (née Cooper)*

first rumble, we went there. We must have stayed there for about half an hour before the teachers fetched us out. When we went back into school we could see flames and smoke going up over the Fauld area.

I always went down to my Auntie's at dinner-time. They lived in the High Street next to where Parrick's Grocery used to be. My Grandfather was working in the mine in the next chamber to the one which blew up. Another cousin came up from Nestles' factory – she wanted to go down to the Dump to see if our grandfather and her father were okay but her mother, my aunt, wouldn't let her go. They did come out okay. Her father worked on the locos which took the ammunition into the mine and luckily he'd just come out again – he felt the blast rattling his trousers. Grandfather Edgar Gent had a lucky escape.

My father, Percival Winson, was working at Gregson's Farm – the Glebe – near the Church. He was one of the rescuers who helped to get people out of the mine after the gas had disappeared. He used to work as a grave-digger with Joseph Cooper who was killed in the mine. He took over the grave-digging and did it for years.

We came home to Hanbury on the school bus at the usual time. We saw Capertition Wood where lots of the trees had gone and then went down by Hanbury Woodend and Top Farm – the Hardwicks'. We could see all the devastation – there were no hedges – nothing but brown mud – most of the trees had gone and some were upside down. The Harrisons' cottage was wrecked and the Village Hall.

Before it happened, I regularly used to walk across the fields to Upper Castle Hayes Farm with Gordon Goodwin. They used to have a billy goat which frightened me to death. I used to say – "I'm not coming through that gate until you've tied that goat up." I did get used to it in the end. It was across three fields to the Goodwins' and I walked home from school with Gordon many times. When I left school the next summer I was fourteen and I went straight to work on Mr Allen's farm – Croft Farm.[34]

The headmaster at Tutbury School, Mr Stevens, who had formerly been the headmaster at Hanbury School, recorded in the School Log Book:

At 11.12 a.m. a terrific explosion at 21 MU R.A.F. Fauld shook the school and the whole neighbourhood, the detonation being heard as far as Coventry and Northampton. Many people (including workers at Messrs Peter Ford's Plaster Works at Fauld) and many horses and cattle were killed. One farmhouse disappeared. Attendance at school adversely affected in the afternoon.[35]

John Cooper's older brother Joe was also at Tutbury School at the time:

The only way I can describe it was that it was like an earthquake. We saw it actually from the school yard. We saw this great black cloud going up. They'd got us out of the classrooms to get us running about. Mr Stevens, who used to teach at Hanbury School, was the headmaster there. He said, "I don't know what you're going to find when you get home but I hope you're going to be all right." We didn't know about my father then. Vicar Crook came across and told us at 11 o'clock at night. I can remember it vividly. It's something which never leaves you. We lived through it.

I remember Jack Gorton who was down the mine and then worked for your Dad [Jeff Hellaby]. Also Horace Utting, he was down the mine [i.e. the Dump]. He was the older brother to Dick Utting. When I worked for Gregsons, I used to walk the sheep down – to dip the sheep at your Dad's.[36]

Tom Allen, Fred Allen's elder brother, also at Tutbury School at the time, recalls:

We went to the far end of the yard and saw all the smoke rising up over Fauld from there. The teachers didn't tell us what had happened. It was getting dark when we got home to Hanbury on the school bus. I've never seen so many trees up-ended in the air. There was mud everywhere. A big lump of clay had come through the back bedroom. The fence round the Water Tower was all lifted up. There was a big hole made by a huge lump of alabaster which had lifted up the fence. We wondered if it was a bomb. It would have been even worse if the Water Tower had been blasted.[37]

Like Percy Winson, Tom also remembers the times he had spent at Upper Castle Hayes Farm with Gordon Goodwin. Additionally he recalls bombs being brought through Hanbury en route to King's Standing Aerodrome. Betty Swain (née Lindsey) also recalls lorries bearing red flags which, after the explosion, continued to carry bombs through the

Tom Allen circa 1946
Photo loaned by Percy Winson

village to Cross Plains airfield at King's Standing near Needwood, which was about four miles south of Hanbury.

Betty and her sister Audrey Cooper were at school in Tutbury and they too returned home to see the devastation in Hanbury. The Lindsey sisters both recall being outside the school and seeing the great black clouds of smoke and debris and dust. Audrey remembers:

The children who went home for dinner came back and said that Hanbury was in a dreadful state. I worried all day about what had happened. My father worked at Peter Ford's – he worked on the plaster boards. He'd worked in the pits first [the gypsum mine] before he went into the plaster works. My brother Fred and cousin Peter were at Hanbury School. Betty and I and all the others from Hanbury went home on the school bus as usual – the village was covered with debris and soil and sludge.[38]

Audrey's sister Betty recalls:

Mother met us off the school bus. She told us that Dad was home okay and that Fred and Peter were alright. We'd expected everyone to be dead at Hanbury School. The house was very dark when we got home because the veranda was covered with all this thick sludge. My Dad's sister and family from Burton came to stay with us. They lived near Christ Church in New Street, Burton and everyone was evacuated from there because the explosion had made the church steeple unsafe. There we were – a family of five – in the midst of it – and a family of four came to live with us.[39]

Wards in the Burton General Hospital, close by Christ Church, were also evacuated following the explosion. Ginny Pilkington told how:

My husband, then aged eighteen months, was a patient in Burton General Hospital having broken his leg. The ward was evacuated as the church steeple nearby developed a crack as a result of the Fauld Explosion. He remembers being carried across the hospital yard in the arms of a man.[40]

Charlie Gibbs was thirteen years old at the time and should have been at school. He recalls:

I was playing truant from Tutbury School that morning. My grandmother was at home and my mother was looking after Mrs Deaville who'd just had a baby daughter, Gillian.[41]

Some years later, Charlie's mother, Millicent Gibbs recalled:

I had got my mother at home. She was doing my washing and I was doing a friend's who'd had a baby and she was getting up that morning. I had just fetched some washing out and all of a sudden there was this big explosion. A neighbour next door came out, she came running out and she said "What's the matter, Mrs Gibbs?" "Oh," I said, "I don't know" and she said, "I think it's that plane that's just gone over." "Oh," I said, "I don't think so, I think it's the Dump's gone up."[42]

Charlie remembers:

Mother came running down to see if I was all right. I was crying my eyes out because a large boulder had fallen on the rabbit hutch. The rabbits were Snowy and Spotty – I tried to dig them out and couldn't find them at all. The gable end of the house and chimney came

down. The washing was covered with dirt. The door wouldn't shut. We went back to the Deavilles' – the blacksmith's. My mother said, "I need to see your father – I need to get to Fauld." They wouldn't let her go. We went up to the Harrisons' – the roof was off. There was a great hole made by a gypsum boulder. The Village Hall was wrecked but the house by the Village Hall where the Shepherds lived – that was barely touched.[43]

Charlie Gibbs junior
circa 1943
Photo loaned by Charlie Gibbs

Later in the day, Charlie's mother, Millicent Gibbs, was waiting for his father's return from the gypsum mine. She had been told that he was safe and was at the air shaft helping to bring up the bodies of his dead workmates but as time went by she became increasingly concerned.

I said to my mother, "I think I shall have to go down to the pits – I can't wait any longer." And I set off walking down the road, but then who should I see but my husband and these two Air Force men bringing him. And, of course, I went to his arms and started to cry. And he started to say that he'd thought everything had gone up in Hanbury. So anyway, I said to the Air Force men, "I'll manage him now" and I brought him home, gave him something to drink and got him to bed.[44]

William Watson had also escaped from the gas-filled gypsum mine. His daughter, Hilda Carter, who now lives in Marchington, recalls:

There were three of us children living at Brickyard Cottages, Hanbury Woodend. I was sixteen at the time and my brother Tom was fifteen. My youngest brother, Maurice, was still at Tutbury School. I was working in the Income Tax Office at Burton and I came home on my bike. Mother wasn't there but I saw all the washing on the line covered in dust. I was told that they'd all gone up to the village and I went up there. Then I learnt that my Dad had got out but he'd been taken to New Street Hospital in Burton and my Mum went to the Hospital. He was all right in a few days – he'd been gassed. He was with Ken Bowring, who didn't get out. Father was born in 1898 and lived to be eighty-one. He never went back down the mine. He was a loco driver and knew Joe Cooper, who didn't get out. He worked on a farm afterwards – it was Needwood farm for Mr Riches. I've never visited the crater.[45]

The village community rallied together as best they could with those whose homes were not too badly damaged providing food and shelter to the homeless. It was nearly midnight before work on endeavouring to recover bodies was eventually called off and the exhausted emergency teams made their way back to their bases. They would return the next day to continue the search.

It was not until a quarter to six in the evening, five and a half hours after the explosion, that the following message was received by Civil Defence Mutual Assistance Control:

Hanbury Village very badly damaged and escaping gases have formed huge craters and thrown clay about in all directions. Nearly all houses in the village badly affected. Civilian casualties estimated between 20 and 30. Military casualties not known. Further information will be available tomorrow.[46]

For Hanbury it was a major catastrophe. Practically every building in the village had received some degree of damage. The response and support provided by the American troops was immediate: they provided tarpaulin sheets to cover gaping holes in damaged roofs and worked to remove dangerous masonry in the many damaged buildings. The war was still going on and a blackout was still necessary through the hours of darkness. There was no power or water in the village and the authorities needed to provide a prompt response with water containers, mobile canteens and voluntary helpers. The support provided by the Women's Voluntary Service was first class. In his Report for the Coroner, P.C. Mackay stated:

I must pay tribute to all these people so tragically affected. None complained during those terrible days. Most of them had lived in the quiet of an English village all their lives and war had seemed very far away for them. Nobly they faced up to disaster and went quietly on obeying instructions and never complained. Many of them, too, had lost someone dear to them but this did not deter them from facing boldly to the trials, peril and difficulties of those dark days.[47]

A reporter in the village recorded:

I stood on a mass of churned earth which had once been a road and looked on a scene which defied description. I have seen nothing like it on the battlefield. Many of the rescuers were veterans of several campaigns from Dunkirk onwards. They had seen towns and countryside blasted by bombs and high explosives but they too had never seen such destruction at one blow. A be-medalled R.A.F. Sergeant said to me: "It looks like hell on earth."[48]

As he left that Monday evening he noted:

When I left last night anxious relatives were still waiting for news of their menfolk. Good tidings reached some. Their men were known to be safe and working with the rescuers. Other women just waited. Roofless houses were being patched with tarpaulins but many people were homeless and had to find temporary accommodation for the night.[49]

On Tuesday 28 November the County Area Officer of the Air Raid Precautions Department visited Hanbury and reported:

One Farm [Upper Castle Hayes] *on the outskirts of the village has been completely demolished whilst a second Farm* [Hanbury Fields] *was almost demolished, resulting in several people killed. Between twenty and thirty houses in Hanbury have received fairly extensive damage, but the Tutbury Surveyor has the matter in hand.*

Two houses are uninhabitable [the Harrisons' cottage and Shelleys' Rock House] *and the residents are being housed by friends. The School has been turned into a mortuary; there is no gas or electricity available, and after consulting with Colonel Pemberton Mr Ballard asked for the Queen's Messenger Service to be sent there to feed the population of about 450.*[50]

The *Manchester Guardian* commented that:

The battlefields of France and Germany are reproduced in this corner of England where a little village was partially wrecked by the force of the explosion.[51]

On Wednesday 29 November the Bishop of Lichfield, Dr E.S. Woods, went to the village and visited some of the bereaved. He toured the damaged area where, in addition to the main huge crater, many subsidiary craters pitted the whole region and they were fast filling up with water.

The Vicar of the village told me that the Bishop "stood aghast at the sight". He slipped into one of the craters but, although plastered with mud, he suffered no injury.[52]

The Bishop, covered with mud and dirt, visited the homes of those who had suffered most and offered consolation. He had recently returned from a tour of the battlefields of Italy and declared:

It is the worst scene of devastation that I have ever seen – worse than anything I saw in Italy.[53]

The Rev Crook meanwhile stated:

I have been living on cups of tea and sandwiches. I have never left the church rooms until everything is clear every night and as far as sleep goes, that is impossible.[54]

A factor which added to the distress of the people of Hanbury in the days immediately following the explosion was the number of low-flying aircraft over the devastated area.

Villagers have complained about the ceaseless roar of aeroplanes zooming down to see the cratered countryside. They said that at times they could count as many as 100 aeroplanes wheeling and diving overhead. They consist of all types, heavy and light bombers, fighters and training aircraft.[55]

A report from the Minister of Home Security dated 30 November noted:

During the afternoon of Wednesday it was reported to me that an abnormal number of aircraft were continually flying low over the scene of the incident, causing distress to the families who had suffered. At my request the Air Ministry agreed to place Fauld and three miles around it out of bounds to aircraft flying. Unfortunately an authorised low flying route lies within two miles of the locality.[56]

On Saturday 2 December and Monday 4 December the Air Ministry authorised flights over the crater, the village of Hanbury and surrounding area in order to obtain an accurate record of the devastation.

The Vicar, meanwhile, working day and night with his parishioners, was becoming increasingly concerned about the effect of the situation on his wife. On Saturday 2 December Mrs Lillian Crook collapsed. At the village Memorial Service, on Sunday the third, the Bishop described her as "very seriously ill" and on Monday 4 December she died. Her death was attributed to shock following the explosion and she appears on the memorials as one of its victims. The vicar and his wife had been in Hanbury for seven years. They had two sons, one of whom was a Major in the Royal Corps of Signals in Italy at the time and the other a chaplain to seamen in Australia.

The *Daily Herald*, under a headline of "Relief Squads Bring Life Back to Bomb Village", reported from Hanbury:

Their homes have been smashed by the gigantic explosion at the R.A.F. maintenance depot. Their clothes have been torn to shreds; many have lost everything but their lives. A mobile food column has just [Thursday] *driven into the village. Under the trees in the vicarage garden a tiny marquee has been erected. A field kitchen is sending up clouds of steam and Irish stew is bubbling in containers.*

Along the road walks R.A.F. Sergeant Bill Hall from South Shields with a mine detector in his hand and earphones on his head. Soon Sergeant Hall gives the "All Clear" to this village. It seems the roads are safe again.

And all the time down at the ammunition dump and the wrecked plaster works, the rescue work goes on hour by hour.[57]

Many of those who had been at school at the time remember visiting the crater in the days immediately following. Audrey Cooper (née Lindsey) recalls:

The next weekend we walked over to the crater and in the fields before we got there I looked down and realised I was standing on a cow – it was partly buried in the field. There was this tree which was upside down – its roots were up in the air. It was all so alien. The crater was so steep you couldn't see the bottom of it. There was water in the crater and another one on the side. There was no-one to stop you going. All of the village would go I guess. It must have been dangerous.[58]

In his 1945 New Year's message to his parishioners, the Rev. James Crook wrote:

The task of writing this New Year's message to you all is the most difficult problem that has faced me since I came to Hanbury. I wish it could have been written by someone else. The vacant chairs in so many homes and the fatherless children will always be a reminder of November 27th.

Before I close this letter, I should like it to be placed on record how much the village owes to the noble band of our own men and women who, from the first, so willingly and unstintingly gave themselves in the service of rescue, also to the Police who have been wonderful, and our best thanks to our American brethren for their kindness in sending men and material to cover up many of our damaged roofs; this generous act we shall not forget.[59]

The vicar went on to record the church's loss:

Our Church will be the poorer for the passing of W. Slater [mine-safety man at the ammunition dump], *treasurer to Draycott Church; G. Rock* [Botham's farm worker], *Verger and Chorister; J. Cooper* [gypsum miner] *and H. Carter* [plaster-worker at Ford's], *Sidesmen and Mrs Crook* [vicar's wife], *enrolling member of the Mother's Union. It is impossible to realise at present what their loss will mean to our Church for each in his or her own way gave loyal and devoted service and the blank caused by their departure must be regarded as a call to others to come forward and help in this our greatest hour of need.*[60]

One of the sidesmen on duty for January 1945 would be Charles Gibbs. George Rock's wife would be responsible for *"Flowers for the Altar on Sunday, January 7th"*. Mr Harry Botham of Hanbury Field's Farm, in addition to being the church organist, had been the vicar's warden. It was at this time that my father, Jeff Hellaby, became the vicar's warden. Marjorie Snow (née Hellaby) can recall the vicar speaking with her at Sunday School and telling her that he had found his new churchwarden.

In the village of Hanbury with the hamlets of Fauld and Coton-in-the-Clay, together with the neighbouring villages of Newborough, Hoar Cross, Marchington and Marchington Woodlands, thirty- one people lost their lives as a result of the explosion.

In the weeks following the disaster, when bodies were still being recovered up until the time of the Inquest held on 6 February, 1945, people locally were very seriously concerned regarding the possibility of further explosions. Endeavouring to allay their concerns, the Coroner contacted the Honourable J. F. Gretton M.P. on 29 December, 1944 regarding the publication of a statement that there was no likelihood of a further explosion. However, the Air Ministry could not provide any such assurance. In a copy letter from Lord Sherwood, Under Secretary of State for Air, dated 10 January, 1945 it was stated:

Although we have every sympathy with the Coroner's desire to assure the local residents that all danger of a further explosion has passed, I am sure you will appreciate that it is not possible to issue a public statement of this kind.

The removal of various explosives in this area is a hazardous task and will take some considerable time. I can, however, assure you that all possible precautions are being taken to lessen the risk of a further explosion, and that the work is proceeding as expeditiously as possible.[61]

Meanwhile, there was no school for over three months for the children of Hanbury and while Joseph Foster, the Manager at Peter Ford's Mine and Plaster Works, was engaged in the grim task of identifying bodies and then attending funerals, his grandson Joe Foster had his own story to tell.

No school for weeks but lots to do. On one occasion we boys found a bomb in a crater so we dug it out. As it hadn't exploded we thought it was evidently a dud. We put it on Christopher's trolley cart and took it down to a hut which the R.A.F. was using. We knocked on the door and a Sergeant opened the door. We asked him where we should put the bomb. He went white and yelled "RUN!" Later we found that the bomb had a live fuse in it. We could have been killed.[62]

NOTES

1 The *Manchester Guardian*, 29 November, 1944.

2 As recalled by John Cooper of the time when he was nine years old at Hanbury School, *The Guardian*, 27 November, 2004.

3 Extract from Hanbury School Log Book, 27 November 1944. Ref. Staffordshire Record Office: D4346/1/3, accessed at Burton Library.

4 As recalled to the author by Tony Deaville, 8 October, 2011.

5 As recalled by John Cooper to local radio, the local press and to the author who renewed contact with him on numerous occasions during 2011 and 2012.

6 As recalled to the author by Jim Woolliscroft on 11 September, 2011.

7 As recalled to the author by Bill Moore on 9 September, 2011.

8 As recalled to the author by Brian Cooper on 9 September, 2011.

9 As recalled to the author by Bill Moore on 9 September, 2011.

10 As recalled to the author by Fred Allen on 8 October, 2011.

11 As recalled to the author by Celia Rutter (nÉe Johnson) on 8 September and 25 October, 2011.

12 As recalled to the author by Peter Harrison on 8 September, 2011.

13 As recalled to the author by Ida Roberts (née Harrison) on 8 September, 2011.

14 As recounted to the author by Peter Ede on 8 August, 2011.

15 Recalled by Margaret Nicklin on 31 August, 2011.

16 As recalled by Joe Foster in an email to the author dated 28 September, 2011.

17 As recalled by Pat Polley (née Foster) in a letter to the author dated 15 October, 2011.

18 Rev Crook as reported in the *Burton Daily Mail*, 28 November, 1944 and the *Daily Telegraph* 29 November, 1944.

19 John Hardwick, unpublished handwritten record.

20 The National Archives Ref AIR 17/10.

21 The National Archives Ref AIR 2/6966.

22 As recalled to the author by Tom Moore on 26 October, 2011.

23 As recalled to the author by Celia Rutter (née Johnson) on 8 September, 2011.

24 *Manchester Evening News*, 28 November, 1970.

25 *Daily Telegraph*, 28 November, 1944 and also the *Daily Herald* and *Daily Mirror* of the same date.

26 *London Daily Mail*, 29 November, 1944.

27 *Derby Evening Telegraph* November 27, 1944.

28 *Manchester Guardian*, 29 November, 1944.

29 *Gazette*, 28 November, 1944.

30 As recalled to the author by Margaret Nicklin (née Cooper) on 31 August, 2011.

31 As recalled by Betty Fradley (née Astle), September 2011.

32 As recalled by Audrey Hardwick (née Bridges), 9 September, 2011.

33 As recalled by Margaret Winson (née Bowring), 11 November, 2011.

34 As recalled by Percy Winson to the author on 11 September, 2011.

35 *The story of Mr Wakefield's School at Tutbury 1733-1990* by former head-teacher R.W.Pye.

36 As recalled by Joe Cooper to the author on 10 September, 2011.

37 As recalled by Tom Allen to the author on 8 October, 2011.

38 As recalled to the author by Audrey Cooper (née Lindsey) on 24 October, 2011.

39 As recalled by Betty Swain nee Lindsey on 24 October, 2011.

40 As recalled to the author by Ginny Pilkington, a volunteer at the Magic Attic archive in Swadlincote.

41 As recalled by Charlie Gibbs on 25 October, 2011.

42 BRMB radio documentary from Birmingham produced by Brian King, 1983.

43 As recalled by Charlie Gibbs on 25 October, 2011.

44 BRMB radio documentary from Birmingham 28 November, 1983.

45 As recalled to the author by Hilda Carter on 20 October, 2011.

46 Staffordshire Record Office F4/1C/G.

47 P.C. Mackay's Report to the Coroner.

48 *Derby Evening Telegraph*, 28 November, 1944.

49 Ibid.

50 Letter from ARP County Area Officer, 28 November, 1944. Staffordshire Record Office F4/1C/G.

51 *Manchester Guardian*, 29 November, 1944.

52 *Derby Evening Telegraph*, 29 November, 1944.

53 *Burton Daily Mail*, 29 November, 1944.

54 *Derby Evening Telegraph*, 29 November, 1944.

55 *Derby Evening Telegraph*, 30 November, 1944.

56 National Archives Ref AIR 17/10.

57 *Daily Herald*, 1 December, 1944.

58 Audrey Cooper (née Lindsey(, 24 October, 2011.

59 Hanbury Church Parish Magazine, January 1945.

60 Ibid.

61 Copy letter from Lord Sherwood, Under Secretary of State for Air, to the Hon J.F.Gretton M.P.

62 Record provided to the author by Joe Foster.

CHAPTER SIX

WITNESSES AND VICTIMS AT THE DUMP

"My immediate impression was one of horror. There was a column of black smoke billowing out of the entrance to the mine. In the forefront a stack of boxes containing incendiary bombs were blazing furiously. All over the area were isolated patches of fire. I could see an airman and a civilian lying face downward at the side of a brick building. They must have been killed instantly."[1]

"I was thrown against a wall in the mine. The lights went out and there was another explosion which was worse than the first. This time I was thrown to the ground. There was a rush of wind and dust flying about. It was complete darkness."[2]

At eleven o'clock on the morning of 27 November, a farm labourer was laying a hedge on the edge of a field not far from the entrance to the R.A.F. ammunition dump when, to his complete amazement, the cows in a nearby field became quite frantic and raced across the grass. They continued to behave in a totally bizarre manner for a number of minutes. He shouted to his nearby workmate:

What's the matter with them cows? They can't be gadding at this time of year![3]

Minutes later the reason became all too clear. Dump worker Tom Archer, who was working only ten yards from the entrance to the mine where the bombs were stored, reported:

There was a tremendous glare of light behind us in the heart of the galleries underground [caverns and tunnels of the mine where bombs were stored] *where many men would be working. I ran for it in a cloud of dust and stones that were pouring out of the galleries in a gale of wind. A man near me stumbled and fell. I got hold of him and helped him out. Behind us was a vast wall of dust and flames.*[4]

In a building within the R.A.F. camp at only a short distance from the mine entrance there were about fifty women workers. Some were hurled through the wooden roof by the explosion although none were seriously injured. In the N.A.A.F.I. canteen Mrs Lily Flint and other women workers threw themselves to the floor while the building rocked. *Masses of stuff was flying overhead and crashing into the ground roundabout us. All we could do was hold tight until the "earthquake" ceased.*[5]

Reg Payne circa 1944
Photo loaned by his son Harry Payne

Meanwhile, sixteen-year-old Harry Payne, who had witnessed the explosion from the windows of the Nestles factory at Tutbury and whose father, Reg Payne, worked in the mine had arrived on the scene.

On arrival at the Fauld gate I was stopped by the Security Guard, Mr Cross, who I knew. He was obviously in a state of shock and did not react when I pedalled past him and up the road towards the mine entrance.

Some way up the road I saw Dad sitting alone on a boulder

at the side of the road. He didn't express any surprise when he saw me but quietly told me to go home and tell Mum he was O.K. and would be home as soon as he could. I remember looking further up the road and seeing a greenish yellow glow in the side of the hill which I assumed was fire inside the mine.

Until the time he died in 1979 my father never expressed an opinion on how the explosion happened and generally was always reluctant to talk about it. The only real information he gave was that he was extremely lucky to have survived, as he had been called out of the mine to another job only a short time before the explosion.[6]

Earlier that morning Thomas Worsley, at his home in one of the Air Ministry houses on Green Lane, Tutbury, had a decision to make. He was Foreman of Works at 21 Maintenance Unit R.A.F. Fauld, where there were two jobs needing to be done: one was at the mine where the bombs were stored and the other was on the roof at Scropton railway sidings. He made the decision to take his men to Scropton and do the job on the roof because it was a dry and bright day, the first in a long time. Had he decided to do the job in the mine he and his men could well have been killed, but as it was they witnessed the explosion from an impressive vantage point and must have gazed in horror at the sight. His daughter Hazel Ede, daughter-in-law of Dorothy Ede, who was lucky to escape with her life when working as a land girl on Fauld Manor Farm (see Chapter Three), recalls:

One day when I was a teenager, my father told me this story. Taking a picture out of his wallet he told me that his workmen had taken it because they said that they'd had a lucky escape; that it was my father who had saved their lives and that it was because they were on the roof at Scropton when the explosion happened, well out of harm's way, that they were safe. My father had made the right decision on that nice sunny day.

After my father died, I found the photo in his wallet very worn and well-loved where it had been close to his heart. He was a very blessed and lovely gentle man.[7]

Left: Tom Worsley 1945 *Photo from group picture of workers involved in reclamation in the mine after the explosion and loaned by Betty Swain (née Lindsey)*

Right: Tom Worsley with workmates 1945 *Photo loaned by his daughter Hazel Ede*

Also earlier that Monday morning, Sergeant Bill Morton-Hall, of the R.A.F.'s 6211 Bomb Disposal Unit, had set out from Digby in Lincolnshire on a reconnaissance mission to look for a reported bomb in the area of Burton-on-Trent, little appreciating how his day would turn out. Shortly after eleven o'clock, he and his three companions located the blue American practice bomb which they decided had probably been jettisoned by accident since there were no others close by. They had just loaded the bomb onto their vehicle, a Humber-Snipe resplendent with red wings, blue flashing lights and "Bomb Disposal" in red letters on the side, when there was an earth tremor and they witnessed the appearance of a huge volume of smoke to their left.

I knew exactly what it was. I knew the Fauld ammunition dump was over that way. My corporals and I jumped back into the car and headed for the Dump. When we arrived within 15 or 20 minutes an Air Force policeman, seeing the words Bomb Disposal asked, "You didn't start it, did you?"

It was absolute chaos. The four of us quickly became involved as bomb experts. I can't recall much of the first hectic hour. Then other people began to arrive – among them the Salvation Army with a useful mobile bath unit and their tea and buns.[8]

Sergeant Bill Morton-Hall contacted his headquarters and arranged to remain in the area for a further week. He recalled declaring the village of Hanbury safe and was featured in the national press as "The man who gave the all clear".

In May 1977, another R.A.F. Flight Sergeant, Charles Mitchell, revealed that he had had a bird's eye view of Britain's biggest explosion on the morning of 27 November, 1944 when he was the wireless operator and air gunner in a six-man crew of an R.A.F. bomber on a training flight returning from East Anglia to his base at Ashbourne. They were on the approach run-in at about seven thousand feet when he saw the Fauld mine disintegrate below:

It was one hell of a something which obliterated everything but we felt no shock waves. It seemed rather like looking into a blue-arc lamp where the explosion occurred. The whole area was covered in smoke and dust clouds.[9]

Perhaps this was the aircraft which a number of observers claimed to have seen?

On 26 November, 1944 Corporal Lionel Poynton had been concerned about an incident he had observed at the Dump. Before being transferred to Fauld in July 1944, he had spent three years as an armament instructor at R.A.F. Kirkham and fully recognised the importance of taking proper precautions when handling defective bombs. During a routine inspection of the mine he had discovered a flagrant disregard of essential safety procedures. In one of the caverns he had found two armourers, Leading Aircraftmen Bailey and Fairbanks, dismantling defective 1,000 lb bombs under the supervision of an A.I.D. examiner; one of the airmen was chipping out composition explosive from an exploder pocket but the chisel he was using was brass instead of the regulation copper and worse still he was doing this surrounded by other bombs. Poynton had been seriously disturbed by what he saw and his instinct told him that the action should be stopped immediately as the brass chisel could trigger ignition of the bomb and, by a chain reaction, of the many others close by. However, as he had no authority over the A.I.D. inspector he could only warn his R.A.F. colleagues of the danger of what they were doing. However, he was

Sergeant's Mess together with three senior officers at R.A.F. Fauld 1943:
Front row (from left): 3rd Commanding Officer, 4th Senior Warrant Officer Gallaghan, 5th Warrant Officer Cross
Middle row (from left): Sergeant Morrison, 4th Flight Sergeant Torrance
Back row (from left): Sergeant Venables, 3rd Sergeant Richardson, 4th Sergeant Brownlow, 5th Flight Sergeant Neil Robinson, and 6th Sergeant Haynes
Photo loaned by Neil Robinson

sufficiently concerned by what he had observed that he arranged to return to the Dump the following day with his immediate superior, Sergeant Stanley Game, so that he might alert senior R.A.F. officers. For Sergeant Game, it was to be an ill-fated first and final visit to the remote "new" area of the mine.

It was not the most propitious start to the morning of Monday 27 November, 1944 at Fauld. The depot continued to be under extreme pressure and many of its officers were inexperienced in dealing with explosives. The Commanding Officer, Group Captain R.J. Storrar, had not actually had the R.A.F.'s exacting training in dealing with explosives. The post of Chief Equipment Officer, who was required to have the appropriate training, had been vacant since September. In the absence of a permanent appointment Squadron Leader L.H. Anness had been acting Chief Equipment Officer for less than three months. At nine o'clock that morning, the Commanding Officer, Group Captain Storrar, left to go on leave and consequently R.A.F. Fauld was temporarily in the charge of the most senior officer on site, Wing Commander D.L. Kings, the Master Provisions Officer for Number 42 Group. His role of acting Commanding Officer was one which, later in the day, he fulfilled with great courage and distinction. However, for all the many other military and civilian personnel employed at Fauld it was, ostensibly, the start of another normal busy working week.

One Works Department gang had been sent to empty the drainage sumps in the new area and another to inspect the electric light fittings. It was a routine day too for the A.I.D. men and the servicemen detailed to assist them.[10]

Former R.A.F. Flight Sergeant Neil Robinson was stationed at Fauld from the spring of 1943 until January 1945. He was only twenty-one when he became a Flight Sergeant in the R.A.F. Regiment in June 1943. He was in charge of the Italians working at Fauld and they knew him as "Sergeanti Bambino". He vividly recalls the events of that November morning including, he ruefully remembers, being instructed by a senior officer to "*get your Italians off the camp.*" Suddenly they had become "his" Italians![11]

Flight Sergeant Neil Robinson was also regularly required to run "back–up" courses with R.A.F. personnel on topics such as arms drill, rifle-firing, grenades and defence of the camp against invasion. He was involved in leading one of these on the morning when the Dump went up. He also recalls going into the mine with colleagues on a fruitless search for bodies the following day, where the water and mud came up over their boots.[12] He has produced a written record of the day he will never forget.

The day started much the same as the previous one. After an early morning parade, fatigue parties were detailed to their various duties under the supervision of a Corporal or Leading Aircraftman. The party for duty in the mine were marched off by their duty sergeant and disappeared from view as they rounded the bend in the road.

Flight Sergeant Neil Robinson
Photo loaned by Neil Robinson

Other groups dispersed leaving a group of twelve junior N.C.Os and airmen who were temporarily seconded to me and another senior N.C.O. for a course in weapon training and field manoeuvres.

We marched our small contingent down the main road of the camp until we reached our destination – a small lecture room in the Motor Transport Section.

He explained that the first part of the morning passed without incident and after a half-hour break he resumed his lecture at half-past ten.

I had been explaining the theory of small arms fire for about forty minutes when a violent explosion was heard simultaneously with an earth tremor that shattered the window and buckled the walls of the small lecture room. Self-preservation took over and the next instant fourteen terrified airmen were huddled on the floor, all trying to reach the safety of a frail trestle table.

Numerous thoughts pass through one's mind during a crisis, my first recollection was "had a land mine been dropped from an enemy aircraft?" During my dive onto the floor under the table, I saw streaks of daylight appear between the walls, so great was the tremor.

After a short period he crawled outside. He explained that the sight mesmerised him as he looked in the direction of the mine:

From the area of the mine came the now familiar mushroom shape of an atomic explosion. It appeared to be about fifty yards wide and reached upwards almost out of sight. As the top of the "mushroom" began to spread to the left and right I could see large objects appearing beneath the smoke and fall noiselessly to the ground. (It was revealed later that the objects I saw were mounds of earth weighing up to a ton each.) The sky suddenly became dark as the pillar of smoke spread, the daylight disappearing behind the grey haze.

He and all the course members ran the four to five hundred yards up the narrow R.A.F. camp road that led to the mine entrance. En route they were joined by other airmen and by the time they reached the mine area the majority of the camp personnel were congregated there. He recorded:

My immediate impression when I reached the area was one of horror. There was a column of black smoke billowing out of the entrance to the mine. In the forefront a stack of boxes containing incendiary bombs were blazing furiously. All over the area were isolated patches of fire. I could see an airman and a civilian lying face downwards at the side of a brick building. They must have been killed instantly.

Fire-fighting parties were quickly organised and I joined a team busily engaged trying to extinguish the incendiary stack blaze. During this spell I saw a Leading Aircraftman being restrained from entering the mine. Wearing a service respirator he was attempting to enter the mine and search for his friend who had been on duty that morning.[13]

Nearly forty years later, Neil Robinson also contributed to a documentary programme on local radio:

It was coming up to 11 o'clock and all of a sudden it went black. I was knocked on the floor and then all panic let loose. Somebody said the Germans are bombing us and I looked up to see if there were any bombers about but there wasn't. And then all of a sudden this very hot wind came up the valley and we were coughing and as we looked up there were trees, there were bushes, there was turf, there was everything. It all came down – it started to rain down on top of the corrugated roof. The noise was horrendous and I didn't know what it was and one of the men said, "I know what it is – that's the Dump gone up."

We ran to the top of the camp – to the mine entrance – and started helping to put out the fires because the heat coming out of the mine had set boxes of incendiaries on fire. It was just devastation everywhere. There was a chap lying down by the entrance to the mine; he had his head blown off. There were little smoking piles of boxes, lumps of earth everywhere. We were given instructions to draw arms from the armoury and go and have a look where all the cattle had been maimed – and put them out of their misery. So we spent about an hour and a half doing that – shooting sheep and a couple of cows and a horse.

The only way I can explain what the land looked like – it was as if you saw photographs of No Man's Land during the First World War. There was nothing growing there, just soil as far as we could see – but there was all this smoke.[14]

Much earlier that morning, at the administrative base of the R.A.F. camp at Fauld, Squadron Leader L.H. Anness, under three months into his job as acting Chief Equipment Officer, had an urgent problem to solve. Later that day, the regular daily consignment of one hundred 4,000 lb bombs was due to leave from Scropton railway sidings but there were not enough railway wagons available to complete the job. Having dealt with his administrative duties in his office at Fauld, he decided, because it was a bright sunny day, to walk to Scropton so that he could discuss the issue with the transportation officer, Flight

Lieutenant Coles.

Squadron Leader Anness was standing in an open doorway at the transport section at Scropton railway sidings when he witnessed Britain's biggest explosion. At the official Military Court of Inquiry, held between the fifth and eleventh of December, 1944 the Squadron Leader stated:

I saw an enormous column of smoke shooting skywards for, I should imagine, two or three thousand feet and mushrooming out at the top. Black objects were also coming out in this column and shooting out to either side.[15]

The debris which fell, later estimated at around two million tons, was composed of earth, rock and boulders together with the shattered remains of buildings, fragments of machinery, bombs, uprooted trees, dismembered farm animals, soil and dust. It all rained down upon the surrounding area. Topsoil was detected up to eleven miles away. The falling debris and unexploded bombs, together with those which exploded on impact with the surface, created many additional smaller craters in the area between the main massive crater and the village of Hanbury.

Approximately sixty-five thousand square yards of the R.A.F. underground ammunition depot was directly affected by the explosion. This was about a third of the total area. The explosion occurred in the smaller "new" area of the mine, containing some four thousand tons of bombs and other explosives including more than fifteen hundred 4,000 lb bombs, and it was this part which was obliterated. Serious damage was caused to the old mine which had space for up to twenty thousand tons of bombs and shells. Many of the bombs in the old area were covered with debris caused by extensive roof falls so that highly sensitive explosives were mixed with the rubble. At the time, the total stock of bombs in both the "old" and "new" areas of the mine was about fifteen thousand tons or the equivalent of a fifteen-kiloton nuclear device.[16] Had the damage to the larger "old" mine area been greater the resulting devastation and loss of life could have been very significantly greater, extending to larger urban areas.

For a long time, the position was precarious in the extreme. The possibility of the whole going up was considered to be 80% and evacuation of the whole area (Burton, Lichfield, Derby and Uttoxeter) was considered, but the population concerned was too much and a chance was taken which came off.[17]

The effects of the explosion had been felt many miles away. However, unlike the exposed hilltop village of Hanbury, the administrative buildings at the Fauld R.A.F. Camp were shielded by the higher ground of the north-eastern slopes of the Stonepit Hills and escaped relatively unscathed.

On duty at the National Fire Service Company in Burton that morning was Fire Officer Charles Elliot. He had long anticipated a call to R.A.F. Fauld, having previously persuaded the Air Ministry to let him take a crew underground to examine the layout of the Dump as he had been anxious to find out about the safety standards in the mine.

When it did happen, there was no surprise. I was on the telephone in my control room and there was a bang and a strange clump. The building seemed to move, we looked at each other and we knew that what we had feared for years had finally happened and I turned out my appliances without waiting for any calls from anywhere. I'd got three appliances and I turned those out, told the control to notify the Divisional Headquarters as to what I'd done and off I went. Fifteen minutes later I was at Fauld.[18]

The immediate task for Elliot and his men was to work on blazing incendiary bombs which had been stacked outside the mine awaiting transport to Scropton. The entrance to the mine was choked with clouds of dust and lethal carbon monoxide fumes created by the explosion. R.A.F. personnel, with handkerchiefs over their mouths, were making desperate attempts to search for survivors but were constantly being driven back by the noxious gas. Elliot put through a radio call to his headquarters for assistance and then he, with four of his men, put on breathing apparatus and entered the mine.

The scene as we went in was in complete darkness because the lighting had gone and the main tunnel was full of cordite fumes and alabaster dust and you could see very, very little with the light of the breathing apparatus lamps but we struggled on along the main tunnel roadway until we came to a point where it was impossible to go any further. We hadn't seen any casualties up to that point but we found casualties on the way back along the same route so we must have passed them going in. We picked up those two casualties on the way back and brought them out but you could see all these stacks of bombs that had fallen over when you flashed your lamp on them and they made it difficult to make progress.[19]

Meanwhile Mines Rescue Squads had been called. At 11.50 a.m. the Leicestershire and South Derbyshire Coal Owners Rescue Station at Ashby de la Zouch received a call requesting the services of the brigade. At 12.15 p.m. the further support requested by Charles Elliot from the Fire Service arrived and by one o'clock the Mines Rescue Brigade from Ashby de la Zouch had also arrived at the scene.

Mine entrance after the explosion

Photo courtesy of TNA

Approximately ten minutes after the explosion occurred the acting Commanding Officer, Wing Commander Donald Leslie Kings, was the first to enter the mine. He took charge of the first rescue operations and helped prevent fire spreading to nearly ten thousand tons of bombs stored in the neighbouring tunnels of the old mine. He was later decorated for bravery, receiving the George Medal.

He was the first witness called at the Court of Inquiry and stated that:

At approximately 11 10 hours on 27 November, 1944, I heard a tremendous explosion. I was then in the Master of Provisions Office facing the Mine with a clear view right up to the Mine. The ground shook violently, and looking out of the window I saw a tremendous upheaval of smoke, rock and flame going up into the air. The explosion seemed to rumble as a continual roar for some time afterwards, I should say about 20 seconds. I was standing in my office at the time with Flight Lieutenant Dawson and I said to him "The Mine"; we waited for a second or two wondering what was going to happen next, and could hardly realise that the place was still standing and no windows broken. I then realised that as C.O. I had better do something about it. My car was parked outside the office, so I immediately proceeded up to the Mine, the fire picquet going up immediately in front of the car. Flying Officer Clements came out of the other end of the M.P.O. building and I picked him up, I also met Flying Officer Lewin and Mr Pollard [Chief Inspection Officer of the Aeronautical Inspection Department] *on the road going up to the Mine and gave them a lift.*

When we arrived at the control point there were two incendiary fires burning and exploding furiously . . .[20]

At the time of the explosion the people working underground in the caverns where the bombs were stored included military personnel, civilians and Italians. At the end of his statement, having explained how he organised the search for victims, the Wing Commander continued:

Experts at the time indicated that an air raid had taken place, to the extent that one man present said he had seen three aircraft dive into the area.[21]

When questioned further by the court on this concluding statement, he replied that he did not remember the name of the civilian who stated that he had seen three aircraft dive over the Mine.

Having given details explaining exactly what he had done in taking charge of the mine rescue work prior to the arrival of the Mines Rescue Squads he went on to state:

I sent a party of a Warrant Officer and 50 airmen with spades and shovels, who had come over from Church Broughton, round to Ford's Works to assist at that site, as I had then heard that they had suffered extensive damage and casualties. During the afternoon I directed many offers of assistance to Ford's works and Hanbury.

I then went over to the main crater which from my point of view looked nearly half a mile across and decided that in view of the number of small craters all over the place that bombs must have been thrown out of the Mine, probably at great temperature, and must have exploded in the air and on the ground when landing from the great heat. This ruled out to a great extent rumours that the depot had been subjected to air attack; one man had actually said that he saw three aircraft dive over the Mine before it blew up.[22]

The thirty-one other witnesses, military and civilian, who gave evidence at the Court of

Inquiry were very largely providing witness to what had occurred within the "old area" of the mine, tunnels, shunts and adjacent parts. No-one who was in the "new" area at the time escaped alive. Horace Utting, brother of Dick Utting who worked for Jeff Hellaby at Fauld House Farm, worked as a safety man and escaped unscathed. At the time he was in the incendiary area and, as the ninth witness before the court, stated:

On the morning of 27th November, 1944, I was in the Incendiary Area emptying water holes when the explosion occurred. We wondered what this rumbling was and we were put into darkness. We wandered our way outside and found that everything was in a mess. Next thing we did, we made our way to the H.E. [High Explosive] *Area to see if we could help, but we found the gas was too bad and we had to come out again.*[23]

Horace Utting was in one of the parties of men who, in the months after the explosion, worked with Dr Godfrey Rotter (scientific adviser) and Mr Eric Bryant (resident engineer) on restoration at Fauld. Among others, he was awarded the British Empire Medal (B.E.M.).

Joseph Clifford Salt was also in the mine when the bombs exploded. He was the foreman in charge of the civilian staff and on 27 November had allocated about thirty civilian labourers to the task of loading and unloading bombs in the mine. Following the explosion he displayed great courage in helping with the rescue and leading rescue teams through the shattered mine, which became lethal with gas fumes and fire. He was later awarded the George Cross. At the Court of Inquiry he was the third witness and stated:

Horace Utting 1945

Photo from group picture of workers involved in reclamation in the mine after the explosion and loaned by Betty Swain

When the first explosion occurred the lights did not go out, I ran to the door to see what direction the explosion came from. I looked down Ford's level, then up the main line and then back to the office [his office underground] *to fetch my torch. I had just entered the office when the second explosion occurred and blew the lights out. It blew me out of the office with Storeman Cresswell and Airman Still. I tried to find my way back in the dark, civilians and Italians were shouting "find a light". I shouted to Cresswell to find my torch as he was nearer the office than I was. Cresswell came with my torch and I accompanied the personnel out of the mine entrance. As we were coming up the main line out of the Mine, we were almost carried off our feet by what seemed to be blast behind us, coming from what seemed to be the direction of the office. I got the civilians out of the mine entrance, where Warder Simpson was lying injured on the bank, someone helped me to carry him out and we met Flight Lieutenant Lewin and a party with a stretcher. We placed Simpson on the stretcher and sent him to the Medical Room, and then someone pointed to the ground and we saw Warder Skellet under the rubble. We took him out and placed him on the next stretcher and sent him to the Medical Room. I went back into the Mine with Flight Lieutenant Shuttleworth and two mine safety men.* [This was at a time when conditions were still unknown and there were all manner of risks.] *We proceeded to F Loop to see if we could get into the New Area* [the location of the explosion]. *We heard a noise on the left-hand side of F Loop, and I called out to see if there was anyone there, and we found J.*

Woodall, *a janitor. We fetched him out from behind a fall of roof and took him out of the Mine to the Medical Room.*

Joseph Salt continued with his witness statement telling how he and Wing Commander Kings accompanied Charles Elliot's team from the National Fire Service, the first rescue party who had arrived with oxygen masks and equipment, back into the Mine in an attempt to get into the "new area". They climbed over rock falls but some of the rescue party were overcome by gas and had to be accompanied back to the mine entrance. By this time one of the Mines Rescue teams had arrived and Mr Salt again took them back into the mine with Mr Perry, who was in charge of the mines rescue team from Leicestershire and South Derbyshire. He concluded:

By that time I was feeling pretty groggy so I made my way out of the mine, and I was taken to the Medical Room.[24]

Flight Lieutenant J.P. Lewin entered the mine alone and on his own initiative some twenty minutes after the explosion and carried out a prolonged search in the underground workings. Later he entered again with Foreman Coker and searched for a further hour. By this time the gas fumes were becoming extreme and Flt. Lt. Lewin carried Foreman Coker out of the mine and then returned to continue searching on his own again. He only abandoned his search when teams from the Mines Rescue Organisation arrived. He then went to assist in the rescue of miners from Peter Ford's mine and descended the air shaft several times to help the casualties (see Chapter Four), and finally helped Wing Commander Kings in organising the relief measures on the surface. Together with the Wing Commander and Mr Joseph Salt he was awarded the George Medal. Flight Lieutenant Shuttleworth received the British Empire Medal (B.E.M.), as did a number of others of the mines rescue teams and local national fire services.

Wing Commander Kings, Flight Lieutenant Lewin and Mr Salt made repeated attempts to reach military and civilian personnel trapped underground but lack of precise knowledge of exactly where people had been working, absence of emergency lighting and breathing apparatus and the carbon monoxide gas circulating even in the minimally damaged areas made the task impossible. The National Fire Service Units and Mines Rescue Service also found the conditions extremely hazardous.

Corporal Lionel Poynton, who was the last person to escape with his life on the day the Dump went up, was a key witness at the December Military Court of Inquiry. It was because he had been seriously disturbed by his observations during a routine inspection that he had arranged to return to the Dump with his immediate superior, Sergeant Stanley Game, on the morning of Monday 27 November. The two non-commissioned officers entered the mine at ten o'clock and walked the three-quarters of a mile to the remote "new" area. At the Court Inquiry Corporal Poynton stated:

We proceeded into the new area to 27 Road where L.A.C [Leading Aircraftman] Fairbanks and L.A.C. Bailey were working on 1000 lb. MC [Medium Capacity] Bombs, which, I believe, were Unit Returns having been jettisoned. This work consisted of removing nose and tail plugs where possible, and removing the exploder container complete, or when it was not possible removing the C.E. [Composition Explosive] from the exploder pocket and collecting it in an ammunition box. Whilst I was there I saw a bomb with the transit plug in the tail removed set up horizontally on some form of batten about a foot from the floor. <u>*L.A.C. Bailey was chiselling out the C.E. from the exploder pocket. He was using a brass chisel and a hammer.*</u> [The previous two sentences were underlined in the Court of Inquiry Report.] *I do not remember whether the hammer was of steel or brass.*[25]

Corporal Poynton went on to explain that it was while L.A.C. Bailey was doing the dismantling job with the brass chisel that he and Sergeant Game were joined by Mr Sanders, an A.I.D. examiner, who made no observation on the tools used by L.A.C. Bailey. However, the corporal and his sergeant had no authority to overrule the A.I.D. examiner and stop the two airmen and when questioned by the Court of Inquiry he confirmed that the two airmen were working under A.I.D. instructions and not under his instructions. Corporal Poynton continued his statement to the Inquiry (and again this sentence was underlined) saying:

<u>*As I have done quite often previously in connection with similar work in the A.I.D. Compound, I warned L.A.C. Fairbanks and L.A.C. Bailey to take care as this was a dangerous job.*</u>[26]

Corporal Poynton and Sergeant Game left the area where Fairbanks and Bailey were working and went towards the "old" area, stopping on the way to speak with L.A.C. Deucharas, who was in charge of Italian workers stencilling small ammunition boxes for shipment overseas. They continued on towards the "old" area of the mine, walking along the narrow tunnel which took them through the gypsum pillar (Castle Hayes Pillar supporting Castle Hayes Farm) which separated the "new" bomb storage area from the "old" and saw another group of Italians working near the main line with Aircraftman Sheridan. Having travelled through the narrow tunnel separating the "new" area from the "old", Poynton and Game were still only 200 yards from where the two airmen had been working on the defective bombs, when, on the other side of the gypsum barrier, at ten minutes past eleven, 3,670 tons of high-explosive bombs erupted in one huge explosion. Corporal Poynton had just stepped out into the main roadway and Sergeant Game was behind him in the entrance to the cavern where L.A.C. Deucharas had been working with the six Italians. Sergeant Game, L.A.C. Deucharas and six Italians were killed.

Corporal Poynton recalled:

I was on the main road and the Sergeant was in the entrance to the gallery. The ammunition boxes flew around like flies and the lights went out. We were in complete darkness. I remember calling out to Sergeant Game several times but there was no response. I was crawling around in the dark trying to find him – we were then about three-quarters of a mile inside the mine and there was dust everywhere.[27]

Corporal Poynton's statement to the Inquiry concluded with:

On our way to this gang [the second gang of Italians] *there was a blast which hit me in the back. All I remember is crawling around in the darkness calling for Sergeant Game, but I couldn't find him. I remember trying to climb over a pile of boxes* [of ammunition] *when a second blast hit me and knocked me over again. I heard the shout of "Corporal!" and I shouted "Who are you?" and the answer was Sheridan. I can then remember crawling along feeling the rail* [railway line] *until I joined Sheridan, I think it was twenty yards. We then joined hands and feeling the rail crawled along together and contacted three armourers who had been engaged in painting S.A.A.* [small ammunition] *boxes. All five of us joined hands and walked along until we met another airman who had a small torch with him and we proceeded out of No. 2 Entrance* [mine entrance].[28]

These final sentences of his statement, although factually accurate, do not reveal the full horror of the situation they found themselves in surrounded by unexploded bombs. They are remarkable for what they conceal. They were three-quarters of a mile from the mine entrance and for much of the way they were in complete darkness, crawling on hands and knees and feeling their way along the railway lines. This small group of men with Corporal Poynton learned that they were among the last men to get out of the Gallery alive. The body of Sergeant Game was recovered from beneath boxes of ammunition later in the day. The bodies of Caporale Rocco Novello and Soldato Salvatore Trovato were recovered on 1 December and those of Caporale Luigi Scuto, Soldato Emilia Di Paolo, Soldato Aldo Lanzoni and Soldato Salvatore Ruggeri eleven days later on 8 December. They had been buried under tons of ammunition boxes and blasted rock. No trace of the men working in the "new" area would ever be found: in addition to Leading Aircraftmen Bailey and Fairbanks they included A.I.D. examiner Thomas Sanders, A.I.D. viewers James Brassington and Frederick Nicklin, electrician's mate Alfred Shipley, trainee electricians Frederick Campbell and Lewis Frow, together with Charles Hogg, Gerald Mahon, Albert Mellor and Bert Stanley of the Air Ministry Works Department. That section of the mine was sealed and because of the danger of unexploded bombs is likely to remain so for ever.

Not far from Corporal Poynton, Leading Aircraftman Alfred Gibbard had been working labelling ammunition boxes. He told how:

We were lifting the box up and all of a sudden all hell was let loose and there was a massive gush of air. And you just couldn't hear the actual bang – there was no actual bang – just a whoosh and a thud and I was just hurled off my feet and pinned against the roof. And it seemed pretty much to have been a second or two but it seemed an eternity and when I was released from that roof I found I'd caught my knee. I'd knocked my knee up and had a few bruises on my elbow when I came down from the roof.[29]

Corporal Poynton and L.A.C. Gibbard were lucky: many men around them were killed by the blast and flying wreckage including Ambrose Patterson, George Powell and Frederick Slater.

In Lionel Poynton's mind there was no doubt as to what had caused the explosion.

My own conclusion is that one bomb on which they were working had had what's called a flashback from the exploder pocket, it detonated and the detonation wave was sufficient to detonate all of the bombs in the New Area. It was a case of sympathetic detonation.[30]

The explosion, however, could have been of much greater magnitude. The fact that there was a long narrow tunnel from the "new" area, where the explosion occurred, to the "old" area, where over twenty thousand tons of bombs were stored, was probably instrumental in giving a degree of protection to the "old" area. The blast, however, did rush along the narrow tunnel which went through the gypsum pillar between the two areas and created some damage.

The last person to leave the "new" area alive was Leading Aircraftman Michael Watson. Five minutes before the explosion he had gone in search of appropriate skids to load four 4,000 lb bombs onto the railway trucks which would be transporting the bombs out of the mine. He escaped with Ken McLeod, who is the only person still alive who was underground inside the bomb store at the moment when the explosion occurred. He was the fourteenth witness at the Court of Inquiry where, as Leading Aircraftman Kenneth Alan McLeod, he stated:

I am an armourer in "C" Flight, No. 21 MU Fauld. I have been at the unit eight weeks. I have been working at various places i.e. in the Belting Shed, the Mine and in the Compound [A.I.D. Compound].

On the day before and on the day of the explosion I was in the Mine putting steel bands round 0.5 Ammunition Boxes with two other armourers.

The lights went out between the first and second explosion. I was thrown up against the wall at the first explosion. I went to make my way out and was thrown to the ground by the second explosion. The second explosion had a greater effect than the first; there was a terrific rush of wind and dust. It is difficult to say from which direction it came, but it was from the general direction of the New Area. Three of us decided to make our way out in the dark; we felt our way up to the wall until we came to the concrete. Before we reached the concrete we joined up with Corporal Poynton.[31]

Ken McCleod, together with armourer colleagues, was in what was known as a "shunt", a cavern of around one hundred by fifty feet, which lay off the main mine avenue. It was this location which doubtless helped to save his life as the force of the explosion went up the main avenue.

Ken McLeod has provided a written record for the author:

On 27 November, 1944 I was in the mine. At approximately 11.10 a.m. there was a terrific explosion. I was thrown against a wall, the lights went out and there was another explosion which was worse than the first. This time I was thrown to the ground, there was a rush of wind and dust flying about. It was complete darkness. After picking myself up I heard voices. We said "'we have to get out of here." We said we should hold hands and try to feel our way and we then realised we were going the wrong way. We then felt the same things and realised we had all joined hands and were going in a circle. We found our way out by following the rail track, and then in the distance we saw a light; the driver of the locomotive had left the lights on. The first thing we saw when we got out was a dead duty Ministry of Defence policeman

**Leading Aircraftman
Ken McCleod**

Photo loaned by Ken McCleod

[John Skellet]. *The landscape had completely changed. There was mud everywhere and incendiary bombs were going off.*

I helped to collect water bottles from the billets and fill them with clean water and took them to the Station Nurse. Two of us then went to some cottages which had been flooded to see if we could find anyone but we didn't find anyone [The Purse Cottages, homes to the Hills and the Fords].

Emergency services came to the scene including the Mines Rescue. They went into the mine to see if they could find any survivors but they found no-one. I think the four of us who got out together were the last ones to get out alive. One of the Mines Rescue men lost his life. [This was fifty-one year-old James Beard of the Mines Rescue from Ashby de la Zouch, who was gassed.] *I helped to carry him on a stretcher down to the First Aid point.*

Days later four of us escorted the body of Leading Aircraftsman Deucharas to Derby station to send him home to his mother in Crieff, Scotland. Two of the Airmen who got out with me were later medically discharged. It is a day I will never forget.[32]

Ken McCleod had been working in a cavern packed with small-arms ammunition with four Italian former prisoners of war and three of his armourer R.A.F. colleagues. The Italians were feeding boxes of ammunition onto a conveyor belt and the armourers were inspecting it to see if it was fit for use. Shortly before the explosion he had spoken with both Sergeant Game and Corporal Poynton. He told of how a huge lump of alabaster had come off the roof, demolishing all the ammunition boxes. It just missed him and his colleagues. It took them three-quarters of an hour to get out and in the last few yards they were having breathing problems as the gas started to affect them. When they reached the mine entrance they discovered that it had collapsed but they managed to crawl through a narrow gap.

During an interview with Ken McLeod he mentioned that the armourers were not given the right tools with which to work with the bombs and that his first job had been to take an exploder out of a 350 lb bomb with an old barrack-room poker made of iron. Just before the explosion on that fatal Monday morning, when working on ammunition in the "old" area of the mine, he recalled hearing, from the direction of the "new" area, a loud and very anxious voice calling for the "lamp boy". He then saw Lewis Frow, the fifteen-year-old trainee electrician, disappear along the roadway leading to the "new" area. Ken was the last person to see Lewis Frow alive and recalls:

Just prior to the explosion there was an agitated voice – I think it was Sanders [A.I.D. Examiner] *– calling for extra light. I'm convinced that they had found something seriously wrong in the new area of the mine. I would say they were inspecting the bombs, Nicklin* [A.I.D Viewer] *and Sanders, and found something unusual. They couldn't see what it was and sent for the lamp lad and then . . . Boom! That's one possibility. Another possibility is – the two R.A.F. lads, Bailey and Fairbanks, they were in another part of the mine fitting suspension lugs to 4,000 lb. bombs and there's a possibility they drilled too far and that could have started it.*[33]

Five months later, on V.E. Day, 8 May, 1945, Ken McLeod met his future wife, Joyce Frow, at a dance held at the R.A.F. station at Fauld. Lewis had been her brother and was the youngest victim of the disaster.

Fifteen-year-old Lewis Frow was one of the eighteen victims who lost their lives (above and below ground) whose bodies were never found and for whom the Fauld Crater is their grave.

In the yard outside the main entrances to the mine, Air Ministry Policeman Constable Leslie Ingham was on duty. From a small hut near one of the mine entrances he was directing the traffic of bomb-loaded trucks in and out of the mine. At the moment of the explosion he was standing beside one of the hut windows.

There were little pieces of dust coming towards us and then it became gravelly and the little windows were cracking and he [a colleague] *said "the bloody mine's going up!" And then I looked and there was this great mushroom in the sky and it was said in Burton that if*

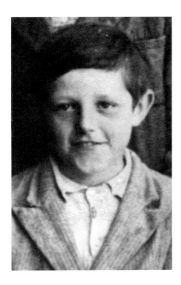

Left: Lewis Frow 1941

Photo loaned by his sister Joyce McCleod

Right: Ken and Joyce (née Frow) McCleod 1945

Photo loaned by Joyce McCleod

ever the Dump went up then God help Burton and I turned and ran. I was scared. I started to run to get to the other side of Burton [sic]. This was true. I had to get to the other side of Burton before the next one came and as I ran the blast – assuming it was the blast – took me into the air. I've thought since, many and many a time, how lovely to be a bird because I floated in the air and the next minute I hit the top of a fence which led into the Air Inspection Department and precipitated over the fence which resulted in me dropping onto the other side onto the railway line and busting my ribs. But that was nothing when I saw what happened afterwards.[34]

Another Air Ministry Policeman on duty that day had his stomach ripped open by the force of the blast. He survived, but his colleague P.C. John Skellet from Rolleston, who was standing closer to the mine entrance, was killed.

Mr John Webb, a professional mine rescue worker, was amongst those responding to a call at ten to twelve requesting help from the brigade. He, together with his Superintendent Mr Perry and colleagues Alfred Parker, James Beard, Leonard George Snape, Cyril John Whetton and William Slater, proceeded to Fauld, arriving at approximately one o'clock. They were the first team of mine- rescue workers to arrive at Fauld and by this time the Dump was so thick with carbon monoxide gas that death could result from just a few seconds' exposure to the lethal fumes. On arrival, they divided into two teams and were given a map of the mine and information on the probable positions of survivors. John Webb led his team of Jim Beard, Cyril Whetton, Bill Slater and Len Snape into the mine. One hundred and forty yards from the mine entrance they established a fresh air base and marked it with chalk. Only four of this first rescue team returned alive. P.C. Mackay took down Mr Webb's statement of what happened:

Leaving the fresh air base at one forty-five p.m. we proceeded along loop "E" and examined several roadways. [See map showing underground tramways in Chapter Two]. We eventually explored a roadway known as "E.L." which was in a state of devastation. During this period an examination of oxygen consumption by the brigade was regularly made. Proceeding along "E.L." we found two dead bodies within a few yards of each other and at this stage decided to return to the fresh air base. This would be about two thirty p.m. An attempt was made to bring with us the first dead body. This was loaded onto the stretcher by myself, Beard, Slater and Whetton. The other members of the team, including Beard, conveyed the body approximately ten yards on the stretcher. Owing to the difficulties of travel, I decided that the risk was too great to recover this dead body and I wrote instructions on a girder in chalk that we would abandon the body and return to base.[35]

Shortly afterwards, due to the gas, James Beard began to experience serious difficulties. He failed to respond to any treatment and the team was forced to leave him behind and proceed to the fresh air base to summon what assistance was available. No further mines rescue teams had arrived by three thirty and all of the members of the brigade, including Superintendent Perry, were overcome by gas and had to be assisted out of the mine by R.A.F. personnel.

John Webb's team had reached safety only just in time. Rescue attempts were suspended while ventilation equipment was brought in in an attempt to clear the mine of gas. All hope of finding anyone else alive had long since been abandoned.

By the middle of the afternoon all forms of help had arrived in the area: Fire Service, Civil Defence, Mines Rescue and medical assistance. Relatives stood in groups waiting for news.

Two other rescue teams failed to locate Beard and at half past ten Superintendent Perry asked John Webb if he was in a condition to lead the Ilkeston Rescue Brigade into the mine and recover Beard.

John Webb's statement concluded:

At eleven ten p.m. I went into the mine again with the Ilkeston team and directed them to the point where Beard was left, finding him about eleven thirty p.m., in the exact position he had been left. He was in a sitting position with the back of his head on a munitions box. He appeared to be dead. The oxygen and reviving apparatus had spent itself out and the light on his hat was just burning out.[36]

The team leaders of the Collieries Mines Rescue Association were awarded Companion of the British Empire medals (C.B.E.) and the Air Council placed on permanent record their high appreciation of the gallantry shown by all team members, saying:

The explosion was unprecedented in character and magnitude, and gave rise at once to highly dangerous conditions throughout the passages and recesses of the storage mine. It was essential to penetrate and explore the mine with the least possible delay, partly in the belief that the lives of workers cut off by the explosion could still be saved and partly in order to control the dangerous physical conditions and guard against the risk of further explosion.[37]

In a letter from the Right Honourable Viscount Stansgate to Air Marshal Sir Grahame Donald, telling of his great pleasure in recommending to His Majesty the grant of Gallantry Awards to certain members of the staff of the Bomb Storage depot at Fauld, it was recorded:

From the accounts of what occurred during those twenty-four hours I can picture to myself the appalling conditions in which Royal Air Force personnel and members of the civilian staff of the Depot entered the mine at the height of the crisis, risking the gravest danger from fire, further explosion, noxious fumes and roof falls. They penetrated into mine workings which were a labyrinth of blocked roadways, past galleries containing thousands of tons of high explosives, some of it crushed under fallen rock.[38]

AIR MINISTRY, LONDON.

Sir,

1st May, 1945.

I am commanded by the AIR COUNCIL to say that it gives them much pleasure to put on permanent record their high appreciation of the gallantry shown by the TEAMS of your COLLIERIES RESCUE ORGANISATION on the occasion of the explosion which occurred at the R.A.F. storage depot at FAULD on the 27th November, 1944.

The explosion was unprecedented in character and magnitude, and gave rise at once to highly dangerous conditions throughout the passages and recesses of the storage mine. It was essential to penetrate and explore the mine with least possible delay, partly in the belief that the lives of workers cut off by the explosion could still be saved, & partly in order to control the dangerous physical conditions & guard against the risk of further explosion.

Rescue teams were brought to the depot with admirable promptitude. The mine was systematically and continuously explored for some twenty-four hours, with further intermittent work during the days following.

Each Team Leader was awarded a Commendation by His Majesty the King, partly for leadership & partly in token of the gallantry of the individual members of the team under the leader's direction.

Subjoined are two lists; one, of the Active Teams, i.e. of the men who entered the mine and went into the danger area with full rescue and breathing apparatus; the other, of the Stand-By Teams, i.e. of the men who responded to the call and stood-by, ready to take the full risks if required in support of their comrades.

The Air Council desire to pay their tribute of honour and respect to these men, and in particular to the memory of JAMES BEARD who sacrificed his life in the operations.

I am, Sir,

John Robertson, Esq. O.B.E., J.P.
Chairman, Leicestershire & South Derbyshire
Collieries Rescue & Fire Station,
Ashby-de-la-Zouch, Leicestershire.

Your obedient Servant,

Permanent Under-Secretary of State.

Active Teams.

LEADERS –
Herbert James Hall
Arthur Hazell
Albert Hunt

Harold Insley
James Kendrick Twgy
John Webb

MEMBERS –
John Thomas Adcock
Job Arnold
James Beard
William Percy Bills
Clifford Bradford
George Henry Broadhurst
Eric Burton
Wilfred Corner
Harry Crowder
Frank Alonzo Garland
Wilfred Hart
Roland Hill
Percy Hogg
Walter Harold Haughton
George Edward Ison

John Thomas Kenny
Joseph Francis Lee
Kenneth James Mousley
Frank Poxon
Samuel William Preston
William Slater
Leonard George Snape
Frederick Francis Starkey
Joseph Storer
Arthur Augustin Tompkin
Timothy Toon
Willis Ward
John Cyril Whetton
Stanley John Wright

Stand-by Teams.

Frank Beadsmore
Stanley Billings
Harold J. Boulstridge
Cecil Albert Boulton
Alwyn Brown
Harold Brown
Samuel Brown
Bertie Chipman
Jack Clamp
Frank Corner
John Cowley
Francis Dennis
William Foley
George Gamble
Leonard Gilliver
Howard Leslie Goacher
Charles Donald Harvey
Sherud Jervase Joyce

Charles William Lane
Harold Lunn
William Malpass
William Millington
Harry Milson
George Lawrence Moore
James Moore
Alfred Parker
Hubert Noel Poole
Frederick W.W. Redfern
James William Rice
George Smith
Jim Smith
Albert William Walton
Frank Harry Webb
Frederick B. Whetton
Thomas Mathew Wilson
Bernard Wykes

Written out on the 10th May, 1945, by M.C. Oliver, A.R.C.A. London.

Letter from the
Air Ministry

Photographed from the framed original at the Magic Attic archive

119

The rescue attempts were heroic but ultimately hopeless. It was the poison gas which defeated the rescuers, the same noxious gases which had also caused the death of five miners in the neighbouring gypsum mine. The loss of life at the ammunition dump at Fauld totalled fourteen civilians, six military, six Italian military and one mines rescue worker. It was less than a third of the total loss of life that day.

NOTES

1 Reported by former R.A.F. Flight Sergeant Neil Robinson and recalled to the author on 20 March, 2012.

2 Recalled by former R.A.F. Leading Aircraftman Ken McCleod to the author on 18 August, 2011.

3 P.C. Mackay incorporated a number of "queer happenings" into the end of his report to the Coroner.

4 *Daily Mail*, 28 November, 1944.

5 Ibid.

6 Memories of Harry Payne lodged in the Tutbury Museum. Whilst researching this book the author spoke with Harry Payne on 19 August, 2011.

7 Letter from Hazel Ede, 21 October, 2011.

8 *Burton Mail*, 19 October, 1993.

9 *Burton Mail*, 18 May, 1977.

10 Reed, *After the Battle* (1977).

11 As recalled by Neil Robinson to the author on 20 March, 2011.

12 Ibid.

13 Report of former Flight Sergeant N.W.Robinson which he wrote during the 1960s.

14 BRMB documentary broadcast from Birmingham written and produced by Brian King, 28 November, 1983.

15 National Archives, Ref AIR 17/8 Inquiry at R.A.F. Fauld Explosion at No. 21 Unit, Fauld 27 November, 1944.

16 Trevor Jones, "The Great Fauld Explosion", *Staffordshire Studies* Vol. 1 (1988).

17 Papers of P.C. Mackay.

18 BRMB documentary broadcast from Birmingham produced by Brian King 28 November, 1983.

19 Ibid.

20 National Archives Ref AIR 17/8 Inquiry at R.A.F. Fauld Explosion at No. 21 Unit, Fauld 27 November, 1944.

21 Ibid.

22 Ibid.

23 Ibid.

24 Ibid.

25 Ibid.

26 Ibid.

27 Former Corporal Poynton reported by the *Burton Daily Mail* after the Inquiry of December 1944 was made public in November 1974.

28 National Archives Ref AIR 17/8.

29 BRMB local radio documentary recording from Birmingham 28 November, 1983.

30 Ibid.

31 National Archives Ref AIR 17/8.

32 From Ken McLeod as told to the author on 18 August, 2011.

33 Ibid.

34 BRMB radio documentary 1983.

35 Statement given by John Webb to P.C. Mackay, Coroner's assistant, 1944.

36 Ibid.

37 Letter of Commendation from the Air Ministry to the Teams of Collieries Rescue Organisation.

38 The National Archives Ref AIR 19/523.

CHAPTER SEVEN
SECRETS AND RUMOURS

"I must caution you not to show any of these works, even to your friends, before they have been submitted to us by the censor."[1]
"I appreciate the Coroner's anxiety to give as much information as possible, but I am afraid that it is not possible at this stage to say anything about the cause of the explosion."[2]

Secrecy, security and censorship were central to all activities at M.U. No. 21 R.A.F. Fauld following its establishment in the late 1930s, especially as it became Britain's major ammunition depot serving Bomber Command during World War Two. Secrecy was maintained after the explosion with the Air Ministry's refusal to make any official statement as to either the cause of the major explosion or the likelihood of further explosions. The secrecy of war allowed conspiracy theories to flourish. Rumour suggested sabotage and the theory was given credence by the fact that former Italian prisoners of war were working at the Dump. There was also a rumour of spying based on reports that four German prisoners of war had escaped from the American base at Sudbury on the previous day. A further rumour, suggesting that a V2 rocket deliberately targeted the site, was believed by many at the time and strongly supported in some quarters. There were even wild rumours of a "super bomb" or early nuclear bomb or V3 and of three planes seen diving near the site before the explosion. There was even a wild theory that the I.R.A. was involved.

For thirty years afterwards spy and saboteur theories abounded. When the findings of the Court of Inquiry, which was unable to determine a definitive cause of the explosion, were made public in 1974 the rumours and speculation did not cease. They have continued into the twenty-first century.

From the outset, the Air Ministry was concerned to maintain secrecy regarding all activity at M.U. No. 21 R.A.F. Fauld. In 1937, when arrangements needed to be made to transport vast quantities of bombs to airfields across the country, it became necessary to purchase several acres of land for a transport depot at Scropton railway sidings. The farmer who sold the land "was advised to state, if asked, that his land had been requisitioned for the construction of a government oil depot".[3]

Early on in the war, in a letter dated 23 February, 1942, the War Office commissioned artist David Bomberg to make a painting of the underground bomb store for a fee of 25 guineas.[4] In a letter to Bomberg which followed, the precise location of the bomb store was not stated and there was no specific mention of R.A.F. Fauld. However, the crucial importance of secrecy and security precautions was emphasised. It stated:

It will be necessary to submit all your preliminary sketches and studies, as well as the finished work, for censorship. I must caution you not to show any of these works, even to your friends, before they have been submitted by us to the censor.[5]

The Bomb Store painting of 1942 was Bomberg's single commission as an official war artist. His biographer, Richard Cork, described the painter's depiction of the underground caverns housing the vast arsenal as *"strange, haunting and distinctly ominous places"*, representing the store as:

A dark eerie chamber permeated by intimations of the human tragedy that these bombs would inflict when they were unleashed on historic cities and on the helpless citizens who became the victims of remorseless night raids.[6]

David Bomberg's portrayal of the bomb store does have an extraordinarily prophetic quality. Bombs from Fauld certainly were unleashed on German cities. However, less than three years after the painting was executed, the blazing destruction predicted was, with a terrible irony, borne out on a devastating scale in the cataclysmic explosion in the ammunition depot itself. Richard Cork wrote:

Full details of the disaster were hushed up at the time and neither Bomberg nor Lillian [his wife] *ever seems to have heard about it.*[7]

Bomberg's painting has been described as:

A powerful painting executed in difficult conditions, an historical document of a place now destroyed and a revealing insight into the atrocities of war.[8]

Although the existence of the bomb store was supposed to be secret and Government security during wartime demanded that all developments and activity at No. 21 Fauld Munitions Unit were conducted in absolute secrecy many people in the local area were aware that the disused mines were being used for bomb storage. John Hardwick, who

Painting of Bomb Store by war artist David Bomberg, 1942

Painting in a private collection, London and reproduced here in black and white with permission of the owner

farmed at Hanbury, recorded the following:

For hundreds of years alabaster has been mined in an area between Tutbury and Hanbury, and some disused mine workings proved an ideal place for the R.A.F. to have a "target" ammunition store. It was started about 1937 and by 1944, at the height of the allied bombing campaign, a train load of bombs was moving on a daily basis from Fauld by narrow gauge railway over the River Dove and from there, to airfields in Lincolnshire. All the bombs were not jettisoned [i.e by the R.A.F. when on bombing raids over Germany]. Some were returned to Fauld where they were de-fused before returning to store. The usual practice was for testing to take place and we were used to hearing small controlled explosions most days.[9]

The 3,670 tons of bombs which did explode in a rural area of eastern Staffordshire on 27 November, 1944 was three times greater than the amount dropped on London on the worst night of the Blitz of 10 May, 1942 and six times greater than the bomb tonnage dropped on Coventry during its fiercest wartime raid of 14 November, 1941. However, the Fauld explosion was a disaster of the Second World War which had nothing to do with enemy action. Nevertheless, at a quarter to nine on the evening of 27 November, Lord Haw Haw (William Joyce, announcer on the English-language propaganda radio programme *Germany Calling* broadcast by Nazi Germany) was on the air claiming that a German V-weapon had hit an ammunition dump. The next day Reichsmarschall Goering, who was in charge of the Luftwaffe, also claimed that the explosion was caused by a V2 bomb.[10] Two days after the explosion, Propaganda Minister for the Third Reich, Joseph Goebbels, claimed that it was caused by a direct hit from a V2 rocket. His official news agency sent out this story under a faked Stockholm dateline:

With reference to reports that an R.A.F. munitions depot blew up, it now transpires from London that this explosion was the result of a bombardment with a German V weapon.[11]

By the end of the week further exaggerated claims were being put out by enemy propaganda:

Enemy radio is now "asking" if the catastrophe was caused by a V3. One station of enemy origin said: "Doubt has been thrown on the theory that it was a V2 rocket bomb that hit the bomb depot. Something else must have done it – perhaps some new V3 German secret weapon. It is most probable that some new weapon caused the detonation of the bomb depot."[12]

The requirement for strict wartime security and secrecy regarding both the location and severity of a major accident at Britain's largest arsenal remained paramount. However, in the immediate aftermath of the explosion, the desperate need for an immediate response by the National Fire Services, the Mines Rescue Organisations of local collieries, Hospital and Ambulance Services, the Women's Voluntary Service and by the United States Forces stationed locally dictated a much greater urgency.

Wing Commander Kings, the Commanding Officer at Fauld on the morning of the explosion, had emphasised his concern for security when, in response to a question at the Court of Inquiry, he stated:

A press reporter had got into the Unit on the back of a fire tender, and Flight Lieutenant Shuttleworth had him held pending a decision on what to do with him. I told F/L Shuttleworth to instruct the reporter not to make any statement on the accident until news was officially released by the Ministry of Information. I also asked F/L Shuttleworth to telephone the local press agency representative to broadcast a local warning against publishing stories of the explosion.[13]

The warning went unheeded. The explosion was reported in the local and national press in addition to being picked up by the German Ministry of Propaganda. The authorities could not hope to hide the massive amount of devastation and the following day the Press Association reported:

The whole area surrounding the dump is a desert. Hundreds of cattle are lying dead in the fields. The grass has been scorched and the ground is pitted with bomb craters.

Although newspapers did cover the story the strict security of wartime meant that all but the barest details were censored and the valiant efforts made by the authorities to prevent any specific reference to R.A.F. Fauld were largely successful. There were very real fears that once the site was known the chances were that attempts to bomb it would be made by the enemy.

It hit the headlines in the local press on the same day. In the final edition of the *Burton Daily Mail* of Monday, 27 November the front page carried the following report:

BURTON AND DISTRICT ROCKED BY GREAT EXPLOSIONS
Service Personnel and Civilians Killed and Injured
MEN BURIED AND CRUSHED WHEN UNDERGROUND WORKINGS CAVE IN
CASUALTIES FEARED HEAVY [14]

And the front page of the *Derby Evening Telegraph* of Monday, 27 November had headlines of:

MANY KILLED AND BURIED BY EXPLOSION
Ammunition Dump Disaster Traps Men Underground: Countryside Blitzed [15]

But the War continued and the biggest explosion ever to occur in Britain competed with other headlines on the same front page:

All Front Advance Deeper into Reich
and
Munich Heavily Bombed

The front page headlines of the *Daily Express* on 28 November were:

Allied Blitz touches new peak: Luftwaffe loses 236 in two days. War's biggest fighter battle.

It does, however, also report on its front page:

Bomb Dump Explosion entombs 37 [16]

On 28 November *the Times* reported:

MANY DEAD IN R.A.F. EXPLOSION [17]

And the *Daily Telegraph*:

90 KILLED IN R.A.F. BOMB DUMP EXPLOSION
MIDLAND TOWNS ROCKED [18]

In *The Times* on 29 November, the news from the war front was:

R.A.F. Bombers in great strength on Monday night struck two blows at key German railway centres behind the Western Front

And on the home front:

It was believed last night that the death roll caused by the explosion at an R.A.F. depot and dump near Burton-on-Trent amounted to 160 and that over a 100 men were still buried in the ammunition store.[19]

In the *Burton Mail* of 2 December, 1944 the Coroner was reported as saying:

By exaggerating the numbers we are helping the enemy and by saying they are too small we are raising false hopes among the general public.

Our enemy is trying to gain some kudos for this, which is entirely unproven and unlikely. On the other hand, to minimise is only raising false hopes.[20]

The press estimates of the number of deaths were highly speculative and exaggerated. Figures in excess of 200 hit the headlines in the *Daily Mail*, leading to Government criticism that the national press were damaging public morale. The Government would clearly have preferred to keep all news of the disaster out of the public domain, and the way it was seized upon by the Nazi propaganda machine made their reasoning crystal clear. Lord Haw Haw not only claimed that it was caused by one of their V2 flying bombs but also fuelled the rumours of sabotage by suggesting that it could have been set off by one of the Italian former prisoners of war.

At the secret Court of Inquiry, Wing Commander Kings had stated:

I sent the Italian Co-operators back to Hilton Camp and placed them under guard for the time being, the reason being that one or two people were making unpleasant remarks about having Italians on the Unit.[21]

Rumours that the explosion resulted from sabotage by the Italians started to circulate immediately and it was not until after the Inquest of February 1945 that the rumours were firmly scotched. There were six Italian workers who lost their lives that day. One of the Italians who should have been with them in the mine had reason to thank his senior officer, Lieutenant Luigi Silvestri, who had placed him on a charge for some misdemeanour: it was a charge which saved his life.[22]

Wartime secrecy shrouded the cause of the explosion in mystery but some of the stories in the local, national and international press speculated on the possible causes of the huge explosion. The *Derby Evening Telegraph* reported on its front page on Tuesday, 28 November, 1944:

In the opinion of a Royal Engineers officer, who held an important post at the ammunition dump, what appears to have happened "is that one bomb exploded and the rush of air acted as a detonator for all the bombs in the Dump". He said that it was this detonating wave underground which caused the earthquake effect which was felt for miles.[23]

Under a headline of: "*It Was Worse than Hill 60*" [Ypres 1917] the *Daily Express* reported:

Mr Thomas Fell, two of whose brothers are missing, told me: "All six of us brothers went through the last war and came out alive. I was at Hill 60. This was worse."

Thomas Fell's missing brothers Edgar and Benjamin both lost their lives in the explosion. They had been working as "stone-dressers'" at Peter Ford's Works.

The Vicar of Hanbury, the Rev. James Crook, was also reported as saying:

"I was in the Silvertown [London] *explosion in 1917 but it was not as terrible as this." (The Silvertown explosion in a high explosive factory killed 69 people and was heard 100 miles away).*[24]

Most of the national and some of the international press had picked up the news of the disaster by Tuesday 28 November. The French language newspaper *Dépêche Algerienne*, under the headline below, reported that in the region of Burton, which was described as "near London", a violent explosion in an R.A.F. munitions depot had resulted in the death of 220 people:

PRES DE LONDRES

L'explosion d'un depot de munitions aurait cause la mort de 220 personnes[25]

It later came to light that it was also published in the German Nazi Party newspaper *Völkischer Beobachter* ('The People's Observer') two days after the explosion. Under the headline below it was reported that an English bomb store had exploded leaving hundreds dead and suggested that a V2 rocket was the cause.

Englisches Bombenlager Explodierte

Hunderte Von Turten/V2 Ursache?[26]

On the fiftieth anniversary of the Fauld explosion, the *Burton Mail* produced a commemorative edition which included a story recalled by a former prisoner of war, Mr George Gardiner, of Stapenhill, near Burton-on-Trent. Mr Gardiner, who was aged seventy-three when he recounted his story to the *Mail*, was held in a British work camp at Auschwitz after being captured in Tunisia in 1943. He told of how, while fetching medical supplies from a chemist in occupied Poland, he had pocketed a cutting from the German newspaper, dated 29 November, 1944, describing the explosion. The following is a translation of how the news was reported to the German public, including an ill-supported suggestion that the Nazis had successfully targeted Fauld with a long-range missile.

More than 200 civilians were killed, according to English newspaper witness accounts, in a terrible explosion in Burton-on-Trent. The number of soldiers and workers who lost their lives has not been made known.

In the explosion of the R.A.F. bomb store near the Midlands town of Burton, the bomb provision for many hundreds of air attacks was blown up, the military has reported.

The cause of the explosion given was that a smaller bomb exploded and detonated the whole bomb store. Few people, however, believe this explanation. They point out that bomb stores are, as a rule, laid out in such a way that in the case of part of the store blowing up, the damage is limited to a certain room. It is, therefore, not surprising that the Burton catastrophe is being linked with the V2 (rocket).

A worker, taking part in the rescue operation, gave the following description of the explosion:

"It was terrible and incredible. The earth swayed as if the ground had been taken from under your feet. A whole hill was swept away and another rose in its place. It was impossible to get near to the site of the explosion, but we could look into the huge crater."[27]

Mr Gardiner told of how a fellow prisoner translated the newspaper clipping and that when he told the guards that he knew about it they said that it was a V2 rocket which hit Fauld. He agreed the story could well have been propaganda but kept an open mind in view of the guards' statement.

The Air Ministry had full knowledge of the findings of their own secret military Court of Inquiry, which was set up to try to determine the cause of the explosion and which was conducted between 6 and 11 December 1944. If, however, they revealed that the court had not been able to determine with absolute certainty exactly what had caused the explosion, they feared increasing the level of public apprehension and anxiety regarding the possibility of further explosions. The result of this strict maintenance of secrecy placed the Coroner at the Inquest, held in early February 1945, in a very challenging situation. Additionally, the rigid adherence to secrecy allowed further rumours and speculation to run riot.

The Coroner, Major J.L. Auden, was being pressed to hold the Inquest into the cause of death of the victims of the explosion as soon as possible but he did not intend to do so until he was confident that as many as possible of the bodies had been recovered. When the Inquest opened on 6 February 1945 forty-nine bodies had been recovered and nineteen were "missing presumed dead". Prior to the opening of the Inquest the Coroner had expressed his concern that it would not be sufficient for him to bring in a verdict of "accidental death" but he was expressly forbidden by the Air Ministry from examining the cause of death of the victims of the explosion. He was prevented from examining the one thing that everyone wanted to know. Why had the Dump exploded? In the event, the bland and unsatisfactory verdict of accidental death was given. Lord Sherwood, the Under Secretary of State for Air, wrote to the local M.P., Mr J.F. Gretton, with a copy to the Coroner saying:

I appreciate the Coroner's anxiety to give as much information as possible, but I am afraid that it is not possible at this stage to say anything about the cause of the explosion.[28]

Also prior to the Inquest the Coroner had expressed his concern about a number of questions he knew he would be asked and to which he did not wish to provide ambiguous answers. He pointed out that:

Local inhabitants in the devastated area have behaved most admirably and quite naturally they are anxious to have some information, and expect me to furnish it.[29]

Although the Coroner was not allowed to say anything about the cause of the explosion, or to give any assurance that further explosions were unlikely, he was informed by the Air Ministry that he could give assurance on three of the rumours which had been circulating. These were that the accident was not due to sabotage, that the ex-Italian prisoners of war were not involved and that it was not due to blasting in the neighbouring Staton's works. At the Inquest the Coroner stated that the whole district was alive with rumours. He offered an apology to Italians to whom sabotage had been attributed by some people and expressed strong disapproval of the rumour which had been circulated. He stated:

The Italians did not ask to be sent to the dump. They only did their duty there. Following the explosion their lives became somewhat unpleasant in the district owing to what I can only call pot-house gossip. They were no more to blame than the I.R.A.[30]

The Commanding Officer at Fauld, Group Captain R.J. Storrar, although not present at the time of the explosion (he returned from leave, which had commenced at nine o'clock on 27 November, at 3.00 p.m. that day), was present at the Inquest. He confirmed that, although the official investigation was not complete, he too was in a position to say that the cause did not arise from sabotage.

In 1946, the Americans were also interested in pursuing information on the Fauld explosion but they did not find the Attlee Government cooperative. On 11 June, Air Commodore K.J. Collier C.B.E., Director of Equipment at the Air Ministry, Woburn Place WC1 received a letter from Colonel Frank Reed, United States Military Attaché at the American Embassy, London. The letter requested information regarding the Fauld explosion. The details requested were quite specific:

Depth at which the explosion took place

Area occupied by explosion

Dimensions of the crater

Damage to structures by earth shock if any

Damage by blast

Any other effects that were observed

Interestingly this letter, which is now in the National Archives, reveals pencilled marginalia giving data regarding answers to the first three of the above, namely: 90 ft.; 65,000 sq. yds.; 915 ft. by 720 ft. plus.[31] However, the Government decided not to disclose any information to the Americans.

Rumours continued to circulate. In January 1947 the Government stated that the Fauld explosion was the largest ever to occur in the British Isles and although they did not consider it was due to enemy action they were still not prepared to say anything further.

On 17 January, 1947, the *Derbyshire Advertiser* reported as follows:

BOMB DUMP EXPLOSION BIGGEST EVER IN BRITAIN

H.M. inspectors of explosives, in their annual report for that year (1944) published last night as a White Paper, state that the explosion [at Fauld] *was not due to enemy action. Further than that they do not go.*

The *Advertiser* also reported that the White Paper stated that:

This sixth year of war has been noteworthy for by far the biggest explosion ever to have occurred in these islands.[32]

The *Daily Graphic* reported as follows:

BIGGEST DUMP EXPLOSION RIDDLE UNSOLVED

The mystery of Britain's biggest explosion disaster in which 68 people were killed [two others died afterwards] *and 22 injured was still unsolved when the report of H.M. Inspectors of Explosions was published in a White Paper last night.*

An underground Dump at Burton-on-Trent blew up in November, 1944, devastating a wide area of countryside. Next day Goering claimed that the explosion was caused by a V2.

The report denies that it was due to enemy action but gives no clue to the Air Ministry Inquiry findings. Considering that 3,000 tons [3,670] of explosive was involved the loss of life was light, says the report.

The previous biggest explosion was at Silvertown, London, in 1917, when 69 people were killed and 400 injured.[33]

In 1944, the public were denied access to official documents for fifty years. In 1962, the Earl of Harrowby (whose home was in Staffordshire and who had visited the site in the days following the explosion)[34] raised a question in the House of Lords. The Hansard extract of 12 December, 1962 notes:

The Earl of Harrowby asked Her Majesty's Government whether an explanation can now be given as to the cause of the 1944 explosion with its serious loss of life and of munitions at the Fauld alabaster mine in Staffordshire and whether the report of the inquiry can now be made available.

The First Lord of the Admiralty (Lord Carrington) replied:

"The cause of the explosion at Fauld in 1944 was never established.

"It is not the practice to publish the reports of Royal Air Force boards of Inquiry and

notwithstanding the lapse of time <u>*it would not, in my opinion, be in the public interest to*</u> <u>*make an exception in this case.*</u>*"*[35]

It is very interesting to note that the Hansard record underlines in red the final eighteen words of this statement. Filed with this Hansard extract at the National Archives is a report from a *Daily Telegraph* reporter under a headline of:

BOMB STORE SECRET

The Earl of Harrowby said yesterday that he is to ask the Government to lift the security *"black out" on the cause of an explosion in which seventy people died in 1944.*[36]

In 1967, the embargo on public access to official documents was lowered from fifty to thirty years. The Earl of Harrowby continued to press for early release of the findings of Court of Inquiry and the *Sunday Times* of 16 February, 1969, picked up the story under the headline:

Biggest blast will remain a mystery[37]

The Ministry of Defence continued to state that:

"It would not be in the public interest to make an exception in this case" and the Earl, *who had already raised the issue in the House of Lords without success commented*:

"I feel the whole story is extremely fishy. The fact that the report will never be published *is a very serious thing. I cannot help feeling that there is more behind it."*[38]

Thirty years to the day, the government released the findings of the Court of Inquiry. All the Air Ministry files and associated papers relating to the explosion had been classified as "SECRET" until 27 November, 1974. The court found that an airman using the wrong tools on a defective bomb was to blame. It was revealed that the most likely cause of the explosion resulted from bombs being primed for use and stored with the detonators still installed. However, they could not provide a definitive cause of the explosion and were forced to use the words "in all probability" and this was based on the evidence of only one witness. Others who might have been able to provide confirmatory evidence had died in the mine and all evidence had been destroyed in the blast.

The *Burton Daily Mail* of 27 November, 1974 had as its front page headline:

FINDINGS OF INQUIRY INTO 1944 FAULD BOMBS EXPLOSION

AIRMAN WAS USING BRASS CHISEL ON HUGE BOMB

Regulations "not fully observed"

Rumours and speculation about the cause of the huge explosion in the R.A.F. Underground *Bomb Store at Fauld thirty years ago – including the suggestion that there was sabotage by* *Italian Prisoners of War working in the mine – have at long last been ended.*

The lifting of the 30-year "secrecy ban" also discloses another fact – that the explosion *could have been ten times greater, possibly even wiping Burton off the map, had it spread* *to the main area where many more bombs were stored.*[39]

The Court of Inquiry of 6 to 11 December, 1944, which had been ordered by Air Marshal Sir Grahame Donald, Air Officer Commander in Chief of R.A.F. Maintenance Command, concluded:

<u>*In all probability*</u> *the work of chipping out the C.E.* [Composition Explosive] *Exploder* *from a 1,000 lb. M.C.* [Medium Capacity] *Bomb, using a brass chisel, was the cause of the* *initial explosion. It is known that C.E. will explode easily if struck between brass and steel*

surfaces. This bomb was one of a row of 1,000 lb. bombs which were presumably exploded by sympathetic detonation or by fragments. Subsequently the whole (or the greater part) of the content of the New Area (of the mine) exploded.[40]

The Court also found that although current regulations and standing orders were adequate they were not fully observed.

There are obviously mitigating circumstances during wartime when urgency is a keynote, man power is of poorer quality and quantity, and more work is expected of a Unit than that for which it was designed.

Some relaxations can be made with safety, and there must have been a tendency to extend relaxation locally owing to "familiarity breeding contempt".

The findings also stated that:

It appears from the evidence of Witness No. 30 [Corporal Poynton] *that an airman was permitted to perform a dangerous operation in the Mine. This indicates negligence on the part of the A.I.D.* [Aeronautical Inspection Directorate] *supervising staff present in the Mine, due either to lack of knowledge, lack of a proper sense of responsibility, or a lack of proper direction from senior authority.*

Neither the Chief Inspection Officer (A.I.D.) [Mr Pollard] *nor the Acting Chief Equipment Officer* [Squadron Leader Anness] *can be entirely absolved from all responsibility; as they do not appear to have been sufficiently aware of the work undertaken in the Mine Area, nor to have adequate records or control of such work.*[41]

In response to the latter finding, Air Marshal Sir Grahame Donald observed that there appeared to be a lack of a clear determination of responsibilities between the A.I.D. and the R.A.F. and commented:

From the evidence it would appear that at 21 M.U. there is a lack of a clear cut definition of responsibilities between the Chief Equipment Officer and the Chief Inspection Officer. It is my impression that elsewhere in the Group the allocation of responsibility is clearly understood, although the dividing line may be thin. I am taking action to remedy this fault.

In the second finding it will be observed that the Court cannot entirely absolve the acting Chief Equipment Officer and the Chief Inspection Officer (A.I.D.) from all responsibility. It might seem therefore that an opportunity should have been given to Squadron Leader Anness and Mr Pollard to be present during the proceedings and to cross question any witness. The court however did not arrive at any conclusions regarding the responsibility until the whole evidence had been placed before them.[42]

The finding which did not absolve Squadron Leader Anness and Mr Pollard from all responsibility, when neither was allowed the opportunity to defend himself at the Court of Inquiry, suggests a seeking out of the proverbial scapegoats. The "blame game", however, is a sterile debate. Alternatively, it could well be argued that it was a systems failure: it was the divided responsibilities, as remarked by the Air Marshal, which was the weakness in the system and it was a system which was operating under tremendous pressure and at full stretch. With manpower shortages and limited training, shortcuts were taken. The need to ensure the safe defusing of jettisoned bombs was operational at the same time as the need to respond to the demand for weapons. These demands were at a constantly high level with round-the-clock bombing of German cities and industries, by the R.A.F. with their

Lancasters at night and the U.S.A.A.F. with their Flying Fortresses by day.

Additionally, the Court had found:

No evidence that any aircraft or bombs fell in the area of the mine on 27th November or that any enemy action was involved. The Court also examined the possibility of sabotage, but found no evidence in support of this. Any stories or rumours concerning the above two points can therefore only be considered as without foundation.[43]

Also released thirty years on was the official confirmation that not only was the explosion the biggest to have taken place in Britain but the actual amount of tonnage which exploded, as precisely as it was possible to estimate, was confirmed. In papers attached to a Hansard minute of 30 November, 1944, the Secretary of State for Air, Sir Archibald Sinclair, had revealed that the total tonnage of bombs exploded was approximately 3,670 (3,470 high-explosive bombs and 200 incendiaries).[44] The Secretary of State had expressed his deep regret that the disaster 'has been attended by severe loss of life and damage to private property'. (The Under Secretary of State for Air, Lord Sherwood, had made a personal tour of the area ravaged by the explosion.)[45] The Secretary of State also, in his oral answer before the House of Commons on 30 November, 1944, had stated that 'the total loss of bombs is less than 4,000 tons, no more than has been dropped on a single raid on Germany.'[46] This, however, was somewhat disingenuous: a single raid over Germany would cover a wide area whereas at Fauld the explosion of bombs was concentrated on one small area. It has subsequently been pointed out that the underground bomb explosion was significantly greater than that in Flanders during the First World War when, in June 1917:

The British Army had detonated nineteen underground mines under the German lines in the Wytschaete-Messines sector in an attempt to straighten out the Ypres salient. In all, a million pounds of explosive was detonated over the six-mile sector, killing an estimated ten thousand German troops. At Fauld between six and a half and seven million pounds had blown up within a single small sector.[47]

A question remains as to why Britain's biggest explosion, which was reported in the Press and picked up by Nazi propaganda, remains relatively unknown outside the local area? A partial answer may lie in the fact that it had to compete with many other items reported and also, occurring in a sparsely populated area, resulted in a lower loss of life than if it had occurred in an urban setting. However, why was the secrecy, which allowed rumours to flourish, maintained for thirty years in spite of questions raised in Parliament over twenty years after it had occurred? It could reasonably be argued that the serious problem lay in withholding from the public the conclusions of the Court of Inquiry. However, in the more paternalistic age which prevailed in the middle of the last century the authorities were able to hide behind the statement that "it was not in the public interest".

In the years which followed the revelation in 1974 of the findings of the Court of Inquiry a number of alternative theories regarding the possible cause of the explosion continued to surface.

At the time of the fiftieth anniversary in November 1994, the daughter of one of the witnesses at the official inquiry revealed that her father knew more than he was prepared to say.

"They weren't supposed to be smoking," said Mrs Ann Denne, daughter of Tom Mylotte who worked as a storeman. "They were searched before they went in but there's always

a way." She said that at the Court of Inquiry her father was asked if he was keeping something back. "He said unless you can bring someone out alive to say otherwise I am saying nothing."[48]

A close examination of the written record of the full statement made by Thomas Mylotte, the twentieth witness at the Inquiry, together with the questions put to him and the answers given, does not confirm the above suggestions.

Former R.A.F. serviceman Malcolm Kidd was stationed at Fauld in 1944 and at the time of the explosion was working on bombs in the mine. In May 1993 he wrote from his home in Cheshire to the then landlord of the Cock Inn at Hanbury, saying:

Contrary to regulations, two 1,000 lb bombs from a crashed aircraft arrived in the mine. My Sergeant told me to stencil on them "for dumping in deep water". I did this and went out of the mine for the 10 a.m. break. Whilst in the rest room a civilian said "I will get some stillsons [wrenches], take the noses off those crash bombs and we can send them out again." Fortunately for me I was ordered to return to a part of the mine some distance away from the bombs.

Whilst working on some sea mines which were dropped by parachute, I heard a boom, the lights went out, there was a rush of air, dust everywhere, a second rush of air and then silence. Fortunately I managed to find a torch which I kept for emergencies and leading my party out got out of the mine to find blazing boxes of incendiary bombs which had been jolted by the blast.

I was present at the inquiry but not called to give evidence and shortly after posted to Italy and ended up in Yugoslavia helping Tito until the war ended.

There is no doubt in my mind that the civilian had put a wrench on the nose pistol, turned it, crushed the detonator inside, exploded the bomb which then caused a sympathetic detonation throughout the new area, which, unconcreted, allowed the blast to go up and take the top of the hillside with it.[49]

Fifty years on Malcolm Kidd visited the scene of the explosion in November 1994 and his recollections of his experiences on that fateful morning were taken up in the local and national press. He reiterated that he had been sent to deal with two 1,000 lb bombs which had been recovered from an R.A.F. crashed bomber and that he had been ordered to stencil each bomb with "For Dumping in Deep Water" as they were due to be jettisoned at sea. He remained convinced that the explosion had been caused by the civilian munitions worker trying to unscrew the nose pistol on one of the 1,000 lb. bombs. Confirming that he was present at the Court of Inquiry although not called upon to give a witness statement, he now regretted that he had not intervened.

But I was very young and very junior. My father had been in the Guards and I was taught to carry out orders and not to question anything. I was just an ordinary aircraftman. It wasn't my job to say "don't do that".[50]

However, he insisted that he was telling a true story and wished to put the record straight. A Ministry of Defence spokesman said:

The inquiry presumably conducted its business to the satisfaction of the government of the day. This is now a closed affair and all the papers are at the Public Records Office. However, if someone has a different story to tell in the media, it is perfectly legitimate to do so.[51]

Malcolm Kidd's letter to the landlord of the Cock Inn was also recalled just prior to the sixtieth anniversary of the explosion and was printed in the *Derby Evening Telegraph* in December 2004.

Interestingly, P.C. Mackay's papers, which did not come into the public domain until 2006, reveal the following with reference to some bombs which were returned to Fauld.

They brought them back to their dromes, from whence they were sent back to Fauld, WITH THE FUZES AND DETS STILL IN THEM.

By a grave oversight, they went back into the Mine, where they were subsequently noticed to be "alive".

People who were not engaged inside the Mine at the fatal time have told me what they knew and saw. They saw one man (who died) removing such fuzes and dets. [sic] from bombs he had found "alive". Apparently he found "a wrong-un".[52]

One of the theories regarding the cause of the explosion, which was discounted in the findings of the Court of Inquiry but had been widely believed at the time, related to the possibility of a German attack with a V2 rocket. It was a theory which refused to die a death and as recently as the first decade of this century was still being promoted by Alec Savidge, whose father had had a job as the senior electrician at Fauld. He said his father, Tom Savidge, had seen something hit the hillside and smoke rising from the trees directly above the mine several seconds before the main explosion. He maintained that this was a key piece of evidence that showed it was a V2. Alec Savidge also examined the official photographs taken by a Mr W.H. Horsley between 1 and 8 December, 1944 and claimed that one of these showed the wrecked rear section of a typical German V2 rocket missile of the type which was regularly being fired at the south-east of England.

A major problem with Alec Savidge's theory was that the V2s did not have the range or guidance system to hit Staffordshire accurately. On 15 March, 2004, a spokesman from the Science Museum in London, speaking on a BBC radio programme, *In Loving Memory: Fauld*, stated:

From what I know about the V2 programme and the range of the V2 and the likely state of readiness of updated V2s, I would conclude that it was highly unlikely, almost impossible, that any type of V2 would have reached Staffordshire.[53]

Alec Savidge was also interviewed on the above radio programme, where he introduced an even more controversial notion when he suggested that it could have been a uranium bomb. However, as Germany was nowhere near making a nuclear bomb by the end of the war there is nothing to back up his theory, which was based on the evidence of a local farmworker, John Bowley. Bowley, who was also interviewed for the programme, maintained that he had bought what turned out to be a Geiger counter at an auction sale of surplus military gear and that whilst ploughing in the vicinity of the crater, with the Geiger counter strapped onto the front of his tractor, it had started to tick violently. However, as the producer of the programme pointed out, 'there are many difficulties with John Bowley's story and one of them is that a Geiger counter wouldn't detect uranium very well'.[54]

The true cause of the Fauld explosion can never be proven with absolute certainty. The most likely cause which is now most generally accepted is that of bad practice and negligence. However, the notion that it could have been an atomic explosion refused to die and was still being quoted on the internet in 2012.

It would appear that the Fauld Disaster resulted from the accidental detonation of a small atomic bomb. It is similar to a slightly larger blast that occurred, also in rock tunnels, on the German island of Heligoland when it was under British control in 1946.[55]

There had been thirty years and more in which rumour and speculation had run riot. The secrecy of war, which allowed conspiracy theories to flourish, robbed the Fauld victims of true recognition that they also died for their country. The Fauld Crater, which is the last resting place of those victims who were never found, is indeed a war grave like no other. It is a grave they share with an unknown quantity of unexploded bombs.

NOTES

1 E.M. O'Rourke Dickey to war artist David Bomberg, 23 February, 1942, Imperial War Museum, quoted in *David Bomberg – a biography* by Richard Cork (Yale University Press, New Haven and London, 1987).

2 Copy sent to the Coroner, Mr J. L. Auden, of a letter from Lord Sherwood, Under Secretary of State for Air, to Mr J. F. Gretton M.P., 7 February, 1945.

3 N.J. McCamley, *Disasters Underground* (Pen and Sword Military 2004).

4 E.M. O'Rourke Dickey to David Bomberg, 23 February, 1942, Imperial War Museum Archives, quoted in Richard Cork's biography of the artist.

5 The Director General of the Ministry of Information to David Bomberg, 23 February, 1942, collection of the artist's family and quoted in *David Bomberg – a biography* by Richard Cork.

6 Richard Cork, *David Bomberg – a biography*.

7 Ibid.

8 Description provided by Bonham's auction house.

9 Unpublished record of John Hardwick.

10 Claim reported in the *Daily Graphic*, 17 January, 1947 in an article entitled 'Biggest Dump Explosion Riddle Unsolved' following the report of HM Inspectors of Explosives in a White Paper of 16 January 1947. The report denied that it was due to enemy action but gave no clue to the Air Ministry Inquiry findings.

11 *Daily Express*, 29 and 30 November 1944.

12 *Derby Evening Telegraph*, 2 December, 1944.

13 National Archives Ref AIR 17/8: Inquiry at R.A.F. Fauld Explosion at No. 21 Unit, Fauld 27 November, 1944.

14 *Burton Daily Mail*, 27 November, 1944.

15 *Derby Evening Telegraph*, 27 November, 1944.

16 *Daily Express*, 27 November, 1944.

17 *The Times*, 28 November, 1944.

18 *The Daily Telegraph* =, 28 November, 1944.

19 *The Times* 29, November, 1944.

20 *Burton Mail*, 2 December, 1944.

21 National Archives Ref AIR 17/8.

22 Neil Robinson to the author 20 March, 2012.

23 *Derby Evening Telegraph*, 28 November, 1944.

24 *Daily Express*, 29 November, 1944

25 *Dépêche Algerienne*, 28 November, 1944.

26 *Völkischer Beobachter*, 29 November 1944.

27 *Burton Mail*, 28 November, 1994.

28 Letter from Under Secretary of State for Air to J. F .Gretton M.P. Copy to J. L. Auden. This copy letter was loaned to the author by John Cooper, who has conducted his own research into the Fauld explosion.

29 Copy letter from J. L. Auden to the Hon J.F. Gretton, also via John Cooper.

30 *Derby Evening Telegraph*, 7 February, 1945.

31 The National Archives Ref AIR 17/12.

32 *Derbyshire Advertiser*, 17 January, 1947.

33 *Daily Graphic*, 17 January, 1947.

34 The Rev. Crook, in speaking at the opening of Hanbury Memorial Hall, made reference to the Earl's visit to Hanbury following the explosion.

35 National Archives, Ref AIR 2/6966.

36 National Archives, Ref AIR 17/12.

37 *Sunday Times*, 16 February 1969.

38 Ibid.

39 *Burton Daily Mail*, 27 November, 1974.

40 National Archives, Ref AIR 17/8.

41 Ibid.

42 Ibid.

43 Ibid.

44 National Archives, Hansard 30 November, 1944.

45 *Burton Daily Mail*, 2 December, 1944.

46 National Archives, from Hansard extract (Official Journal Of Parliamentary debates, oral answers, vol. 406, col. 66, 30 November 1944.

47 Trevor Jones ,*The Great Fauld Explosion* (Staffordshire Studies Vol. 1) 1988.

48 *Derbyshire Advertiser*, 30 November, 1994.

49 Copy of letter in the Magic Attic archive, Swadlincote.

50 *Express and Star*, 24 November, 1994.

51 Ibid.

52 Mackay Papers.

53 BBC Radio 4 documentary radio programme *In Living Memory: Fauld* produced by Jolyon Jenkins 15 March 2004.

54 Ibid.

55 Internet site: 'The Fauld Crater near Hanbury', Flickr (http://www.flickr.com/photos/7382107@ N04/459935896/), accessed 21 August 2012.

CHAPTER EIGHT

AFTERMATH

"The earth, once green pastures, was scorched as if in pain. A devastated site where once men toiled, women baked and children played."[1]
"For years this was a moonscape because the topsoil had gone and there was no end of attempts to drain the fields, only nothing worked. They were trying to make land out of something which wasn't land any more."[2]

A wasteland beyond all imagining, a devastated, ravaged, tortured and dystopian land was the scene viewed by Air Vice-Marshal A. Lees when, together with other members of the R.A.F. Court of Inquiry, he visited the crater and surrounding area in the fading light of the afternoon of 5 December, 1944. The alien scene meeting their eyes was reminiscent of the worst conditions on the Western Front nearly three decades earlier. It was a scene where human remains and an unknown quantity of unexploded bombs lay hidden and where the search for victims had been on-going over the past week. The search continued for more than two and a half months. It was not officially abandoned until 10 February, 1945, four days after the Inquest into the cause of death of the victims, at which time there were still nineteen persons missing presumed dead.

The Bishop of Lichfield, Dr E.S. Woods, had also viewed the disaster area and spoken with many of the bereaved. On Sunday 3 December he had conducted a memorial service in Hanbury parish church and addressed the large and representative congregation:

I was glad to come here during these days, and yesterday afternoon I was taking part in the funeral services of some of those who lost their lives, but I can but reflect that the deaths of these good folk are an integral part of the war casualties. They would never have had to give up their lives if it had not been for the war and the chances of war which have been brought to this corner of England.[3]

Almost forty-five years later Byron Rogers of *The Guardian* spoke with survivors Roy Gregson and John Hardwick and also visited Hanbury Church. He recorded:

In the church there is a framed list of those who died in the Second World War. Seven names, the sort of toll you might expect in a place of this size, but then after these comes the three long parallel rows of those who died on November 27 1944. The Coroner recorded a verdict of "Accidental death caused by an explosion on Government property", and not a word suggests what it was like when for a few minutes a small village became a war zone.[4]

On 1 December, 1944 Lord Sherwood, Under Secretary of State for Air, had viewed the area and seen the rescue work in progress at the Dump and Ford's Works. He also met people in the village of Hanbury where he was reported as saying:

I have come out here to see for myself this damage, and am very impressed with all the efforts everyone has made.[5]

Three days after the explosion a decision was taken locally to launch an appeal across the land to help support the bereaved.

NATIONAL APPEAL FUND

The members of the Rural District Council, inside whose area the explosion at an R.A.F. maintenance depot occurred, have been quick to decide measures to help the dependants of the victims and at a special meeting at Burton-on-Trent yesterday afternoon it was decided unanimously to launch a national appeal under the designation "Staffordshire Explosion Relief Fund".[6]

The clerk to the Rural District Council was secretary to the distress fund that was established and by 31 January, 1945, £5,000 had been donated. However, the Air Ministry were dragging their feet regarding official compensation for the dependents of the victims and the Rev. Crook was reported in the *London Daily Mail* under the headline below saying:

VILLAGE WAITING FOR AID

Mr Gretton, our parliamentary representative, has been arguing the case of the villagers with Lord Sherwood, Under Secretary of State for Air, but the Air Ministry seem to be terribly slow in getting things settled. Weather conditions are adding to the hardships being endured by the people of the village. Something must be done to help out these people quickly.[7]

Meanwhile, the immediate urgency following the explosion had been the safety of the bomb store and removal of explosives. This meant the removal of bombs from the "old" area of the ammunition dump. The "new" area, where the explosion had occurred, was completely inaccessible and part of the "old" area was damaged. In the "old" area around 15,000 tons of high explosives remained with 4,000 tons in the damaged portion. Within this area the possibility of a further explosion remained high, and if this occurred it would have the potential to cause damage over a significantly wider area.

The 3,670 tons of high-explosive bombs which had gone up on 27 November, 1944 completely obliterated the "new" mine. This area had had a total storage capacity of 8,000 tons of explosives. It has been estimated that there was 5,000 tons of explosives in the "new" area at the time of the explosion.

The exact quantity of ordnance in the New Store at the time of the accident is not known, but is estimated at 5,000 tons. However, the shape of the crater and the fact that the ordnance in the Old Store remained intact indicate that there is a significant quantity of ordnance in the remaining gallery system of the New Store.[8]

Left: Bombs in the mine under a rock fall after the explosion *Photo courtesy of TNA*
Right: Bombs in the mine after the explosion *Photo courtesy of TNA*

The authorities determined that clearance of the "old" area should be initiated with all possible speed but it was soon discovered that the damage here was greater than had at first been anticipated.

Reports now show that the damage to the main mine is more extensive than the "light damage" at first believed.[9] [One fifth of the "old" area had been affected by the explosion.] *In this damaged area various sensitive explosives are mixed up with debris; serious roof falls have occurred, and rock from the vaulting and pillars is partly supported by stacks of explosives. The clearing of this area is charged with great risk.*[10]

In the remaining four-fifths (about 40,000 square yards) of the "old" area of the mine the damage was deemed to be negligible although roof falls could be expected.

There are about 15,000 tons of explosives in this undamaged area, in which also is housed the magazine [11]

It was decided that the whole of the mine stock of bombs and explosives should be removed from the undamaged "old" area and transferred to R.A.F. Tatenhill, known as the "Needwood" camp, a flying unit six miles away.

On 23 December, 1944, the following was reported to the Under Secretary of State for Air:

In order to reduce the chance of another explosion and damage over a wide area, it has been decided that the whole of the mine stock of bombs and explosives in the undamaged part of the mine must be removed as quickly as possible.[12]

The report stated that evacuation work was proceeding with thirty men (one day shift of civilian volunteers and two night shifts of airmen) and that they were clearing around three to four hundred tons a day.

The new area is still unapproachable and much of the old area is still unsafe. The intention is to empty the old area of stores and day and night shifts have been working on this.[13]

Former Leading Aircraftman Ken McCleod, who was among the last to escape from the mine on 27 November, recalls:

It must have been over a week later when I went back into the mine after it had been decided that it had to be emptied of all the unexploded bombs. They decided to put the civilians on the day shift and the R.A.F. on night duty. We had to check that the bombs were safe before they were removed to Tatenhill. I remember I went to see if my tunic was still where I'd left it when I'd escaped from the mine. I found it still hanging on the nail where I'd left it but the blue cloth had turned green – probably from the gas. And my wallet – it was tan coloured, camel skin – was still in the pocket. The wallet had turned black with patches of green and some pound notes had also turned green with all the gas and sulphur. The knapsack of one of my mates was also still hanging there. His bicycle lamp was still in it. If he'd gone back for it we would have escaped from the mine much more quickly.[14]

The Air Ministry's expert adviser on explosives, Dr Godfrey Rotter, volunteered to take charge of the operation to remove bombs although concerns were expressed within the Ministry regarding the dangers of removal in the damaged part of the "old" area.

I am very sorry to hear that the damage is so much worse than we feared at first. Before Dr Rotter is requested to undertake the dangers for which he has volunteered, I should be obliged if you would carefully consider other alternatives and send me an appreciation of the risks involved. Might it not, for example, be better to blow up the remaining explosives

Above: Godfrey Rotter and Eric Bryant
Photo taken from group photo and loaned by Betty Swain (née Lindsey)

Left: Dr Godfrey Rotter in the mine
Photo courtesy of TNA

rather than risk precious lives in trying to retrieve them? Would not the work of retrieving them mean an immense expenditure of skill, labour, time and material? If the roofs are, in some cases partly supported by stacks of explosives, will they not have to be shored up before the explosives are removed?

What is the final estimate of the loss we shall have suffered through this explosion? Does it dangerously affect our reserves of any particular bomb or explosive?[15]

Meanwhile, the war continued and the R.A.F. at Fauld still had a responsibility to respond to the demands of Bomber Command. However, it was inevitable that the Unit could not be fully functional in the months immediately following the explosion.

The removal of bombs was carried out under the guidance of sixty-six-year-old Dr Rotter who, before being called out of retirement by the Air Ministry at the beginning of the war, had been director of explosive research at the Woolwich Arsenal. Resident mining engineer Eric Bryant, who had advised on the original conversion of the mine into a bomb store, was in charge of structural restoration work. It was demanding and dangerous work and it was not until 25 March, 1945 that all of the high-explosive bombs from the undamaged four-fifths of the "old" mine area had been recovered.

The Air Ministry Director of Works reported that he was:

Extremely grateful for the services of Dr Rotter not only for the safety of the whole establishment of 21 M.U. but also for the safety of some large towns in the neighbourhood which might readily be involved if there were to be another explosion, the natural traverse having disappeared.[16]

The clearance from the remaining fifth of the "old" area, where there had been serious damage and where the risk of a further explosion remained, was much more hazardous. It was estimated that there was about 6,000 tons in this damaged portion of the "old" area. An Air Ministry file dated 12 January, 1945 noted:

The stock in the damaged portion is about 6,000 tons. No estimate can be made for some time as to how much of this might be salvable, but if none were recoverable it would not dangerously affect any of our reserves.[17]

It was early April before Dr Rotter and a small team could embark on the clearance of the damaged portion.

Dr Rotter considers that in view of the danger and delicacy of this latter work, it may be desirable that he and two or three others alone should undertake it.[18]

On 7 April the Air Ministry approved a proposal for clearing the damaged area of the mine and five months of challenging and dangerous work, under the "hands-on" guidance of Dr Rotter and Mr Bryant, was undertaken by a team composed mainly of civilians.

Dr Rotter stated:

There was constant danger of further explosions, but I've had a magnificent team of men to help.[19]

On 11 September, 1945, four months after the war in Europe had ended, R.A.F. Maintenance Command was able to report to the Air Ministry (on the basis of a report from Dr Rotter) that the clearance of the damaged area was almost complete.

With the exception of one cavern, which is believed to contain only S.A.P. [Semi-Armour Piercing] bombs not exceeding 70 tons, all explosive stores have now been removed from the mine; in all 23,000 tons have been removed, of which 4,000 tons were recovered from the damaged area. [Additionally, 9,000 tons of rock debris had been removed.] The one area which remains to be cleared is filled with mud which has entered from above; its complete clearance will not be effected for some weeks. Apart from the somewhat improbable presence of a cluster bomb which may have been deposited there by a freak of blast, the handling of S.A.P. bombs should not entail any abnormal risk; the principal risks to be encountered are those normal to quarrying in unsound rock and to the mud.[20]

It was a year to the day after the explosion, 27 November, 1945, that the last of the bombs was finally removed. However, in October, in recognition of the outstanding service given in the removal of the bombs left in a critically dangerous condition, Gallantry Awards were granted.

The situation required from Dr Rotter and Mr Bryant not only the best scientific and professional knowledge but personal courage sustained day after day throughout the months of physical exploration and constant risk. But these two alone could not have carried on the work without the teams of men who contributed the most careful and efficient service, characterised throughout by a similar gallantry.[21]

George Medals were awarded to Dr Godfrey Rotter and Mr Eric Bryant. Dr Rotter's example was outstanding and, says the citation:

His enthusiasm for the work, the risks of which he fully appreciated, was inspiring.[22]

Mr Bryant was the first to enter the damaged portions of the mine and had to crawl on top of overlying explosives in a dangerous state and to crawl under roof which was liable to fall.

His confidence and judgement, says the citation, inspired all concerned to carry on with the dangerous work.[23]

Mr Sydney Walter Maxted, scientific adviser to the Ministry of Supply, and Mr George Edward Fox, leading storeman, had led a small party engaged in the precarious work of recovering damaged explosives. *"Great care was needed as it was not known if the safety devises of certain damaged stores were still intact."*[24] Maxted was made a Member of the

British Empire (M.B.E.) and Fox was awarded a British Empire Medal (B.E.M.). Mr Ernest Parker and Mr Horace William Utting *"worked fearlessly, shoring up a bad roof which might have fallen on more explosives."*[25] Both were awarded the B.E.M. Thirteen others, many of whom had worked at the dump or at Peter Ford's mine and plaster works previously, were commended for their brave conduct.

In the official announcement of the awards it was recognised that urban centres further afield had been in serious danger had there been a further explosion in the damaged portion of the "old" area where removal of bombs and restoration work took place.

DERBY PERIL IN DUMP EXPLOSION

In the words of the official announcement of awards a "further explosion might well have caused damage to the town of Derby, and would most certainly have damaged towns and villages in the neighbourhood, since a natural protecting traverse had disappeared in the explosion on November 27th."[26]

Ernest Parker
Photo taken from group photo loaned by Betty Swain

By October 1945 work was also under way to construct an access to the working gypsum mine, which had been damaged as a result of the explosion. Also from October 1945 the reconstruction work in the "old" area continued through 1946 and R.A.F. Fauld continued handling many thousands of tons of bombs after the war.

The Fauld 'Clear Up' Gang
Back row (left to right): Ernest Parker, Tom Worsley, Fred Lindsey, Unknown, Unknown, Walter Kirkland, Bagnall, Horace Utting, Joe Ford **Middle Row** (left to right): Unknown, Unknown, Zonnie Yates, George Fox, Mr Saunders, Dr Godfrey Rotter, Eric Bryant, Malcolm Andrews, Unknown, Tom Downing, Bill Causer **Front Row** (left to right): Locker, Bill Green, Unknown, Tom Wainwright, Unknown, George Whittaker, Tom Ashmole, Unknown

Photo courtesy of Betty Swain (née Lindsey)

On 31 July, 1945, the Air Ministry had visited Fauld and a report was prepared to consider whether the site could be made fit for continued bomb storage. As the "new" area had been totally destroyed by the explosion, the site now comprised the three areas of the "old" area, known as the H.E. (High Explosive) area, the incendiary area and the detonator area, all three of which were separated by earth barriers. The report revealed that:

The outskirts of HANBURY (the Cock Inn) are 975 yards from the nearest edge of the H.E. area and 1100 yards from the Incendiary area. The TUTBURY road is 550 yards from the Incendiary area and the fairly substantial buildings of FAULD HOUSE, FAULD HOUSE FARM, MANOR FARM and FAULD HALL are all within 700 yards. The derelict works of Messrs Fords are only a hundred yards from the Incendiary area, and at a lower level, so that the amount of earth cover at this point is small and must rule out completely any reconstruction of the works when category Z explosives [explosives having mass explosion risk with serious missile effect] *are stored there.*[27]

The Safety Panel on underground storage sites recommended that the Fauld site could be repaired for the storage of certain explosives *"up to a net explosive limit of 2000 tons in any sub-area providing the sub-areas are barricaded sufficiently to prevent simultaneous explosion of the contents of more than one sub-area."*[28] It is interesting to note that the panel also recommended that *"the above ground area within a radius of 1050 yards to be kept free from further civilian building or works."*[29]

This report did not come into the public domain until 1974 and bombs continued to be stored at Fauld until the winter of 1971/72. Fauld House, Fauld Manor and Fauld Hall, the six Fauld Cottages on the Fauld Lane part of the Tutbury Road and the eastern outskirts of the village of Hanbury were not aware that they remained in potentially vulnerable locations within the 1,050-yard recommended radius throughout this time.

In the event, due to prohibitive costs, the total amount of reconstruction work undertaken in the bomb storage area had been minimal. The most important work which was done was the construction of barriers in order to stem the flow of mud and water from the crater area together with strengthening weakened areas of the roof.

On 9 January, 1947, when the construction work on providing access to the gypsum mine was almost complete, the Fauld explosion claimed what might be deemed to be yet another victim. The under-manager of Staton's gypsum mine, George Astle, was killed by a rock fall and Eric Bryant, the resident mining engineer in charge of the reconstruction, narrowly escaped the same rock fall.

The Ford and Staton companies later became British Gypsum, which continues today as a large-scale operation supplying eighty per cent of the U.K.'s gypsum and anhydrite (the latter is calcium sulphate without the water content of gypsum). The Duchy of Lancaster and British Gypsum had wished to have the names of the thirty-one men who had lost their lives at Peter Ford's inscribed on the stone lintel above the new mine entrance. However, the Air Ministry did not consider this appropriate and refused to agree.

During 1946 and 1947 Henry Hand, who had joined the Royal Air Force in 1937, was at the underground explosives storage unit of R.A.F. Harpur Hill near Buxton, where he worked with German prisoners of war on war-surplus bombs stacked along runways at the disused airfields of Ashbourne and Darley Moor. Eleven years later in 1958, as a qualified

Inspector of Explosives instructing at R.A.F. Kirkham, he visited R.A.F. Fauld and told how:

The course included a visit to RAF Fauld, primarily to see the facilities for testing ammunition and pyrotechnics. But we were also taken underground to see what remained of the bombs storage at the edge of the vast crater, where a very large brick wall sealed off the devastation behind, altogether an eerie and unpleasant experience.

Then we were informed that a possible cause of the Explosion might have been unstable main explosive fillings of some bombs, thus susceptible to detonation during movement and handling, and triggering off all the hundreds of bombs in the mine, which of course is what actually happened. However, this was conjecture, and I wonder whether the exact cause has ever been established? [30] [The exact cause can never be determined beyond all doubt as the evidence was destroyed with the victims. Only a "probable" cause was ever established.]

In 1960, when the ammunition store at Harpur Hill near Buxton closed, their stores were moved to Fauld. When R.A.F. Fauld closed down during the winter of 1965–66 some 9,000 tons of explosives were moved to R.A.F. Chilmark in Wiltshire.

In 1966 the depot was leased to the American Army in order to house ammunition expelled from France following de Gaulle's decision to withdraw from NATO. In January 1967 the U.S. Army moved in.

Stockpiling began in January this year when the ammunition was moved from France, under orders of General de Gaulle, and came from London by rail to Scropton Sidings where it was offloaded direct to the depots. [31]

However, during October that year, the Air Ministry decided that the Fauld depot was no longer viable and the U.S.A.A.F. was offered and accepted an alternative site in Caerwent, South Wales. A two-year evacuation programme was drawn up. Fauld by this time had just 41 officers and men and 140 civilian employees. On 16 February, 1969 the *Sunday Times* reported:

On the site still owned by the R.A.F., the US Air Force now sees the remaining four caverns as ordnance storage for conventional ammunition. The area is fenced in and patrolled by MoD constabulary and dogs. But villagers from Hanbury easily climb through the fence to stare into the crater and nobody seems worried. [32]

The Americans left Fauld empty in the winter of 1971–72 and they, like the R.A.F., centralised their U.K. ammunition storage.

It was a number of years later before the crater area was securely fenced off and marked with warnings to visitors not to trespass because of the sudden drop and unexploded bombs. Speaking of the crater, John Cooper, formerly of Hanbury School, who went on to become the mining engineer in the gypsum mines where his father lost his life, comments:

It's a bit ironic really. It wasn't fenced off until much later. Before that, as young lads, we all played down there! [33]

It was twelve years after the explosion, in 1956, that the author took her future husband to view the unfenced crater when the trees, which were planted in 1945, were still very small.

In 1984, it was confirmed that all of the area surrounding the crater edge and within the Ministry of Defence boundary fence had received a clearance certificate. The crater itself had been subjected to a visual search but due to erosion of the sides there could be no guarantee that explosives would not surface at some time in the future as they had done in the past and as they still do on the Western Front nearly a hundred years later.

On 6 August, 1985, the *Burton Mail* reported the following:

Crater "Buried Bombs" Fear – Village Alert

There could still be bombs underneath Fauld crater – and they may be coming to the surface. Forty years after the ammunition dump exploded there is danger from what people have always feared as not all of the bombs may have gone up. According to a letter read out at Hanbury Parish Council meeting the bombs could be exposed to air – and the first unwary walker – because of soil erosion.

Councillor Mrs Diana Brown said today: "This confirms what many people have said for a long time. Everyone who has lived near Fauld for any length of time knows there are explosives still buried there – but officials have never before admitted it."

Up to now, she says, the Parish Council, which has been negotiating with the Ministry of Defence to erect a memorial to the 18 people whose bodies were never found in the blast, has tried to keep quiet about its fears. A party of 50 people went over the fields to look at it last Sunday and the area had never been fenced said Mrs Brown.[34]

Forty-four years after the explosion, in 1988, the R.A.F. looked into the feasibility of gaining access to the previously inaccessible part of the "new" area where the accident had occurred and where it was highly likely there would still be an unknown quantity of unexploded bombs. They requested an assessment from engineers '*on the extent of the engineer work involved in gaining access into the collapsed gallery system of the derelict bomb storage facility at R.A.F Fauld (situated close to the villages of Hanbury and Tutbury).*'[35] The report was produced and stated that the task would be enormous, requiring the long-term excavation of around 270,000 cubic metres of material over a three-year period and, at the time of writing, would cost over half a million pounds in fuel alone. The report's conclusion stated:

It is probable that there is a significant quantity of unexploded ordnance remaining within the collapsed gallery system of the New Store. The ordnance has remained in a stable condition for the past forty-four years since the accident and the RAF EOD department advised, after careful and deliberate consideration, that it is unlikely that it will cause an explosion ordnance hazard in the future if it continues to remain undisturbed.[36]

It was accepted that explosive material does remain and for that reason the underground entrances to the affected area (the "new" area) remain permanently sealed.

After the explosion, in addition to the clearance of bombs, the preparation of the "old" mine area of R.A.F. Fauld for continued use in peacetime as an ammunition depot and also the reconstruction of the entrance to the gypsum mine, urgent attention needed to be given to the huge task of land reclamation. The explosion had resulted in an unprecedented situation in which vast tracts of formerly productive farmland had been either lost or severely damaged. In a preliminary report to the Under Secretary of State for Air, dated 1 December, 1944, it was stated that:

Approximately 320 acres of land outside Air Ministry Boundaries is very severely damaged. Of this area, about 50 acres is a total loss for all time and of the balance of 270 acres many years must elapse before fertility is restored. The Ford Extension [the "new" area of the bomb store] is now a crater of horse-shoe shape some 600 yards by 120 feet deep.[37]

Aerial view of the crater after the levelling of the land
Photo courtesy of the Magic Attic archive

Two weeks later it was recognised that the figures in this preliminary report were an underestimate. It seemed that a figure closer to 400 acres of farmland was either totally lost or seriously damaged in addition to significant destruction to woods and trees. Early in 1945 the R.A.F. determined that they would need to purchase 273 acres of the most seriously damaged agricultural land where the prospects of it ever being put to profitable use appeared to be strictly limited. Much of the ruined land had been the property of the Duchy of Lancaster. The R.A.F. saw little prospect of the bulk of the land ever being successfully restored to agricultural use. Moreover, it was land where the possibility of discovering unexploded bombs and or human remains was still real.

In the period between 28 November and 4 December, 1944 bomb disposal squads had searched the crater and surrounding area, including the multitude of varying-sized craters in the immediate area of devastation, and found no bombs. However, on 4 December, a 300 lb high-explosive bomb was discovered by civilian workmen outside the mine area proper and consequently, at the time of the purchase and restoration of the land, it was not possible to state categorically that other bombs did not exist in the area.

In the immediate aftermath of the explosion, prisoners from Stafford Gaol had been brought in to assist with the land clearance. In April 1945, near to where Hanbury Fields Farm had once stood, the prisoners prepared a site for a memorial service for the nineteen unrecovered victims of the explosion. The memorial service, which was also a solemn service of committal, was held on the evening of Wednesday 25 April and conducted by the Vicar, the Rev J. Crook, and the Rev. C. T. Gill (Methodist minister) of Hanbury. A big parade, marshalled by Wing Commander J.R. Pocock and headed by the R.A.F. band from Cranwell, was formed outside the church. Those taking part included Sir James Ross (representing the Secretary of State for Air and the Air Council), Air Vice-Marshal J. A. Stone, Group Captains Lines, Allen and Storrar and many officers, airmen, W.A.A.F. and R.A.F. personnel, constabulary and civilian workers at the Fauld Unit. The lesson was read by Group Captain Storrar of R.A.F. Fauld. Rescue workers were represented and others included the churchwardens, Mr Jeff Hellaby and Mr William Woolliscroft with the chapel represented by Mr Bert Hardwick and Mr John Mycock. Both church and chapel choirs and many bereaved relatives and friends were present, including Italian Army officer Lieutenant Silvestri.

The procession moved through the village to a prepared site adjoining one of the wrecked farm homesteads, which commanded an awe-inspiring view of the devastated scene.

It was also fitting that the service should be attended by Lieutenant Silvestri, of the Italian Army, for several Italian collaborators lost their lives in the explosion.[38]

The Rev C.T. Gill gave a moving address to the large congregation as they stood on the former farmland of Hanbury Fields Farm and gazed towards the vast crater where Upper Castle Hayes Farm had been:

All must experience a sense of strangeness as they view that devastated site where once men toiled, women baked and children played. The earth, once green pastures, was scorched as if in pain.[39]

In June 1945 the arrangement where the prisoners from Stafford Gaol were providing labour for the land clearance was put on a firm basis. The prison governor agreed to continue to provide free labour for a period of three years and the R.A.F., in return, arranged to provide transport and accommodation. The prisoners were accommodated in refurbished huts which had been used by the United States Air Force as a searchlight site at Draycott-in-the-Clay. It was agreed that an attempt should be made to restore as much as possible of the land to agricultural use and that the crater itself should be planted with trees. The work was carried out in the knowledge that unexploded bombs and human remains could be discovered at any time.

Joe Cooper recalls:

They brought in prisoners from Stafford Gaol to do the clean-up job on what had been the Bothams' farmland. They were billeted at the old searchlight station on the Riddings Lane at Draycott-in-the-Clay. They did a good job in tidying up the land including fencing and digging ditches and dealing with dead cattle. It was not a nice job. There's nothing left there of the Bothams' farm. Not even a brick. It had been just off Featherbed Lane.[40]

Some of those who were young boys in Hanbury village have clear recollections of this major exercise of land reclamation. Tom Allen, who had been at Tutbury School when the dump went up and later went to work for the Gregsons at Church Farm, Hanbury, recalled:

The bulldozers were clearing the land. My brother Philip and I used to sit on them and go down into the crater. It always seemed strange and it was always cold. We went on different bulldozers and we thought it was great. The soil in the crater continued to slip down. They planted trees and they continued growing after the soil slip.[41]

Both Tom Allen and John Cooper recalled that over two and a half years after the explosion the body of Stephen West, a farm worker at Upper Castle Hayes, was found. On 11 August, 1947, a prisoner had been clearing earth and debris when he hit a metal object.

He stopped his bulldozer and, as instructed, waved a red flag to attract his supervisor's attention. The metal turned out to be the remains of a buried tractor and beneath it was the body of Stephen West. Tom Allen recalled:

Steve West had been on his tractor. He'd just gone by Bothams' farm and was on his way back to Goodwins'.[42]

Stephen West's body was discovered about 200 yards from the edge of the main crater. It was within a few yards of where the body of his younger brother John had been found ten days after the explosion. The body and clothing of Stephen were identified by both their elder brother, Joseph of Mill Farm, Cubley, and also by a long-standing friend, Horace Edwards of Cottage Farm, Boylestone. Stephen West had been one of the nineteen deemed "missing presumed dead" at the time of the Inquest of 6 February, 1945. At the inquiry held on 15 August, 1947, the Coroner expressed his satisfaction with the evidence of identification and added that he believed the inquiry was unprecedented. He also added a tribute to the prisoners from Stafford Gaol, who had been carrying out land restoration work when the body was discovered, saying that their help in recovering the body was worthy of commendation. On 13 August, 1947 the prison governor had written to the Coroner informing him that the Secretary of State had remitted 21 days of the sentence on each of the four prisoners who had assisted in the removal of the remains.

For many months, the prisoners involved in the land reclamation attended Evensong at Hanbury Church. The author recalls the sea of prison-grey uniforms occupying a complete aisle of the church and the many bass voices swelling the singing of the choir and congregation. The governor at Stafford Gaol, together with a number of prisoners engaged in the land clearance, was also present at the annual explosion memorial service held in 1946.

Some 50 R.A.F. officers and men from the Fauld depot attended the service, together with the Governor and a number of prisoners from Stafford Gaol, who are engaged in re-cultivating the land.[43]

The reclamation was finally completed in April 1949 but towards the end of 1948, when the difficult work was almost complete, a tribute was paid by the Home Secretary to the work done by the prisoners.

EXPLOSION SITE

Almost back to normal after four years

For some time after the explosion it was thought that the land could never be reclaimed but by now the seemingly impossible has almost been achieved. For the past three years prisoners from Stafford Gaol have been clearing the site and have moved many thousands of tons of earth.

In London last night a tribute was paid to those prisoners by Mr Chuter Ede, the Home Secretary, who said that although they worked in the open not one had attempted to escape.[44]

Fifty years on, John Hardwick recorded:

The crater itself is now a place of great beauty. All on its own, without interference from man, it has shed its moonlike appearance and taken on a fully natural beauty with trees and shrubs, flora and fauna. Unfortunately, a fence has been erected at the perimeter to finally meet safety requirements but tree planting and undergrowth clearance are undertaken on a continuing basis.[45]

Sixty years on from the explosion, claims were made regarding the findings of two other bodies between 1948 and 1952.

PROBE CALL ON HIDDEN BODIES

Relatives of the victims of the biggest explosion in British history are convinced that two bodies still lie in fields near the crater. Now, on the 60th anniversary of the Fauld Explosion, a group of survivors and relatives are hoping to gather enough evidence to persuade the Government to excavate the area. The campaign has been mounting support since farmer John Bowley claimed in a radio interview that he had discovered two bodies while ploughing fields. Mr Bowley said he had unearthed the bodies in fields between Hare Holes Farm, Hare Holes Rough and Lower Castle Hayes Farm between 1948 and 1952. He claimed that he and a fellow worker were instructed to re-inter the bodies secretly on official orders and to remain silent about their findings and illegal re-burial at pain of 25 years' prison under the Official Secrets Act.[46]

Sign at crater's edge warning of
unexploded bombs
Photo by the author

Mr Bowley was subsequently interviewed in a BBC documentary but his allegations were somewhat vague and in part contradictory. Over sixty years on it appears unlikely that the allegations will ever be verified.

During the 1980s and early 1990s new fears were raised when underground caverns which, up until the early 1970s, had been used for bomb storage, were used for the storage of fireworks. There were protests locally and Hanbury Parish Council had objected to the application by Fireworks International, which sub-let to Feistel and Benwell, to house the store at Fauld. The local press reported:

Fireworks Explosives Bid

Villagers Haunted by Blast Horror

A macabre irony has brought major fireworks manufacturers to the site to make use of purpose-built wartime bunkers for storage. The fireworks have been here for years but now a Tutbury farmer, who rents the bunkers from the Ministry of Defence, has won a license to repair fireworks, and for the possible storage of other explosives.[47]

Three years later an explosion, where fortunately there was no injury to staff, occurred on 10 August, 1992:

Firework Explosion

Echoes of 1944 Disaster

An underground bunker containing 14 tonnes of fireworks and packaging exploded at Feistel and Benwell Ltd's underground store at Fauld.[48]

In 1999 fears were raised that the Fauld crater, which had been declared a site of "geological interest", was not protected from development such as landfill. Understandably, the suggestion was highly controversial and when the County Council declared that the site could still contain "live ammunition" the issue was reported in the local press:

Fauld site "could still contain explosives"

The site is owned by the Ministry of Defence and has been officially designated as a war grave. It is already protected from development and is likely to be protected in the future. But if someone considers developing the site nobody could give a guarantee that there isn't live ammunition down there. For any potential developer it would be a very hazardous operation.[49]

NOTES

1 Rev C.T. Gill at a service for the unrecovered victims of the explosion conducted within view of the crater on 25 April, 1945, *Burton Chronicle*, 26 April, 1945.

2 John Hardwick reported in the *Sunday Telegraph*, 27 November, 1994.

3 Dr R.S. Woods at a memorial service at Hanbury parish church, 3 December, 1944.

4 *The Weekend Guardian*, March 11–12, 1989.

5 Lord Sherwood, Under Secretary of State for Air reported in the *Burton Daily Mail*, 1 December, 1944.

6 *Burton Daily Mail*, 1 December 1944.

7 *London Daily Mail*, 31 January, 1945.

8 Major A. P. Burnside, R.A.F. Fauld, Ref. *Royal Engineers Journal* April 1988, Vol. 102 No 1.

9 The National Archives Ref AIR 19/523 A.M.S.O. Minute Sheet dated 6 January 1945.

10 Ibid.

11 Ibid.

12 The National Archives Ref AIR 19/523 Minute Sheet F414.

13 The National Archives Ref AIR 29/981.

14 Ken McCleod to the author, 18 August, 2011.

15 The National Archives Ref Air Ministry File No S2553 Minute Sheet dated 9 December , 1945.

16 The National Archives Ref AIR 19/523.

17 The National Archives ref Air Ministry File Minute Sheet dated 12 January, 1945.

18 Ibid.

19 *London Daily* Mail, 3 October, 1945.

20 Copy letter to the Air Ministry from Maintenance Command dated 11 September, 1945.

21 Copy letter from Viscount Stansgate to Air Marshal Sir Grahame Donald dated 3 October, 1945. The National Archives Ref AIR 19/523.

22 *Burton Daily Mail*, 3 October, 1945.

23 *Daily Herald*, 3 October, 1945.

24 *Daily Herald*, 3 October, 1945.

25 Ibid.

26 *Derby Evening Telegraph*, 3 October, 1945.

27 The National Archives Ref AIR 17/12 Report of Safety Panel visit to R.A.F. Fauld in 1945.

28 Ibid.

29 Ibid.

30 Letter from Henry Hand to the author received 26 June, 2012.

31 *Derby Evening Telegraph*, 24 November, 1967.

32 *Sunday Times*, 16 February, 1969.

33 As recalled by John Cooper on one of the numerous occasions when he spoke with the author.

34 *Burton Daily Mail*, 6 August, 1985.

35 *Royal Engineers Journal*, April 1988, Vol. 102 No. 1. Article entitled 'R.A.F. Fauld' by Major A.P. Burnside of the Royal Engineers.

36 Ibid.

37 The National Archives – Preliminary report to Under Secretary of State for Air.

38 *Burton Chronicle*, 26 April, 1945.

39 Rev C.T. Gill at a service for the unrecovered victims of the explosion conducted within view of the crater on 25 April, 1945, reported in the *Burton Chronicle*, 3 May, 1945.

40 As recalled by Joe Cooper, 10 September, 2011.

41 Tom Allen to the author, 8 October, 2011.

42 Ibid.

43 *Burton Daily Mail*, 4 December, 1946.

44 *Burton Daily Mail*, 30 November, 1948.

45 John Hardwick record.

46 *Burton Daily Mail*, November 2004. During the week of the sixtieth anniversary of the explosion the newspaper produced a number of articles of which this, appearing on Day 4 of their "Fauld Special", was one.

47 *Derby Evening Telegraph*, 19 August, 1989.

48 *Derby Evening Telegraph*, 11 August, 1992.

49 Spokesman for Staffordshire County Council quoted in the *Burton Mail*, 12 March, 1999.

CHAPTER NINE

SITES OF MEMORIES AND REMEMBRANCE

"Until the day breaks and the shadows flee away we will remember them."[1]
"For years afterwards you only had to glance at each other to know you were with someone who had witnessed the explosion. There was this common bond between people. This is a very special village to live in."[2]

It was some weeks after the explosion before Father took my mother, my sister Marjorie and me to see the crater. We walked across our fields beyond the tramway which had carried the gypsum, over the protective hill which had saved our farm, by the tortured and devastated woods where we had picked anemones and bluebells and on up the hill towards where the familiar home of my childhood friend, Upper Castle Hayes Farm, had been. I knew that I would never see Marie's home ever again but nothing prepared me for the site of desolation and horror as we gazed across an unrecognisable landscape and into the depth of that vast, raw crater where once we had played in a tree house in the orchard. As a child I had no words to convey my thoughts and feelings and as an adult I remain incapable of finding words to convey the deep sense of loss. A loss, albeit, which was as nothing compared to that experienced by Marie and her brother Gordon or, indeed, by many others of my former classmates and their families.

Now the Hanbury village website records:

Today the scars in the landscape have healed. Birch and pine trees have colonised the crater and it is a place of peace . . . If you visit this place always remember that it is a war grave, and remember that here a small community lost part of itself.

When I visited the crater in the late summer of 2011 perennial sweet peas were flowering as they scrambled through the shielding wire fence with its harsh signs warning of a steep drop and unexploded bombs. The sight of the flowers was a poignant remembrance of the Goodwins' garden and the vanished world of childhood.

The crater in
August 2011
Photo by the author

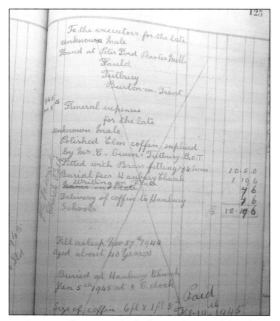

From William Marler's funeral record book
Now in the possession of his grandson Geoff Marler

The handwritten funeral records of former Hanbury village wheelwright, joiner and undertaker, William Marler, reveal that nineteen of the Hanbury parishioners were laid to rest in the graveyards of St Werburgh's Church and the Methodist chapel from the beginning of December 1944 to early February 1945. At the church, they included one unnamed man around 40 years of age, where four of the Hanbury parish councillors, George Ede, Jim Heathcote, Jeff Hellaby and Leslie Shotton were the pall-bearers.[3]

Sixteen of the victims of the Fauld explosion were from Tutbury and combined funerals for six of them were held at St Mary's Priory Church, Tutbury. Harry Payne, whose father Reg Payne had worked as a munitions inspector at the Dump, recalls:

A most lasting memory of this disaster was during a visit to Tutbury Parish Church a few days later [i.e. after the explosion] *to see that several pews at the back of the church had been removed and the floor space occupied by rows of coffins containing victims of the tragedy.*[4]

In addition to the many funerals which took place in Hanbury, Tutbury and surrounding villages and towns including Uttoxeter, Burton-on-Trent and further afield, the Italians were laid to rest, initially in a mass grave in Stapenhill cemetery, Burton-on-Tent, and

Left: This memorial to Corporale Liugi Scuto in Stapenhill cemetery, Burton-on-Trent, one of the six Italians who lost their lives on 27 November, 1944 **Middle:** Former Flight Sergeant Neil Robinson at the Italian memorials, Stapenhill **Right:** Memorial to R.A.F. Corporal Alan Durose, Stapenhill *All Photos by the author*

later individual memorials were erected. The peaceful cemetery at Stapenhill is also the last resting place of R.A.F. Corporal Alan Durose, who was working above ground at the Dump when he was killed.

Anniversary memorial services continue to be held in St Werburgh's Church, Hanbury on the closest Sunday to 27 November and, until the sixtieth anniversary in 2004, services of remembrance have also been held at the unique war grave of the crater itself. The memorial services are attended by representatives of the R.A.F. in addition to villagers and relatives of the victims. There have been suggestions made that the Fauld commemoration should be combined with those of Remembrance Sunday but for many in Hanbury this does not seem appropriate.

The Village Memorial Hall is a memorial to those who lost their lives. Shortly after the explosion, the people of Hanbury had determined that the old Services Recreation Hut which had been flattened by the explosion should be replaced by a Memorial Hall and, following over four years of inspired and determined commitment by the local community, a temporary village hall was opened on 23 July, 1949.

All the local press reported the opening:

HANBURY MEMORIAL HALL

OPENING OF TEMPORARY BUILDING

The official opening on Saturday of the newly erected Hanbury Memorial Hall brought sad memories to a large number of families in the Hanbury and Uttoxeter districts who were bereaved when the explosion at the Fauld R.A.F. Ammunition Dump occurred on November 27, 1944, and 81 people were killed, missing or injured – 27 killed or missing at the main dump and ten injured and 41 killed or missing and three injured at the plaster and cement works nearby.

The ceremony was performed by Mr Rowland Ford of Colwyn Bay, formerly of Uttoxeter, a former director of Messrs Peter Ford and Sons, of Fauld, and their associate companies, whose plaster, mine and cement works was destroyed in the explosion.[5]

Memorial to Victims of War and Fauld Explosion

Beautiful weather favoured Saturday's opening of Hanbury Memorial Hall. This hall is a memorial, not only to those who gave their lives in both World Wars, but also to those who perished in the Fauld Explosion of November 27th, 1944, when 81 people were killed, missing or injured. All the names are inscribed on the Roll of Honour which has been placed in the temporary hall, allocated by the National Council of Social Services.[6]

A service before the opening ceremony was conducted by the Vicar of Hanbury, the Rev. R. Osborn. The Rev. J. Crook, Vicar of Morton, Newport, Salop, who had been Vicar of Hanbury at the time of the explosion, was invited to unveil the plaque commemorating those who had died. In doing so he:

. . . recalled one morning of November 27th, 1944, at ten minutes past eleven and said that the names would always stand in his memory. He would mention Mrs Cox, Mr Shotton and Mr Foster, who did yeoman service, and his wife for saving the Hanbury children. But for her timely help and thought perhaps some of the children's names would be on the plaque.[7]

The Rev. Crook was referring to his second wife who at the time had been Miss Fardon, head-teacher of Hanbury village school.

In moving a vote of thanks to Mr Rowland Ford, Mr Leslie Shotton, Chairman of the Parish Council, also thanked:

Major H.L. Newton, High Sherriff of Derbyshire, for his generous gift of the site, and Mrs Evans and the National Council of Social Services. He also recalled the great spade work of Mr C. Gallimore [of Fauld Hall], *who, unfortunately could not be with them to see some of the results of his work.* [Charles Gallimore was in South Africa at the time.] *They also thanked Mr W.S. Thompson (hon. treasurer), who also was not present, and the Duchy of Lancaster (through their agent Mr Hague).*[8]

Rowland Ford was presented with a buttonhole by fifteen-year-old Gordon Goodwin and his twelve-year-old sister Marie presented Mrs Ford with a bouquet.

For Marie and Gordon, that Saturday in July 1949 must have been so very hard. It was a day I also recall with very mixed emotions. Following the opening ceremony of the Memorial Hall, my mother suggested that Marie and I might wish to go for a walk through the village. It was a walk which I recall took us away from the new Memorial Hall towards the re-built Cock Inn, but before passing the Cock we took sideways glances at the footpath which we used to take to Upper Castle Hayes. We continued walking on towards the top of Hanbury Hill. It was, had I then appreciated the true meaning of the word, poignant for all that was not said.

Dedication of the Memorial Window at St Werburgh's Church, Hanbury in November 1949 (left to right) Eric Skeet, Valerie Hardy (née Hellaby), Joseph Foster, Maud Foster, Miss Williams, Ida Hellaby, Rev Osborne, Unknown, Rev Crook, Leslie Shotton, Unknown (possibly the Rural Dean) *Photo loaned by Jill Woolliscroft*

On the fifth anniversary in November 1949 I was present at the unveiling of the memorial window at Hanbury Church. The opportunity was taken to use some ancient stained glass which for many years had graced the window in the vestry where few could appreciate its beauty. It reads:

The ancient glass was placed in this window in memory of those parishioners who died in active service during the Second World War 1939–45 and all those who lost their lives in the Hanbury Explosion November 27th 1944.[9]

On the right-hand side of the memorial window is a plaque on which the names of those who lost their lives are inscribed. The window and the framed plaque are in the right-hand aisle of the church and it is a part which I recall as the Children's Corner where Sunday school was held. It is a corner of remembrance where, to the left of the memorial window, is a picture of the Nativity in memory of Mark Jeffery and Sarah Louise Hardy, our own children.

Opening of Memorial Hall in November 1962 (the picture hangs in the Memorial Hall)

At the front (left to right): Mr Richard Bamford, Wing Commander Andrade (RAF Fauld), Mrs Andrade, Mr Peter Ford, Mr David Gibb (Staffs Rural Community Council), Mrs Thompson (opener), Mr John Hardwick (Chairman), Mrs Ford, Mr Crawford (Gypsum Mine Manager), Mr Bill Thompson, Mr Roy Marler (Secretary)

At the back (middle): Mrs Audrey Hardwick, Mr Jeff Hellaby, Mrs Ida Hellaby

At the back (far right): Mr Joseph Foster and Mrs Maud Foster

Photo - a copy of that which hangs in the Memorial Hall

Right: Roll of Honour in the Memorial Hall

Photo by the author

Roll of Honour

~ In memory of those who lost their lives ~

1914 - 1918		Fauld Explosion		1939 - 1945
		27th November 1944		
Bennet. W.	Marler. J. W.	Sgt. S. G. Game.	Ford. W.	Abberley. S.
Bennet. S. G.	Martin. M.	Cpl. A. S. Durose.	Ford. Mrs W.	Hassent. B.
Brough. E.	Nash. J.	LAC. J. T. Bailey.	Frow. L. D.	Rushton. E.
Broughton. E.	Pegg. J.	. H. Fairbanks.	Gent. W.	Stonier. R.
Buckley. E. H.	Richardson. J. S.	. W. Deucharas.	Gilbert. O. A.	Upstones. L.
Carter. H.	Richardson. T.	Appleton. J.	Goodwin. M.	Whittaker. G
Causer. G.	Robinson. H. E.	Barker. E.	Goodwin. Mrs M.	Brace. E. F. F.
Evans. S. C.	Robinson. J. Y.	Beard. J.	Harris. A.	
Harris. W.	Smith. W.	Bell. J.	Harrison F. W.	
Harris. T.	Sowter. J.	Bowring. F.	Hill. H.	
Harrison. F.	Tipper. A. E.	Brassington. J.	Hill. Mrs H.	
Harrison. J.	Upton. W.	Carter. H.	Hogg. C. E.	
Leadbetter. R.	Watson. T.	Cartwright. F.	Hudson. T	
McBean. E.	Wheat. B.	Cartwright. R.	Kidd. W.	
Marler C. E.		Campbell. F.	Mahon. G. A.	
		Chawner. S.	Mellor. A. W.	
Pickering. S.	Sanders. T.	Cockayne. L. G.	Miles. G.	Slater. F. W.	West. J. W.
Powell. G. H.	Shepherd. H.	Cooper. J.	Nicklin. F.	Smith. Miss E.	West. S.
Priestley. G.	Shepherd. W.	Cooper. P.	Page. E.	Smith. G.	Woolley. E.
Redfern. J.	Shipley. A. A.	Daniels. G.	Page. G.	Stanley. B. H.	Worthington. I.
Rock. G.	Skellett. J. W.	Fell. E.	Page. P.	Wagstaff. R.	
		Fell. B.	Patterson. A.		

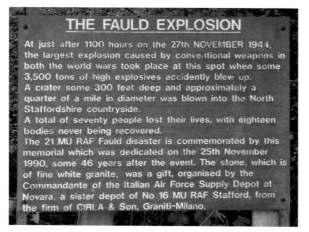

THE FAULD EXPLOSION

At just after 1100 hours on the 27th NOVEMBER 1944, the largest explosion caused by conventional weapons in both the world wars took place at this spot when some 3,500 tons of high explosives accidently blew up.
A crater some 300 feet deep and approximately a quarter of a mile in diameter was blown into the North Staffordshire countryside.
A total of seventy people lost their lives, with eighteen bodies never being recovered.
The 21 MU RAF Fauld disaster is commemorated by this memorial which was dedicated on the 25th November 1990, some 46 years after the event. The stone, which is of fine white granite, was a gift, organised by the Commandante of the Italian Air Force Supply Depot at Novara, a sister depot of No 16 MU RAF Stafford, from the firm of CIRLA & Son, Graniti-Milano.

Above: At the crater's edge near the memorial

Left: Memorial stone erected November 1990

Below: Inscription on memorial stone

All Photos by the author

IN MEMORY OF THOSE WHO LOST THEIR LIVES IN THE FAULD EXPLOSION
27th NOVEMBER 1944

THE FIRST EIGHTEEN PEOPLE NAMED HAVE NO KNOWN GRAVE
AND THIS CRATER IS THEIR RESTING PLACE

J. Brassington	G.A. Mahon	
F. Campbell	A.W. Mellor	T. Sanders
F. Cartwright	J.R. Miles	A.A. Shipley
L.D. Frow	F. Nicklin	Miss E. Smith
C.E. Hogg	J. Redfern	B.H. Stanley
	F.G. Rock	R. Wagstaffe
L.A.C. J.T. Bailey	L.A.C. H.C. Fairbanks	

	E. Fell	
J.H. Appleton	Mrs. N. Ford	P. Page
E. Barker	W. Ford	A. Patterson
J. Beard	W. Gent	S. Pickering
J. Bell	A.O. Gilbert	G. Powell
F.C. Bowring	M. Goodwin	G. Priestley
H. Carter	Mrs. M. Goodwin	H. Shepherd
R. Cartwright	A. Harris	W. Shepherd
S. Chawner	F.W. Harrison	J. Skellett
L.G. Cokayne	H.J. Hill	F.W. Slater
J. Cooper	Mrs. S.L. Hill	G. Smith
P. Cooper	T. Hudson	J.W. West
Mrs. L.E. Crook	W. Kidd	S. West
E.W.G. Daniels	E.A. Page	E. Woolley
B. Fell	G.E. Page	N. Worthington
Sgt. S.G. Game	Cpl. L. Scuto	Pte. R. Novello
Cpl. A.S. Durose	Pte. E. Di Paolo	Pte. S. Ruggeri
L.A.C. W. Deucharas	Pte. A. Lanzoni	Pte. S. Trovato

WE WILL REMEMBER THEM

Eighteen years after the explosion, on 24 November, 1962, Hanbury's new Memorial Hall was opened by Mrs Thompson, formerly of Hanbury Grange, whose husband Bill had been generous in his contribution to the temporary Memorial Hall.

Fauld Explosion: Hall memorial to victims

Hanbury's new memorial hall, which replaces the one destroyed by an explosion at the Fauld Ammunition dump on November 27th, 1944, was opened by Mrs W.S. Thompson of Little Haywood, on Saturday. About 80 [sic] people lost their lives in the explosion, and the new hall is intended as a memorial to them and to local people killed on active service.[10]

On the fortieth anniversary in November 1984 the R.A.F. provided floodlights around the church in Hanbury.

R.A.F. joins in tribute to the victims

The service was attended by villagers and relatives of those killed and a contingent from Royal Air Force, Stafford. The choir from St Mary's Church, Tutbury joined the Hanbury choir and music was provided by the Royal Air Force Midlands Band. The preacher was Squadron Leader the Rev Paul Plumley from the R.A.F.[11]

It was forty-six years after the explosion before a permanent memorial was erected at the crater. On Sunday 25 November, 1990 over five hundred people attended the Fauld Explosion Memorial Dedication Service held at the site. The sides of the crater were now partially clothed with trees but the earliest memorial, stones of white gypsum in the shape of a cross placed in its depths many years before, could then still be detected. The permanent Memorial Stone of Italian diorite, a gift of the Italian Air Force, was donated by Cirla and Son, Graniti, Milan and transported by the R.A.F. It commemorates and is a tribute to all of the seventy people, including six Italians, who lost their lives in the Fauld explosion of November 1944. Among those attending the memorial dedication service were many relatives of those who were killed and these included Maurice Goodwin's ninety-one year-old brother. Also present was a niece of one of the Italians who perished in addition to some of those who had taken part in the rescue operations. The Hanbury Parish Council laid a dozen red roses at the memorial.

The fiftieth anniversary was marked in 1994 and John Hardwick recorded:

The hurt lasts for decades. A look is sufficient to recall the event and its subsequent effect on those of us who lived through it. Soon it will be fifty years since it happened. We hold a memorial service at the crater at 11.00 a.m. on 27 November and a service in church on the Sunday nearest to the 27th. The service is always dignified by the presence of the R.A.F.[12]

In 2002, Hanbury Parish Council adopted a plot for a memorial stone at the National Memorial Arboretum, the U.K.'s Centre of Remembrance at Alrewas, near Lichfield, Staffordshire which had been opened in 2001. Five trees were planted, three of which were the unusual red-flowering Midland Hawthorn. The memorial stone is a simple massive block of Fauld gypsum and bares a stark inscription.

In memory of the 70 people who lost their lives in the underground explosion at Fauld Munitions Store near Burton upon Trent 27th November 1944

It was dedicated at a memorial service held there on 27 November, 2002 and was attended by representatives of the R.A.F., the parish council and relatives and friends of the victims.

Services of commemoration at the crater, to *"remember those who died and give thanks for the qualities of those who survived and rebuilt their community"*,[13] continued until 2004. Annual memorial services at St Werburgh's Church still continue to be held on the nearest Sunday to 27 November but the last of the annual commemoration services at the crater itself, organised by the Hanbury Parish Council, was held on 28 November, 2004. Parish councillor Ida Roberts, who as Ida Harrison had delivered the post to Upper Castle Hayes and walked with the Goodwin children to school on the morning of 27 November, 1944, said:

Not many people are left in Hanbury who had relatives who died in the explosion. It is sixty years now and we felt it was time to hold the last one.[14]

Memorial Stone at the
National Memorial Arboretum

Photo by the author

John Cooper at the crater in 2004

Photo: Christopher Thomond, courtesy of The Guardian

The Guardian of 27 November, 2004 reported:

Today John Cooper will stand at the edge of a huge crater in rural Staffordshire and remember the mighty blast that killed his father Joe, exactly sixty years ago.[15]

Nine years before this last memorial service was held at the crater in 2004, the Brewhouse Drama Group in Burton-on-Trent had put on a play in the summer of 1995 which involved local people recalling their experiences and memories of the Fauld explosion. John Cooper was an advisor for the production of the play which was entitled *For Dumping in Deep Water*. It was what today might well be described as a docudrama.

On 3 May, 1995 the *Burton Mail* reported:

A survivor of the wartime Fauld explosion says he will travel from Cheshire to Burton to see a play about the disaster – Britain's biggest explosion – and cannot understand the attitude of villagers who plan to shun the drama.

Local residents say they will not see the play because it will bring back painful memories of the day in November 1944 when an underground bomb store exploded, killing 70 people and devastating the village.[16]

The survivor was retired local government officer, seventy-year-old Malcolm Kidd, whose job, as a nineteen-year-old airman in the mine in November 1944, had been to paint 'For Dumping In Deep Water' on shell casings to identify unsafe bombs (see Chapter Seven). He said:

There are only a few survivors left now and it's important the facts are preserved for posterity. I feel very lucky to be alive after what went on.

Their sincerity is to be admired and I will be coming along to see the play.[17]

The play was performed at the Brewhouse Arts Centre on 20 June, 1995 in Burton. One of those who saw it and subsequently wrote to the producer was the late Vera Jeffery of Aston

House, Sudbury who, as Vera Shelley, had been born at Upper Castle Hayes Farm before living at Rock House in Hanbury and teaching at Hanbury School.

This letter was forwarded to John Cooper and is in his papers to which the author was granted access. It is reproduced here with his permission and with that of Vera's daughter Rosalie Vicars-Harris.

I was born at the farm "Castle Hayes" that disappeared completely at the time of the Fauld Explosion 1944.[18]

Vera was requesting copies of some of the photographs used in the production and went on to say:

There was one of the kitchen at Rock House where I lived later, and one of the damaged church (Hanbury) where I was married.[19]

In response, the play's producer, Steve Bull, in addition to recommending that Vera should contact John Cooper, wrote:

Since our performance, we have met several people with memories of the times which do not seem to have been well documented, and it is vital that this local history is not lost.[20]

For Dumping in Deep Water was a dramatic presentation of the Fauld explosion over half a century after the tragedy. More than a decade into the twenty-first century it has become the stuff of fiction, referred to in Leah Fleming's novel *The Captain's Daughter*, which was published in 2012 and where she wrote:

Ella's students were being clumsy this November morning, none of them grasping what she was demonstrating. All they could talk about was the huge explosion that had rocked the Midlands two days before, shattering windows everywhere, causing people to fear a rocket attack. Someone said an arsenal had been bombed. Others said a whole city had been blasted away. Lichfield shuddered with its impact as if an earthquake had struck, but there was nothing reported on the news.[21]

Leah Fleming, who lived in Lichfield for thirteen years, set an earlier novel there and for this she:

. . . researched very carefully but no mention was made of the explosion in any of the local papers. It was all hush hush.[22]

Letter from Vera Jeffery

In the second decade of the twenty-first century, the story of Britain's biggest explosion, told through the voices of those who experienced it, is rather like looking at events through the wrong end of "time's telescope". The voices of ordinary people who have told of their personal experiences of an extraordinary event can now be seen more clearly and in a wider context.

The events recounted here do not pretend to be an academic history of the Fauld explosion. Whilst also using primary sources, this is primarily oral history and has focused on the memories of those who were there at the time. Their voices are no longer silent.

NOTES

1 From the Song of Solomon (Can. 2. 17) and quoted by the Rev. J. Crook at the opening of the Hanbury Memorial Hall on 23 July, 1949. Reported in the *Uttoxeter Advertiser*, 27 July, 1949.

2 John Hardwick, reported in the *Express and Star*, 10 November, 1994.

3 The funeral record book kept by William Thomas Marler was shown to the author by his grandson Geoff Marler on 26 October, 2011.

4 Papers loaned to the author by John Cooper include this record written by Harry Payne dated 13 May, 1999.

5 *Uttoxeter Advertiser*, 27 July, 1949.

6 *Burton Daily Mail*, 25 July, 1949.

7 *Burton Chronicle*, 28 July 1949.

8 *Uttoxeter Advertiser*, 27 July, 1949.

9 Undated newspaper cutting from Ida Roberts.

10 *Derby Evening Telegraph*, 26 November, 1962.

11 *Burton Mail*, 27 November, 1984.

12 John Hardwick, unpublished record.

13 *Express and Star*, 19 November, 1994 reporting at the time of the 50th anniversary.

14 *Uttoxeter Advertiser*, 29 November, 2004.

15 *The Guardian*, 27 November 2004.

16 *Burton Mail*, 3 May, 1995.

17 Ibid.

18 Copy of a letter from Vera Jeffery which was forwarded to John Cooper.

19 Ibid.

20 Response from Steve Bull, producer of the play *For Dumping in Deep Water* to letter from Vera Jeffery (copy letter in papers kindly loaned by John Cooper).

21 From *The Captain's Daughter* by Leah Fleming (published by Simon and Schuster, 2012), page 490. Extract quoted with permission of the author.

22 Leah Fleming to the author on 30 April, 2012.

About the Author

Valerie Hardy (née Hellaby) a farmer's daughter from the middle Dove valley of the Staffordshire/ Derbyshire borders, who experienced the immediate aftermath of the Fauld explosion of 1944, was educated at Hanbury village school and Uttoxeter Girls' High School before reading Geography at the University of Leeds. She then studied Education at Bristol and Nottingham Universities and taught in Leicestershire and Derbyshire before going into Educational Administration in Sheffield, Cumbria and Gloucestershire followed by work for the European Business School, London.

Valerie, who now lives in the Cotswolds, is a frequent visitor to the land of her roots where she researched for her first book *Old Derbyshire and New Worlds* and captured the memories and eye-witness accounts for her second, VOICES FROM THE EXPLOSION.

INDEX